Current Topics in Early Childhood Education

Volume III

Editor
LILIAN G. KATZ

Associate Editors
Charlotte H. Watkins, Moral A. Quest,
and Mima J. Spencer

ERIC Clearinghouse on Elementary and Early Childhood Education
University of Illinois at Urbana-Champaign

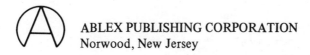

ABLEX PUBLISHING CORPORATION
Norwood, New Jersey

The material in this publication was prepared with funding from the National
Institute of Education, U.S. Department of Education, under Contract No. 400-78-
0008. Contractors undertaking such projects under government sponsorship are
encouraged to express freely their judgment in professional and technical matters.
Points of view or opinions do not necessarily represent the official view or opinions
of the National Institute of Education or the Department of Education.

ISBN 0-89391-057-0   ISSN 0363-8332
ISBN 0-89391-066-X pbk.

ABLEX Publishing Corporation
355 Chestnut Street
Norwood, New Jersey 07648

Contents

Preface

This third volume of *Current Topics in Early Childhood Education* brings together the work of contributors from five nations—Australia, England, Ireland and West Germany as well as the United States—discussing a variety of issues of interest to researchers and practitioners in early childhood education. Many of these papers were presented at a conference in observance of the International Year of the Child, held in Champaign, Illinois, in November 1979 under the sponsorship of the ERIC Clearinghouse on Elementary and Early Childhood Education, the Office of International Programs and Studies at the University of Illinois, and the ABLEX Publishing Company.

A European view of television, and its role in the environment of the developing child, is offered by Klaus Schleicher of West Germany. Philip Gammage of Britain gives us a current perspective on the development of school curriculum in that country. Gerald Ashby describes the development of pre-school education in the state of Queensland, Australia—a process with some constraints unique to that state, and other features common to many other parts of the world where schools must serve widely dispersed, rural populations. Anne McKenna of Ireland reports new research on a topic of universal concern: The development of the young child's verbal sophistication.

The papers prepared by American authors reflect two streams in early childhood literature. Two of them belong in a category we might call "perennial" in that they take up topics of recurrent or constant concern to each successive generation of practitioners as well as to researchers in the field of early childhood education. The role of emotions in the early education of young children, discussed by Fogel, is of continuing interest to those who care for the young.

The differentiation of mothers' and teachers' roles in the young child's life, explored by Katz, becomes a salient issue periodically in the light of shifting role definitions in the larger society and the resultant changes in pressures exerted on each role taker.

Four of the papers deal with topics which can be classified as "emergent" in that they represent concerns, theories, or research styles that are presently attracting increasing attention. Birch's paper focuses on a concern about child development that, though not new, has acquired a new sense of urgency. Eiduson's research reflects an emerging acknowledgment and acceptance of the reality that an increasing number of mothers are raising children alone. The Phyfe-Perkins paper emerges from more than a decade of research on environmental and ecological determinants of experience. The paper by Travis and Perreault reminds us that as more and more mothers of young children work outside the home, day care programs can serve as an important psychological and social resource for them and their families.

Together these papers present more evidence of the complexity and the diversity of the field of early childhood education.

Lilian G. Katz, Ph.D.
Director, ERIC Clearinghouse
on Elementary and Early Childhood Education

1

The Role of Emotion
in Early Childhood Education

Alan Fogel
Purdue University

When the word "affect" is mentioned, most educators tend to think of the distinction which has been made between "affective" and "cognitive" goals or objectives. This division of the learning process into two distinct realms has helped teachers build into their curricula concepts such as appreciation, self-confidence, value, and enjoyment, and thus has expanded our concept of teaching beyond the pure transmission of knowledge. There is another way in which affect or emotion enters into the educational process: via the direct emotional experiences of teachers and children as they go about their work and play. These emotional experiences, whether we are aware of them or not, have a profound effect on the outcomes of education. As Jacqueline Sanders (1977) has written, ". . . forces we do not usually attend to have as strong an effect on our minds and on the minds we are trying to influence as forces to which we normally attend."

By "emotional experience," I do not mean attitudes, thoughts, or concepts which a teacher may hold about a child, or vice-versa: These are primarily cognitive. "Emotional experience" refers to the actual feelings a person has in relation to attitudes, concepts, persons, or events. There seems to be a general consensus among investigators of emotion that humans possess a relatively small set of discrete emotional states (Ekman, et al., 1972; Izard, 1971; Tomkins, 1962). Our "basic" emotions include enjoyment, interest, excitement, surprise, fear, sadness, disgust, shame, and anger. There is evidence that the facial expressions which correspond to each of these emotions are present in newborns or very young infants (Charlesworth & Kreutzer, 1973), and they have been observed to occur in a wide range of cultural and ethnic groups

1

(Eibl-Eibesfeldt, 1971). Emotions are transitory phenomena, and any attempt to consider them in the educational process requires a level of analysis which is more fine grained than the level of analysis to which we refer when discussing terms like attitude, concept, or value. Emotions are the phenomenological building blocks of our more enduring conceptions of "self" and "other."

In this discussion, I have delineated three areas in which to explore some of the emotional factors in the educational process. One major area of emotional experience in the classroom is related to the child's response to the content of what is being taught. Any novel situation, and in particular a situation in which new information and ideas are being presented, may evoke strong emotional reactions ranging from excitement to fear. These reactions, and the way in which they are handled by the teacher, may influence learning and retention. The second, and perhaps the most important area, is the set of feelings which are inherent in the teacher-child relationship. These feelings—both the teacher's and the child's—cannot help influencing what is learned, what is taught, and what is retained. Finally, emotion enters into the classroom as content. Most adults believe, whether they admit it or not, that it is "good" for children to experience strong emotions—both positive and negative—in a protective context, in order to learn about the self and about the self's ability to feel and to cope with the vicissitudes of life.

Unfortunately, even when these areas of emotion are pointed out, they are rarely elaborated in a way that would be useful to teachers. In their recent text, McClinton and Meier (1978) suggest that ". . . the most widely read child-care authorities agree on several points, notably a child's needs for loving attention, interesting surroundings, respect, discipline and freedom of emotional expression." In this paper I hope to provide some theory and research which supports and elaborates this frequently expressed viewpoint.

EMOTIONAL ASPECTS OF EXPOSURE TO NEW SITUATIONS

Psychologists have long been aware that it is impossible to separate cognition and affect. Each step in the intellectual process of approaching and solving a problem is accompanied by a unique kind of emotional experience. For example, when something attracts our attention and we orient ourselves to that event, the affect we feel is interest—and possibly excitement. If a problem is too difficult, we may feel frustrated or angry; if it is threatening, we may feel afraid or bored; and if we solve it, we feel enjoyment and satisfaction.

Does it make a difference to learning whether the child experiences fear, frustration, or enjoyment as a result of an encounter with new content? How can we tell which emotions are likely to arise from a given task or from a particular child? While a major determinant of our own knowledge about a specific child's tolerance for novelty and stress is our prior experience with that child, there are two general principles, fairly well substantiated by recent research, about the environment-affect relationship. One principle has to do with the child's *familiarity* with the new content: How novel or discrepant does the task appear to the child? The other principle is related to the *context* in which the new content is presented: Who presents it, where it is presented, and when (in relation to other content and other events) it is presented.

The first factor, discrepancy vs. familiarity of new material, has been studied in great detail by Jerome Kagan. His studies have focused on children aged zero to five years, but his findings reveal a universal process of human cognition which seems to hold for all ages. According to the findings of Kagan and his colleagues (1978), people become interested and attentive to new information when it is "moderately" discrepant from past experience. If an event—and this could be any kind of stimulus event such as touch, smell, sight, or sound; words, pictures, or real objects—is too novel or completely unfamiliar, the child will not attend to it for very long. If the event is very familiar or identical to what has been experienced before, the child will not attend to it. So children are interested by a moderate level of novelty; they may be bored or frustrated with the same old stuff while they may be afraid of or simply ignore things which are completely new. *The emotion which results from a learning situation depends, in part, on the match between the child's ability and the complexity-familiarity of the task.*

Daniel Stern and his colleagues (1977) discovered that mothers of young infants capitalized on this universal property of human cognition by organizing their behavior into what he called "themes" and "variations." In talking to her infant, a mother will repeat herself many times, either in word or gesture, but the repetitions will not be exact replicas of what went on before. For example, during early face-to-face interaction, the mother of a three-month-old may say "Hi, Christy"; "Hi"; "Christy, Hi"; "Hi!!" in rapid sequence. As she moves from one phrase to the next, there are subtle variations in intensity, pitch, tone, and facial expression. Stern deduced that these variations helped keep the infant's attention at an optimal level. In a peek-a-boo game, the mother of a one-year-old infant will perform all sorts of variations on the main theme of hiding: She may hide her own face and peek out over her hands, from the side, or from between her fingers; or she may hide the infant's face. She may use a variety of objects to hide behind, and she may vary her posture, gesture, and intonation so that no two actions are identical.

One way to look at this is to say that the attention span of infants and young children is very short, and that, therefore, one needs to provide them with a continuous assortment of novel (but not too novel) tasks and variants in order to keep up their interest. In effect, this view defines the teacher's role as that of providing materials to keep the child busy. I do not like this interpretation for two reasons. The first is that it obscures a universal aspect of cognition. The child's cognitive processes, at least according to Kagan, are no different from those of the adult; they are simply somewhat less versatile, somewhat shorter in span, but essentially no different. This concept of sameness between the adult and child facilitates, I think, the adult's ability to identify with the child, and identification is the basis of the adult's ability to empathically tune in to the child's personal experiences (Olden, 1953). The second reason is that this view ignores the emotional aspects of the learning experience. Phrases like "keeping the child busy," "giving the child something to do," "providing materials," "themes and variations" are descriptive of behaviors and actions which the teacher or anyone can observe. By far the more important aspect of the situation is the child's emotional relationship to those materials, themes, and variants. Interest, satisfaction, self-confidence, distress, and fear do seem to be the building blocks of the child's personal experience in learning situations. Kagan's research illustrates that the objective, material qualities of objects and actions are important only insofar as the child can personally relate to them.

It is no less important to understand teachers' emotional experiences in relation to their role as providers of educational materials, one of which may be themselves. There are times when the child's growing enjoyment and satisfaction can produce feelings of self-confidence in the teacher. At these times the teacher hardly notices how much effort is involved in keeping up the rapid-fire pace that children require. But teachers live not only in the child's world but also in the adult's world, which often brings its own set of frustrations and fears, some of which may come from the children. In particular, the very fact of having to keep up the pace, day after day, can itself lead to boredom, frustration, and resentment. I think it is these kinds of feelings which create the conditions under which a teacher may perceive the learning process as nothing more than the arrangement and rearrangement of an endless set of materials. One fortunate aspect of the more open early childhood curricula is the freedom teachers have in changing routines for their own amusement and interest. These variations, very much a part of the adults' desire for cognitive enhancement and enjoyment, feed back into the educational process as a part of emotional refueling; and teachers' liveliness, interest, concern, and affection all help to strengthen the emotional ties between themselves and the children. We shall return to this theme in the next section.

The second major principle regarding the child's emotional relationship to new content is that the *learning context plays a role in the child's evaluation of the content.* Part of the reason for this is that the young child has difficulty disassociating the event from the context in which the event occurs (Piaget, 1973). A classic study which illustrates this phenomenon was done by L.A. Sroufe and his colleagues (1974) with ten-month-old infants. In one experimental condition the infant's mother entered a room in which the infant was sitting. The mother behaved normally in every respect, but she was wearing a mask. This produced a great deal of laughter in the infant. Laughing, like smiling, has been shown to be a reliable index of a positive assimilation of a moderately discrepant event (Kagan et al., 1978; Sroufe & Waters, 1976). In a second experimental condition, after the mother left the room an adult female entered who was unknown to the infant but otherwise friendly. She wore the same mask that the mother had worn; in this condition infants showed fear and distress. Sroufe argued that the mask in the context of the mother was moderately discrepant and therefore enjoyable, but in the context of the stranger, the mask became an object of fear.

Mary Ainsworth and her colleagues (1978) have developed the concept of the mother as the "secure base" from which an infant can explore the world. In her studies, infants from one to three years are better able to play with toys and to explore a strange setting when the mother (or father, or caregiver, or familiar person) is present. If an unfamiliar person enters and the mother leaves, the child ceases to play. A number of psychologists have discovered that some people seem to be better able to learn and create in situations which are familiar and comfortable and in which they feel free from distraction. The importance of these ideas to the present discussion is that they suggest that young children's ability to learn is in large measure a result of their perception of the setting in which learning is to take place.

This is not to say that in "positive" settings learning would always be an enjoyable experience. Mastery can be accompanied by feelings of pain, distress, and frustration. Part of the role of a protective environment is to provide encouragement and support to facilitate the learning process. It is a myth that as children get older they develop a greater tolerance for the frustrations of learning and mastery. Children of all ages experience the same kinds of feelings over and over, each time they are required to learn new material which is challenging. It is also true that some children can learn in the worst of circumstances—in conditions of physical or emotional duress and under extreme forms of discouragement (Rutter, 1979). These "invulnerable" children present a challenge to any simplistic notions about "good" environments for learning. The point is that the contextual factors which affect learning are different for each child and that the same situation can produce a different emotional experience for each child.

Teachers play a major role in the choice of new material, in the sequence of presentation, and in the manner in which it is presented. Ideally, each of these three variables—what to teach, when, and how—should change as a function of the age and temperament of the individual child. Unfortunately, the discrepancy theory and the contextual theory are general statements; they do not provide any insight about the specific aspects of objects, behavior, or environment which will attract a particular child. The process of selecting such variables is often an unconscious or intuitive activity, but it is important to be clear about this: The good teacher organizes materials, sequence, and setting in such a way as to optimize the child's level of emotional arousal to balance interest against fear and enjoyment against frustration. Creating the "right" emotional conditions is the path toward gaining access to the child's capacity for learning.

EMOTIONAL ASPECTS OF THE TEACHER-CHILD RELATIONSHIP

The teacher is of central importance in the pre-school classroom. Through the use of learning materials and contexts, he or she mediates the child's emotional experiences related to learning. Consequently, the child comes to depend upon the teacher for support, encouragement, and stimulation. Young children may not even separate the teacher's learning-related activities from caregiving functions, and ordinarily the child develops a strong attachment to this adult over a period of time. The teacher can and does serve the function of giving emotional support and encouragement when the parent is absent. Recent research shows, however, that the child's attachment to the parent is much stronger and more lasting than attachment to the teacher (Kagan et al., 1978), even in situations in which children spend a great deal more time with professional caregivers than with parents (Fox, 1977).

In a study by Ricciuti (1974), toddlers were observed in stressful and nonstressful situations in the presence of their mothers and/or their caregivers. It was found that children preferred their mothers to the caregivers, when given a choice, in a stressful situation. If there were no choice, the same children unhesitatingly approached the caregiver for comfort. In nonstressful situations, the same children were able to explore a new environment in the presence of the caregiver in much the same way that they would if the mother were present.

This latter phenomenon—the ability of young children to explore new environments or objects in the presence of parents or familiar persons, but not usually in their absence—is well known to students of early attachment. In the Ainsworth (1978) studies referred to above, this is described as the attachment-exploration balance. According to Ainsworth, some infants seem to be able to explore new settings freely—not by ignoring the mother, but on the contrary by soliciting help and affection when needed, and by making independent moves out into the environment, using the mother as a "secure base." These infants, whom Ainsworth has called "securely attached," seem to be able to express their emotions freely and show competence at learning. Ainsworth also identified two other groups of infants. One group stayed very close to the mother in new situations and showed a good deal of anxiety. They could not freely explore, nor did they seem able to derive comfort from their mother's presence and contact. A third group tended to ignore their mothers and spend all of their time engaged with the new toys. Their play, however, was not creatively exploratory, but rather consisted of banging, hitting, and using objects inappropriately. Ainsworth called both of these groups "insecurely attached," and she postulated a link between the infant's relationship to the mother and his or her ability to engage creatively in exploration and learning about new things.

The findings of Ainsworth, Kagan, and Ricciuti, when taken together, suggest that children's attachment to the teacher may be an essential ingredient in their overall orientation to the learning process. Although there are few studies which directly compare individual differences in teacher-child relationships with classroom achievement, the attachment literature does imply a relationship between the two.

Some studies with adults indicate the same general relationship between attachment and learning. Schachter (1959) suggested that uncertainty or ambiguous situations which produce feelings of anxiety can lead one to affiliate with other individuals for help in evaluating one's own situation in order to determine an appropriate response. According to Schachter, since emotions are partly cognitive (a point which I discussed in the previous section), they require, like opinions and attitudes, "social evaluation when the emotion producing situation is ambiguous or uninterpretable in terms of past experience." More recent research has shown that both uncertainty and fear are emotions which usually lead to affiliation (other emotions, such as enjoyment, may lead to affiliation but not as consistently as does fear), and furthermore that affiliation seems to work to reduce fear and distress even in adults (Cottrell & Epley, 1977). This is consistent with Ainsworth's notion of the mother as the "secure base" for exploration.

Learning is a situation in which feelings of uncertainty are generated: How should I hold the brush? Is this the way you make a dog? Do turtles lay eggs? Given that children have feelings of uncertainty, would they not prefer to be with others who are more like themselves—peers, perhaps, who are experiencing the same kinds of uncertainty? Why would children be attracted to teachers for reduction of anxiety? Mettee & Smith (1977) conclude that "comparison information derived from dissimilar others can be more valuable for purposes of self-evaluation accuracy and favorability needs, and therefore evoke greater attraction, than comparison information derived from similar others." Thus children may be drawn to teachers by virtue of their dissimilarity —their greater ability to comfort the child as compared to peers, and because of the prior relationship between the teacher and child which, if we can make an inference from related research, includes elements of familiarity and security.

Recognition that children develop emotional ties to their teachers does not clarify how a teacher should behave in this regard. What are the best ways to foster this kind of attachment? How should the teacher handle children's dependence and independence? Unfortunately, these issues are complex and require a treatment which is beyond the scope of this paper. There is a large body of research on the relationship between parents' behavior and the cognitive, social, and emotional development of their children (see, for example, Clarke-Stewart, 1977). In another paper I have sketched out in some detail the nature of the teacher-child interactions which involve expressions of empathy and mutual affection (Fogel, 1980). In the following paragraphs, I will try to cover the basic premises which, I think, underlie the emotional dimensions of the teacher-child relationship.

First, *human interaction which involves the mutual expression of emotion requires, optimally, the use of empathy.* In order to be empathic we need to be able to experience what another person is feeling, but not only that. We also have to be aware of our own feelings—for example, how the other person is affecting us, how we feel about helping or ignoring the other person, and how we happen to have been feeling before we encountered the other person—in order to be able to make an evaluation of the situation. Cognitive evaluation is as essential to empathy as emotional sensitivity: i.e., we must be able to judge how best to respond to the child given a host of factors including present feelings, the child's and our own, past experience with this child, experience with children in general, and the current social ethos of the society or school (Olden, 1953). This very broad definition of empathy can encompass not only directly meeting children's needs, but also setting limits on children through various kinds of discipline techniques (Fogel, 1980).

Second, *because teachers and children are at different stages of emotional and intellectual maturity, there is a marked asymmetry in the mutuality of empathic understanding.* Mature empathy, at least as I have discussed it in the previous paragraph, requires both emotional experiences and cognitive sophistication. At the very least empathy requires (to use Piagetian language) formal operational thinking. This is because another person's emotions are abstract entities which we cannot experience directly. We have to be able to hold in active memory our impressions about what we think the other feels and at the same time what we ourselves are feeling; and then we must be able to compare these two sources of feeling in relation to each other (reversibility) in order to make an appropriate evaluation. (See Olden, 1953, for a description of this mental oscillation between self and other or between various courses of action, which is characteristic of the empathic process.)

Since formal operational thinking, or the ability to mentally manipulate abstract entities in a reversible manner, does not even begin until adolescence, it would be unreasonable to expect that children could exhibit mature empathy for adults. There are times, however, when children act in ways which seem empathic. Children at very young ages will commonly go to the aid of other children or express affection and comfort to others in ways which are entirely appropriate to the situation.

Hoffman (1975) believes that children are born with mechanisms which automatically orient them to the distress of another person. Newborns will begin to cry when they hear the cry of another infant, a one-year-old child upon seeing another person who is sad may try to comfort that person in the same way in which the child is accustomed to being comforted, for example by offering a toy or a hug. Hoffman believes that these kinds of altruistic reactions are based on a cognitive egocentrism: The child seems to be experiencing the other's distress as if it were his or her own and reacting in ways that he or she would find comforting. This kind of response also presupposes that children think that everyone will be comforted in the same manner as themselves.

Yarrow and Waxler (1975) have observed similar behavior in preschool age children. They found that there are individual differences in the way children react to the distress of others and that such individual differences seem to persist over time. Thus a two-year-old who is very sensitive to another's cry might cover her ears, while at seven years the same child might verbally express her discomfort by saying "I just can't stand that crying." Another child who at two offered his own bottle or blanket to comfort another might later express verbal support such as "don't cry" or "what's wrong?" Other children react to another's distress in aggressive ways such as pushing or hitting at someone who takes a toy away from a sibling, or attacking an adult who is trying to discipline the child's friend or sibling. Each of these forms of expression indicates that children are highly sensitive to the distress of others, and each child reacts in a unique way. Children may be similarly sensitive to other kinds of emotions, but there is little published research on their responses.

It is clear that children, in these early, "pre-empathic" reactions, have not considered all of the constraints of the situation; they seem to be responding rather directly to their own immediate reactions to the other's distress. As children get older and mature cognitively, these early reactions become integrated into a lasting sense of their own and the other person's identity. However, since the love and affection that young children develop for the teacher is likely to be of a qualitatively different nature than the teacher's love for the child, the burden of empathic understanding and genuine emotional support in the pre-school years falls heavily on the early childhood educator.

EXPOSURE TO EMOTIONS FOR THEIR OWN SAKE

In the previous sections I argued that affect was inseparable from cognitive learning so that teachers' awareness of learning-related emotional experience should enhance their ability to teach new concepts. Often, however, teachers find it desirable to expose children to an emotional experience for its own intrinsic value. This is a tactic that raises a good deal of controversy. Most adults would agree that it is valuable to make children smile and laugh, to experience enjoyable feelings. But should we deliberately scare or shame children? Should we try to make them angry or sad with the same zest we use to make them laugh? When the questions are posed in this manner, it is difficult to answer in the affirmative because of the lack of specificity of the context of such learning. If we were intentionally to have the teacher be the object of the child's anger or sadness, we would be defeating our purpose of creating an atmosphere of trust and faith between teacher and child.

In the proper setting, however, the exposure to strong emotions can be an educational experience, and it can be extremely rewarding for both teacher and child. Such an emotional setting would involve play and fantasy—much like the experience we have when we watch a fine movie. A good film, in my view, is one that moves us deeply, one in which we can identify with the protagonist so completely that we share all the sadness, fear, anger and joy of that character's life.

What is it about a good film that allows us to feel powerful, even very negative feelings, and still leave the theater feeling more a complete person than before we went in? Partly it is that the film is not real; it is entirely in the realm of the imaginary. Even if we get so caught up in the experience that we believe for a moment that it is real, we don't ordinarily panic because we know that it will end in a short time; we know we will get up and walk out. A second part of the success of a film has to do with the relative ease of discussing our feelings about the film with other people. It is much easier to share openly our very strong feelings about a movie than it is to share the more personal and real feelings of everyday life. And yet, to talk openly about the movie-related experiences is to talk, at least symbolically, about our own life. After all, we bring our own unique form of perceiving and experiencing from real life into the theater, and we tend to take from the film that which we most need to feel at the moment. The best films allow us figuratively to see ourselves in them, but in a way which is not threatening or aversive.

By analogy, stories and imaginary play can serve the same functions for children. Bruno Bettleheim, in his book *On the Uses of Enchantment* (1977), argues persuasively for this view. He contends that the most important feature of a children's story is that the main character is one with whom the child is able to identify. On the basis of that identification, the child is carried through a series of emotional experiences. Using fairy tales as the model of the "best" kind of story, Bettleheim shows how the story and characters in the fairy tale provide images which suggest some of the beliefs and feelings of the young child. A complex feeling such as ambivalence toward a parent is represented in the story as a clear division between good and bad—the fairy godmother vs. the wicked stepmother. This kind of separation between good and bad aspects of the same person seems artificial to adults. We would like the child to see that each individual is a complex mixture of both good and bad feelings and to appreciate the full mystery and tragedy of life. But according to research on the subject, children are cognitively incapable of integrating the "good" part of an adult with the "bad" part. They may know that the adult at times acts kindly and at other times is mean, but they have not yet established in their world of perception that the adult preserves a continuous identity across all of these transformations. This is because children, until they reach nine to twelve years of age, do not have a continuous and lasting sense of their own identity (Hoffman, 1975).

According to Bettleheim, the fairy tale or story does not *create* strong feelings in the child. The child already has such feelings and the story is constructed in such a way that the child identifies his or her own emotional history in the story. The end result is that the child feels comforted and secure at the end of the story, much like the cathartic experience of the adult after a good movie. The happy ending to the fairy tale also provides the child with a sense of hope that things will ultimately work out. The happy ending may seem unrealistic to an adult who realizes that life does not always work out so neatly, but for the child, the resolution is a necessary protection from that kind of reality.

It is precisely that clear separation of the story from reality which makes it work so well. Although adults can enjoy being torn apart in the theater because they know the experience is not real and will end, children tend to believe the story to be true and real and even part of themselves. Thus, unreality must be systematically built into the story. The happy ending is one way and the opening lines—"Once upon a time . . ." or "A long, long time ago . . ."—help children separate themselves from the actual events of the story (Bettleheim, 1977).

Games, teasing, and joking serve very similar functions for the child. Instead of a story, adults may create a play situation in which they take on a different identity momentarily, and then quickly return to normal. In infancy, the "peek-a-boo" game and the mask game, described earlier, are examples of this activity. The adult creates a situation in which the child experiences a temporary and controlled feeling of loss or fear, after which a very positive emotion follows: The adult appears from behind the mask or out of the hiding place. To use Bettleheim's reasoning, the adult is not creating these feelings out of nothing. Rather, the adult is bringing to the surface the distress and fear which the child already has and may be secretly harboring: The fear and pain of the thought of the adult's loss. When older children imagine, and even sometimes secretly wish for, their parent's or teacher's death, they are trying to deal with their fear of the event. Such fantasies often cause guilt feelings in children, and unless these feelings are dealt with in an appropriate way, the child may continue to feel bad or guilty (Kastenbaum, 1972). The stories and games may help the child to understand that these are acceptable and natural feelings.

With older children, adults play games involving mock emotions: Play fighting, play chasing, tickling, and teasing are some examples. Adults also feign sadness, disdain or anger. Willing credulity leads the child into feeling temporarily those same kinds of emotions or their counterparts. As noted earlier, when an adult pretends to be hurt, a pre-school child will attempt to comfort the adult in the same way that the child has been comforted in the past (Hoffman, 1975). But the adult controls the extent to which the child experiences the feeling and can break out of the game at any moment—with a smile or a hug—before it gets too serious for the child.

Peer play provides even more opportunities for children to dramatize and experience their feelings. Children seem to have a way of regulating the level of affect of their encounters, but fights and hurt feelings often ensue. Here, the teacher must step in to provide the necessary amount of unreality, in essence providing a firm control over the extent to which the children are to carry out their emotional play.

Because emotional experience depends in part on how events and feelings are interpreted, children are in the process of learning what, when, and how to feel. This kind of emotional education is often not made explicit or planned, yet it is perhaps the most pervasive, since the history a child has with respect to a particular feeling will contribute to the interpretation of that feeling. Sylvan Tomkins has written:

> Any affect may be learned to be activated by any object. We may learn to be afraid of anything under the sun, or to be excited by everything we encounter. (1962, p. 324)

Tomkins goes on to explain that sometimes experiences can work to enhance affective states, and at other times they can cause a reduction in or withdrawal from affect. He argues that through control of the child's emotions, socialization for adulthood reduces affect. For example, "if, whenever a child expresse[s] its curiosity and excitement by shouting, this disturb[s] the parents, and the child [is] then shamed into silence, activation of excitement in general can become the activator of the shame response, which thereby reduces the excitement before it can become intense or enduring." This can work to the child's benefit; for example, a child may "learn that whenever one feels distress, another individual will do something to comfort one and thus reduce the feeling of distress" (Tomkins, 1962).

This kind of emotional learning is a constant partner to children's learning of content. The two are inseparable, since nearly all learning in the pre-school occurs in relation to adults and other children. Rather than relegating such essential components of the learning process to secondary, or, worse, unconscious levels, we need to explicitly incorporate them into our methods.

THE TEACHER'S ROLE IN AFFECTIVE EDUCATION

In the preceding sections I have tried to be as explicit as possible about the role of the adult in dealing with the emotions of the young child. Emotions can be the "subject matter" of the educational process, and they are also the natural companions of the child's behavior and cognitions. No matter how emotions arise in education, the extent to which they are understood, fully experienced, and utilized for the benefit of the child is dependent almost entirely on the behavior and attitudes of the adult. The adult's power in the affective domain rests in a large measure on the emotional bond between teacher and child. The emotional security derived from that bond will directly influence the attitudes with which the child approaches new content. Children often do "their" work in order to please the teacher. From the adult's point of view, we might say that such a child is not self-motivated. But children of preschool age have not fully separated their own desires from what they believe to be those of the teacher. To say that children work to "please" the teacher is too simplistic: It rests on the assumption that children want something in return for their efforts.

It is true that children want to feel loved and accepted, but their motivation is not deliberately contrived to win approval. It makes more sense to describe the things children do for us as gifts, genuine expressions of their love for us. Children, in giving their works to teachers or parents, are expressing pride in their efforts as well as showing us how much we mean to them. Pushing them to be self-motivated by refusing their gifts may be counterproductive; our acceptance of their love for us is a primordial educative force.

According to the psychoanalyst Heinz Kohut (1977), a number of factors become integrated over time to form the mature, healthy adult: Self-esteem, empathy, creativity, and wisdom. It seems to me that each of these terms embodies the fullest expression of the unity between affect and cognition. Self-esteem and empathy, while primarily emotional in tone, utilize higher cognitive processes such as judgment and reason. Creativity and wisdom are higher cognitive functions which, as we know from many stories and parables, must be informed by the depth of human emotion. Perhaps we can start children on the road to maturity by approaching them with the wisdom and empathy to recognize the full range of their experiences as they go about the ordinary tasks of living and learning.

REFERENCES

Ainsworth, M., Blehar, M., Waters, E. & Wall, S. *Patterns of attachment.* Hillsdale, NJ: Erlbaum, 1978.

Bettleheim, B. *The uses of enchantment.* New York: Random House, 1977.

Charlesworth, W. & Kreutzer, M. Facial expressions of infants and children. In P. Ekman (Ed.), *Darwin and facial expression,* New York: Academic Press, 1973.

Clarke-Stewart, A. *Child care in the family.* New York: Academic Press, 1977.

Cottrell, N. & Epley, S. Affiliation, social comparison, and socially mediated stress reduction. In J. Suls & R. Miller (Eds.), *Social comparison processes.* Washington, D.C.: Hemisphere Publishing Corp., 1977.

Eibl-Eibesfeldt, I. *Love and hate: The natural history of behavior patterns* (Translation by Geoffrey Strachan). New York: Holt, Rinehart and Winston, 1971.

Ekman, P., Friesen, W., & Ellsworth, P. *Emotion in the human face.* New York: Pergamon Press, 1972.

Fogel, A. On expressing affection and love to young children. *Dimensions,* 1980, *8,* 39-44.

Fox, N. Attachment of kibbutz infants to mother and metapelet. *Child Development,* 1977, *48,* 1228-1239.

Hoffman, M. L. Developmental synthesis of affect and cognition and its implications for altruistic motivation. *Developmental Psychology,* 1975, *11,* 607-622.

Izard, C. *The face of emotion.* New York: Appleton-Century-Crofts, 1971.

Kagan, J., Kearsley, R., & Zelazo, P. *Infancy: Its place in human development.* Cambridge: Harvard University Press, 1978.

Kastenbaum, R. The kingdom where nobody dies. *Saturday Review,* December, 1972.

Kohut, H. *The restoration of the self.* New York: International Universities Press, 1977.

McClinton, B., & Meier, B. *Beginnings: Psychology of early childhood.* St. Louis: C.V. Mosby, 1978.

Mettee, D., & Smith, G. Social comparison and interpersonal attraction: The case for dissimilarity. In J. Suls & R. Miller (Eds.), *Social comparison processes.* Washington, D.C.: Hemisphere Publishing Corp., 1977.

Olden, C. On adult empathy with children. *Psychoanalytic Study of the Child,* 1953, *8,* 111-126.

Piaget, J. *The child and reality.* New York: Grossman, 1973.

Ricciuti, H. Fear and the development of social attachments in the first year of life. In M. Lewis & L. Rosenblum (Eds.), *The Origins of fear.* New York: Wiley, 1974.

Rutter, M. Maternal Deprivation, 1972-1978: New findings, new concepts, new approaches. *Child Development,* 1979, *50,* 283-305.

Sanders, J. A psychoanalytic approach to early education. In J.C. Glidewell (Ed.), *The social context of learning and development.* New York: Gardner Press, 1977.

Schachter, S. *The psychology of affiliation.* Stanford, CA: Stanford University Press, 1959.

Sroufe, L. A., & Waters, E. The ontogenesis of smiling and laughter. *Psychological Review,* 1976, *83* (3), 173-189.

Sroufe, L. A., Waters, E., & Matas, L. Contextual determinants of infant affective response. In M. Lewis & L. Rosenblum (Eds.), *The origins of fear.* New York: Wiley, 1974.

Stern, D., Beebe, B., Jaffe, J., & Bennett, S. The infants' stimulus world during social interaction. In H. R. Schaffer (Ed.), *Studies in mother-infant interaction.* London: Academic Press, 1977.

Tomkins, S. *Affect, imagery and consciousness,* Vol. 1. New York: Springer, 1962.

Yarrow, M., & Waxler, C. The emergence and functions of prosocial behaviors in young children. Presented at Society for Research in Child Development, Denver, 1975.

2

A Functional Approach to Language Development

Anne T. McKenna
University College, Dublin, Ireland

One of the dominant figures in the field of linguistics in the past decade, Noam Chomsky, gave the first adequate explanation for the generative aspects of child language. In so doing he appeared to postulate a return to a simple nativist model of language development in which language is held to be innate, possessed by human beings solely because we are human. When phenomena are established as innate or species specific it is futile to search for influences which will promote or refine their use, and theories of language acquisition grounded on the notion of innateness offer little hope for environmental intervention.

It is now becoming clear that Chomsky's model of language acquisition may be both limited and limiting when applied to the field of early education, as an essential tenet of a teacher's belief is a faith in the importance of the environment for early development. Although Chomsky's model does account for the fact that almost all children appear to extract syntactical rules on the basis of scanty and limited exposure to a nondidactic form of language, it leaves us with the disconcerting reality that there are great differences in language ability from child to child. And so attention has now moved from the acquisition process itself, which almost all children accomplish effectively, to the *use* of these acquired language structures, which all children do *not* accomplish effectively and to which we attribute the language deficiency of many of our preschool children.

RULES OF USE

This change of attention in psycholinguistics which holds such promise for those engaged in early education is a change of emphasis from what has been called the *rules of usage* to the *rules of use,* or a change of emphasis from the rules of syntactical competence to the rules of knowing what to do with language in order to communicate effectively and appropriately (Widdowson, 1979). We might be inclined to think from our experience with other kinds of skills, such as playing bridge or chess, that the child learns the rules and, having learned them, goes on to learn how to apply them. But in what sense is the person who has just learned the rules of the game a good player? The real skill lies not in having knowledge of the rules, but in developing an ability to deploy these in a variety of situations, to create strategies while at the same time reacting and accommodating to the strategies of a partner. Just as familiarity with the use of rules, in addition to mere knowledge of the rules, separates the good from the bad player, so it is with language: The child who is "good at language" is the child who can identify the right occasion on which to use it, who can make language work for him or her appropriately and effectively—in a school situation and out of it (Widdowson, 1979). It is to this question of language use that we now turn our attention rather than to the acquisition of rule-governed sentences or correct speech in young children.

The chronological sequence of learning of rules followed by the application of these rules is one which might be challenged in explanation of language acquisition. In a sense we do not learn the rules first and then put them to use, but just the converse. It is more like being thrown unprepared into a game, and, by dint of playing well or badly, slowly picking up the rules. The infant in the first years of life, having acquired great skill in interacting with others in the family (that is, knowing the nonverbal rules for interacting), picks up very easily the verbal ones that accompany them. As one linguist puts it, children *learn to mean* before they *learn to speak* and only learn to speak because they have first learned to mean (Halliday, 1975).

For instance, if we observe 1-year-old children, it is clear that they are aware that the world is made up of people and nonpeople; that people have plans and intentions but objects in the environment do not; that you can regulate other people by crying or cajoling; but that this is wasted on the cat or the table. These fine existential distinctions pre-date the use of language and indeed are probably the major causative factors in its onset. Building on the ability to recognize "the other" and seeing this other as something that can be communicated with, the child first uses language for the social purpose of interacting with and regulating other people as well as for the purpose of getting them to do what the child wants (Halliday, 1975). In a previous paper I used the analogy of language being the old shoe which the child slips into with ease and familiarity (McKenna, 1977). It fits the child's needs so comfortably for the simple reason that it was made to fit these same needs when it was first created. Its structure is matched to, is isomorphic with, the structure of the nonverbal interaction the child is already engaged upon. For example, recognition of the separateness from others is mirrored in language by the device of switching from "me" to "you" depending on the speaker. Further recognition of another's perspective is signaled linguistically by what are called deictic terms of "this" which becomes "that" or "here" which becomes "there," depending on who is speaking and who is listening. Yet another comfortable fit can be seen between the child's competence in asking, ordering, or pleading and the linguistic device of changed intonation or change of grammatical mood. Language to the child has an almost *deja vu* feeling when first encountered because it was created by our first speaking ancestors from the same mental categories—to suit the same social needs as those possessed by every child and every adult.

LANGUAGE AS DECONTEXTUALIZATION

Language therefore largely derives from social interaction and in its beginning is inextricably bound up with the here and now of such interaction. Nevertheless, its development as a tool of adult thinking and communication depends on its becoming free of any context, of any here and now elements. The decontextualization of language means a lessening of dependency on other, nonverbal aspects of the situation in which communication is happening, like time, place, present perceptual evidence, and—most important—the rush of things inside one's own head. For one of the most constraining here and now elements that the child has to contend with is his or her own private thinking. It is constraining because the child has to learn to make it public for the other person; to specify what is in his or her head for the benefit of others who cannot be privy to this domain of knowledge; to signal to them when previously unmentioned and therefore new knowledge is coming up; to recognize old information that speaker and listener can be assumed to share; and to recognize information that is old because it was mentioned earlier in the conversation. Knowing of the separate existence of the other person and being able to take up the other's perspective is a necessary prerequisite for launching on the language journey. But learning the numerous intricacies and nuances which detail this distinction is a long road which entails gaining control of many linguistic devices which allow you to specify what is in your head for the benefit of others (or by lying to specify *other* than what you are really thinking), until eventually language becomes communicable to anyone at any time. In other words, language and language alone comes to bear the full burden of communication, without gestural, intonational and situational props, culminating in the act of pure linguistic communication as in writing.

It is likely that these linguistic feats are accomplished by the same mental mechanism used in gaining an operational concept of number. As Piaget describes, children learn to "count" by slowly learning to "discount" such irrelevancies as spatial displacement, size, or any other perceptual attributes of the array. As with language we might say that by taking cognizance of their own momentary and idiosyncratic viewpoints, and by degrees slowly cancelling this out of the equation, children are transforming subjective appearance into objective concept. In learning both number and language structure, children take account of their own perspective and view it as one of any number of perspectives; thereby they are able to speak and count as if the private domain did not exist, and therefore they are able to make the private public and communicable.

In a recent study at my own university, we tried to help children appreciate where their private thoughts began and ended, examining the changes brought about by our intervention.[1] Simply put, we compared the children's ability to tell their teacher a story from a picture, under two conditions: (1) when both teacher and child were looking at the picture; and (2) when only the child was looking at the picture, due to the fact that the teacher had her "sore eyes" bandaged. Subjects were a group of 4-year-old children from a disadvantaged background. A previous study had shown that when the picture was perceptually accessible to a child alone, the child produced more complex and compound sentences as opposed to strings of juxtaposed words (Bokus, 1978). Our study examined the nature of these changes, analyzing some of them in detail. We noted that in the situation of nonshared perception, the child strived, and with some success, to speak more explicitly and less ambiguously. The following is an example of a disambiguating phrase which helped to identify information for the blindfolded listener:

/ and a woman *that was looking in the shop,* looked too /
or the following self-correction which helped to clarify the referent:
/ it s/c the cat was looking /.
(self-correction)

Also it was noted that children used the adult device of anaphoric reference, that is, of introducing a new topic by the indefinite article "a" followed by the definite article "the" when next encountering the same topic four times as frequently in the blindfolded conditions than in the shared perception conditions, thus:

/ This day a mammy went up to the bedroom /
/ and the mammy was cross /

and again:

/ Once upon a time a boy tripped over a dog /
/ And he throwed his ball on the dog /

These examples from a nonshared situation show the child's sure control over the mechanisms for introducing new and old information. The use of the in-

---

[1] For details of this and following examples, apply to Department of Psychology, University College, Dublin, Ireland.

definite article in "a dog" introduces this dog as one of many others that it might have been, whereas the switch to the definite article in the next line has a co-referential function in which "the dog" refers to the one just introduced. Likewise, "he" and "his" in the second line also refer to "a boy" unspecified but now identified as the same as the previously mentioned one. Thus in two short utterances we can see how words come to be based on a series of shared assumptions and rules for cooperating in conversation as well as a number of devices for the "stitching together" of text.

Our results show the reserves of skill possessed by socially disadvantaged children in the difficult art of telling and maintaining a good story. It has been suggested that one of the main reasons that children from disadvantaged homes are poor at language is that they fail to recognize their listeners' communicative needs (De Villiers, 1978). This study would appear to show that they are in no way insensitive to these needs, but that they do require extra assistance in recognizing them. For example, they may not respond to the usual need of the teacher of "playing with words," which is what most language lessons really are, but will respond to the teacher when she has a real need, like not being able to see. (It is interesting that on subsequent days, the mothers of these children enquired about the teacher's eye condition, showing that the children had regarded the episode as newsworthy—probably because they felt they had played an active part in helping the teacher.) This study does not give any evidence of whether socially disadvantaged children are better or worse than their counterparts from more privileged socioeconomic backgrounds, but it does show how some of the children were influenced by a changed context which enabled them to call on their own resources and competencies when they perceived a real need for communication. We had managed to create good and bad conditions for the telling of picture stories, and we had identified the good condition. The same child with the same teacher could in fact substantially alter his or her language output when perceiving a meaning and an urgency in the situation. The children in the conditions of shared perception were performing at an inferior level because they presumed that since *some* information was shared, *all* information was shared. Here the discourse lost its communicative intent since the child was led into the trap of believing that since the adult could see the picture, she could also see inside the child's mind. To revert to an earlier distinction, the child possessed the rules of usage, syntactical as well as textual, but needed an opportunity to put these rules to use. We now go further and make the claim (a claim that awaits empirical substantiation) that by giving the children an opportunity to put these rules to use—of having their competence exercised and stretched as it were—we were in fact altering that competence and making the children more assured of the rules. For as we noted earlier, learning the use to which language is put is not merely a by-product of knowing the language, but the most essential, most difficult, and most needed exercise of these preschool years. The children do not merely learn a language and then use it on every possible occasion, but rather vice versa.

They see language working for themselves and for others, and through this they learn its structure and its meaning.

What are the implications of stressing the functional aspects of language and how do we create meaningful situations which afford an opportunity for the exercise of language competency? The first and most simple answer to this question is that we do not need to create such situations in the classroom: They are all around us awaiting our exploitation. Every nursery day provides opportunities for informal interaction between child and teacher—at snack or toileting time, hanging up coats, changing shoes, and doing all the other business of the day's living. Just as the young child learned to speak by learning to mean and to interact with the others in the environment, so too there are many meaningful and familiar situations in which the child is an expert, or interested in becoming one, such as tying laces, fetching a snack, getting ready for "home time," and all the other rituals of school life. And just as with the infant who learns to mean before learning to speak, so it is with the 4-year-old: It is likely that it is out of these familiar and intelligible situations that language will most easily emerge. These are the pivotal activities for language lessons and not mere accidental trimmings to the school day. They have a meaning which is clear to the child, and language under such circumstances comes easily.

Once we fully grasp the principle that language is created and strengthened against a background of living expression, our daily nursery practice takes on a new meaning. For example, allowing children to talk about what has happened at home or outside, asking them for news that we could not have heard but for them, gives them a real feeling of communication. If a child knows something that the adult cannot know and senses a corresponding curiosity on the adult's part, the conditions are set for good conversation. It is in this light, too, that we must examine the question and answer procedures of the classroom. Most frequently the meaning of such exchanges is that of the child guessing what is going on inside the adult-questioner's mind. We know and accept that the eventual mode of teacher-pupil interaction is likely to be that of questioning leading to one particular answer (Sinclair & Coulthard, 1975), but we might ponder the advisability of such a question and answer technique with children of 4-, 5-, and 6 years coming fresh and unschooled from home. True, questions are asked at home, but children ask them of adults just as often as adults ask them of children. What is more, they are always asked on both sides to build up a conjoint meaning in which both are contributing some part. The classroom question and answer session starts off from a plan or strategy in the teacher's head, often from a curriculum plan laid out on a page that can be seen in the mind's eye. For the teacher it has both context and intention: The context of a term's work and the intention of getting from point A to point B. But the children cannot see the plan or strategy along which the adult is progressing, so the situation lacks context and intention for them. It comes out of nowhere and disappears at the end of the lesson, and the children are not quite sure why they are going through this session beyond the conversational rule of trying to follow discourse that is directed their way. Is it any wonder that under such circumstances the children's language often deteriorates to a listless monosyllable and they fail to produce at the level of their true competence?

METALINGUISTIC ACTIVITIES

Much of the life of school is likely to be perceived by children as being of the kind in which it will not make any difference whether one speaks or keeps quiet; a given child's intervention will make no substantial impact. It is likely that the lack of any substantial verbal interaction between teacher and children from disadvantaged homes springs from the fact that, unlike the child in the blindfolded situation, the child in the typical classroom sees no meaningful part to play. Sociolinguists have told us that the children's language is the means by which they are socialized. If the home background is such that conversation is reserved for the utilitarian purposes of eating or sleeping, of switching on or off television, with little manipulation of speech and language for its own sake, for story telling or making verbal games, then the latter activity is not seen to have any use or meaning for the child. A child from such a background has no experience in using words and speech for these purposes or of seeing anyone else do so. Insofar as it is just these same activities of story telling, speech manipulation, and talking about speech which characterize the nursery school day, children from disadvantaged backgrounds will tend to perceive these activities as alien. When young children leave home to enter the world of preschool, they have two considerable adaptions to make: One is to the new group life, in which each child is sharing an adult with a large number of other children rather than having the exclusive attention of an adult as at home; the second is the school way of talking and dealing with talk. But there are many homes where parents, for part of the day at least, do engage in a variety of speech activities, and by giving their children practice in these activities, encourage them to try a variety of speech roles, such as whispering, saying prayers, telling a story, saying a poem, having a little chat, or just "speaking nicely." It would appear that the more home is like school in this way—that is, in giving practice in a variety of speech roles—the easier it is for the child to adapt to school and to the school way of using talk—although the less the child needs to adapt. The more home is unlike school, the more difficult it becomes to switch to alternative speech roles for lack of practice in, for example, switching from whispering to story telling—and the more the child needs to adapt.

Most of our language lessons, and indeed much of our other verbal exchanges in school, are of the type "Say this after me," "Now you tell me a story," "Give Mary a chance to speak." These are what has been described as metalinguistic activities, or talking about talk rather than communicating by means of talk (Mattingly, 1972). We have suggested that some children may hear very little of similar kinds of activity in their own homes. However, it is known that in many homes children as young as 3, and even 2, are beginning to talk about language. Whenever children talk about what you can say or cannot say, what is a "nice thing to say" or a "bad thing to say," they are engaged in metalinguistic activities: They are talking about language instead of by means of language. The following example shows how a 3-year-old makes language usage the subject of discussion. Adult and child are sitting in a relaxed mood, leafing through the pages of a picture book.

C.	Will I read this?	A.	Yes please
C.	(Pretending to read)		
	OK "There's no monkeys"	A.	Is there not?
C.	No, say "Why is there not?"	A.	Why is there not?
C.	Cause, cause they's only		
	Jane and Peter		

The question "Is there not?" asks only for a "yes" or "no" answer, whereas questions in English which begin with "wh" ask for a detailed reply, which in this instance the child had already prepared and intended to deliver. Language structure rather than meaning per se was the central concern in the mind of the child. I think the above example also suggests that young children, once they are embarked on a stretch of discourse, find it easier to follow their own trail rather than engage in a dialogue which demands constant adjustments of perspective and a lack of control over subsequent utterances. (It is for just this same reason that we as adults struggling along in a foreign language can prepare a beautiful phrase for execution but are baffled and disconcerted when our listener, understanding our utterance and totally taken in by the spurious level of fluency, pours forth a response at the same level of complexity.) But although children may not relish a dialogue parter who switches the lines they have written in advance, they do demand more than a sleeping partner. They need an auditor who is at least active enough to show that the message has been received. The following is one of the many stretches of dialogue from our tapes which show the irritation of the child when the adult's standards of attention fall below an acceptable level. The conversation has been going along happily for some five or six minutes, with both partners engaged in passing the ping-pong ball of conversation to and from, when, as so often happens, the adult's attention wanders off, only to be brought back sharply by the child.

	(Child looking at picture)		
C.	"What is that?" said the cow, Betty	A.	Mmmmmmm
C.	What said that brown cow?		
	(What did the brown cow say?)	A.	Mmmmmmm
C.	(answering his own question)		
	"Oh them birds," brown cow		
	(They are birds, said the brown cow)	A.	Mmmmmmm
C.	Well don't speak to me like that		
	Well I'm not your friend.		
	Oh you better not.		

And in this next stretch of dialogue, one can almost hear the satisfaction of the child as he asks for and eventually receives a "Roger over and out" assurance that his message has been received.

C.	Cows, pigs, birds, cows		
	And they liked (Graham/Grain)		
	don't they		
	Aren't they?	A.	They are
C.	Aren't they allowed to get in?	A.	They are
C.	Said "yes" Betty	A.	Pardon
C.	*"Yes"*	A.	"Yes"

It would appear that children ideally need to have an adult available to react to their speech, and being present in the same room is a different thing from being available. But the adult, if he or she wants to prolong the conversation, should not control its direction, as this results in a loss of predictability for the child. The child in the two examples above is striving hard to keep control of the tempo of the conversation, because in this way he can match the mental effort or pace the information processing to his own speed and thus can keep up the verbal exchange with skill and ease.

It might be considered that the kind of verbal interaction described above is descriptive of middle-class children or prescriptive of a one-to-one relationship with an adult, and therefore is of little relevance in the preschool situation. True, a teacher is not the middle class mother, celebrated in psychology textbooks as she brings her child from room to room while doing the housework, setting up little islands of "intersubjectivity" for interactive dialogue. But the preschool classroom is a place where play is seen as of great importance and significance in the child's development, and the kind of verbal activities we have been discussing share many of the aspects of play-in fact are considered by many to constitute verbal play. Just as in play we see an uncoupling from reality, where a doll or a towel rolled up can be a baby, so in verbal play we see an uncoupling from real meaning, an "as if" quality into which the child enters. I would venture to suggest, from my experience of listening to children on tape in a variety of settings, that opportunities like the above for talking about talk are most likely to take place where there is not a great deal of mental exercise going on, or where the information processing demanded is negligible. This would describe the child's activities in ritualized make-believe conditions. The occasions when the child is most likely to play with language appear to be during those apparently aimless and desultory exchanges between adult and child which appear to provide security and psychological space for the child to wander linguistically. We do know that children from disadvantaged social backgrounds very often have great difficulty in playing in make-believe activity. But shouldn't this deficit now be the focus of our attention? All children from all backgrounds have, at least in rudimentary form, a life of the imagination. As well as relying on the meaning of real life, the teacher can call on that second order of meaning known as make-believe and imagination, a life that may be limited by the child's background but which nevertheless is available to every normal child after the age of 12 months.

Does the foregoing argument, stressing the functional aspects of play as well as the ability of the teacher to use the child's make-believe capacity for verbal play, imply that the teacher cannot prepare in advance a program of action, but must always react to the child's behavior in a catch-as-catch-can fashion? We are now back in the familiar territory of structured versus child-centered programs. A reading of the literature and a knowledge of personnel in the field would lead us to conclude that most early educators would decline to come down on one side or the other, feeling a need for the security of a structure which allowed preparations in advance, while at the same time desiring a modicum of nonstructuring to ensure them the freedom of reacting to the needs of the children and the opportunities of the moment.

We could predict that any program which did not contain both these elements would stand little chance of surviving beyond the initial enthusiasm accompanying any novel venture. The recently published program of the United Kingdom National Foundation for Educational Research appears to contain both elements in judicious proportions (Curtis & Hill, 1978). A collaborative effort of 150 teachers plus a research team, it calls itself *My World: A Handbook of Ideas,* an obvious attempt to avoid either the suggestion of a structured prescribed program or the ad hoc effect of a series of "cook book" suggestions. The five interrelated activities of *Talking Points, Linked Activities, Individual Activities, Suggested Rhymes and Songs,* and *Users Own Ideas* center around nine themes such as *Myself, My Family, Food,* and *Clothes;* and each theme is further sub-divided into sub-themes, each of which is treated under the headings of the five interrelated activities. Each item of activity has an identifying symbol indicating the focus of development in which it is involved; thus, Self Awareness (😊); Language and Listening Skills (♫); Intellectual Development (?); Social Skills (✝✝); and Perceptual Skills (⊑⊐). This preschool program purports to be a complete curriculum rather than simply a language program, but the functional approach to language which we have been discussing could not be attempted without inclusion of at least the range of developmental skills outlined above. In summary, this program would appear to be acceptable to the demands of the preschool practitioner and to offer scope for a functional approach to language development—qualities I suggest we should demand of any language program for our preschools.

PUTTING LANGUAGE TO GOOD USE

What then might we conclude from recent psycholinguistic insights which has relevance to the preschool program? The first and most important message is that the child be allowed to use language in the creation of meaning, in working out with the adult a problem that is felt as real by both. We noted that when children had to make the system work for them in the blindfolded situation, the structure content of the system improved on several scores: Language became more precise and detailed, referential communication became more accurate and the child exercised more contextual skills. In a practical extension of this work we must examine the customary practice of arranging our classroom before a language lesson begins, so that it is laid out for pupil and adult to see. Is it possible that our practice is actually impoverishing the communicative opportunities by misleading the child into thinking that the existence of some shared information means all information is shared?

I am not quite sure of the implications of this for classroom teaching, but it might imply some questioning of our assumption that a child with nothing to say will be helped by our asking for a description of a picture, an object, or event which both we and the child can see. Instead we should seek, by all possible means, for communicative intent, where the child wants to and means to tell us something. It would also suggest that in listening to and collecting children's speech for purposes of evaluation, diagnosis, and remediation we will get different levels of complexity depending on the conditions prevailing at that time regarding the child's communicative intent.

There is one obvious conclusion to be drawn from this insistence on child and adult engaging in mutual meaningful activities; in fact it is so obvious that I hesitate to make it. It is that any administrative set-up or preschool structure which keeps the teacher from "rubbing against" the child in the course of the day is contra-indicated. If the teacher is regarded as a learning specialist or program specialist in the narrow sense, with ancillaries to do the caring task, or if the classroom numbers are so large that the teachers cannot rub shoulders with the child in the course of the day, the situation is not a promising one for the development of early language skills and their use. Any attempts to move away from the traditional model of preschool as part care and part school, as a half-way house between home and school, should be resisted on the grounds that this traditional system appears to be nearer the psycholinguistic desideratum, offering as it does a semistructured setting in which children may create their own meaning.

I have also suggested that schoolroom question and answer sessions are often totally outside the experience of the young child. When the questioner obviously knows the answer, he or she does not need any help, and supplying the answer is not going to alter the situation in any way. What children have to learn, and this takes time, is that ours is a conventionalized way of asking questions where the normal rules are suspended—a kind of game played by teacher and pupil. The trouble with question and answer games, however, is the trouble with most verbal games: They penalize the children we are most anxious to help. Children from homes with a linguistic or cultural background different from that of the school will, by definition, have difficulties in adjustment to school practice.

But children from a cultural background in which language is not a subject for discussion, to be played with and dissected, will have the added handicap of being inexpert at adjusting or switching codes. We have seen from the evidence of our tapes how children revel in the game of talking about talk, and we have tried to identify the kind of play situation where this activity might emerge. It is sometimes said that children from socially disadvantaged backgrounds are primarily in need of a structured program, having little structure or ritual in their own homes. If we add to this the fact that out of school they appear to have a great deal of time for free and unsupervised play, we might be tempted to conclude that they do not need any opportunity for classroom play. But is it possible that street games or games involving physical activity are not such rich sources for the life of the imagination as puppets, drama, and make-believe verbal games? One thing we do not know, and we need to know, is how to best foster the life of the imagination in all our children, a human accomplishment no less than that of language. In looking over the transcripts of our children's narratives, it occurred to me that it was just this aspect of language that we had failed to capture. The stretches which occasioned us the most amusement and respect, and caused us to lose sight of our count of indefinite articles, were those that sober psycholinguistic science had failed to grasp. This is not to conclude on an obscurantist note, but rather to recognize and rejoice more abundantly in the phenomenon of our children's language. For in what sense could a count of disambiguating phrases or a description of socioeconomic deprivation capture the drama of 4-year-old Edward's story:

> A little girl's mammy put the little girl in the bed
> And the teddy bear was looking
> and she was talking to the doctor and the doctor said
> "You'll have to stay in bed
> You'll have to keep that little girl in bed for two months
> Don't let her go to school and don't let her out to play
> Just, just put new pyjamas on her"
> and he went
> and that's the end of the story.

REFERENCES

Bokus, B. Effects of adult-shared versus non-shared perception of a picture on its description by the three year old child. *Polish Psychological Bulletin 9*, 1978, *4*, 239-243.

De Villiers, J. C., & De Villiers, P. *Language acquisition.* Cambridge, Mass.: Harvard University Press, 1978.

Halliday, M. A. K. *Learning how to mean: Exploration in the development of language.* London: Edward Arnold, 1975.

McKenna, A. *Child language: Old shoe or magic slipper.* Lecture delivered at XV International Congress of l'Organisation Mondiale de l'Education Prescolaire (OMEP), Warsaw, 1977.

Mattingly, I. G. Reading, the linguistic process and linguistic awareness. In J.F. Kavanagh & I.G. Mattingly (Eds.), *The Relationship Between Speech and Reading.* Cambridge, Mass.: MIT Press, 1972.

Sinclair, J. McH., & Coulthard, R. M. *Towards an analysis of discourse: The English used by teachers and pupils.* Oxford: Oxford University Press, 1975.

Widdowson, H. Rules and procedures in discourse analysis. In T. Myers (Ed.), *The development of conversation and discourse.* Edinburgh: Edinburgh University Press, 1979.

3

Experiential Determinants
of Children's Food Preferences

Leann Lipps Birch

University of Illinois at Urbana-Champaign

Food preferences are important determinants of young children's consumption patterns and nutritional status. This is particularly true in the higher income countries, where the ready availability of a large array of alternative foodstuffs provides opportunities for many food choices. From the broad set of diverse factors that appear to have an impact on the formation of children's food preferences, three categories of influence can be defined: (1) beliefs, attitudes, and knowledge about food imparted to the child by the culture, including food taboos and avoidances, prestige values of foods, and nutritional information; (2) physiological mechanisms, particularly the sensory systems of taste and olfaction, that give rise to sensations forming the basis of the child's perception of the organoleptic characteristics of foods; (3) factors arising from elements of the child's immediate and direct experiences with food. The discussion that follows is restricted to the third category of influence. Factors that are present in the child's direct and immediate experience with food and that are involved in the formation of food preferences include characteristics of the food itself, characteristics of the individual, and the social-affective context in which the experience with food occurs. In addition, the cumulative effects of the child's experience with food on the formation of food preferences will be discussed.

THE ROLE OF EARLY EXPERIENCE IN THE FORMATION
OF FOOD AND TASTE PREFERENCES

Early experience has been assumed to be particularly important in the formation of children's food preferences, and there is some evidence that there may be
sensitive periods early in life that are critical for the formation of food preferences
and aversions (Burghardt & Hess, 1966; Garb & Stunkard, 1974). In addition,
it has been suggested that food preferences established early in life persist
throughout the life span, influencing preferences and consumption patterns
during adulthood (Beauchamp & Maller, 1977; Greene, Desor, & Maller, 1975).

Garb and Stunkard (1974) reported that the onset of food aversions was
greatest during early childhood. Based on this evidence, they suggested that
there may be a critical period during childhood for the acquisition of food
aversions. Their data were cross-sectional and based on the retrospective reports of approximately 700 individuals interviewed at different points in the
life span, ranging from the preschool period through retirement. In order to find
experimental evidence on the existence of critical periods in the formation of
food preferences, it is necessary to look to work with organisms other than man.
For example, Burghardt and Hess (1966) fed young snapping turtles one of
three diets, then changed to a second diet for an equivalent period. The order
of the diets was counterbalanced across groups. In a subsequent choice situation,
16 of the 20 animals showed a preference for the diet first experienced, indicating that the earlier experience was more important in the formation of
food preferences than the later experience.

In reviewing the evidence on the role of early experience in the formation of food preferences in man, Beauchamp and Maller (1977) pointed out
that in an early study by Davis (1928) on the consumption patterns of newly
weaned infants, there was a perfect relationship between experience with fruit
juice and preference for it by her sample of three children. However, Beauchamp
and Maller also indicated that the effects of early experience were confounded
with frequency of exposure in Davis' research, and that an unequivocal answer
to the question regarding the existence of sensitive periods awaits the results
of experimental studies.

When Desor, Greene, and Maller (1975) compared the taste preferences
of children and adults for sweet and salty solutions varying in concentration,
the adults showed larger individual differences than the children in the concentrations of sugar they preferred, varying by as much as eight-fold in preferred
concentration. The authors interpreted these results as evidence for the importance
of experience in the development of individual differences in taste preference.
The role of experience in the formation of taste preference was explored further
by Greene, Desor, and Maller (1975), who obtained preferences for several
concentrations of sweet and salty solutions from both monozygotic and di-
zygotic twins. Because individual differences in preference existed and herit-
ability estimates were low, they speculated that early experience was important

in the development of preference but did not entertain a critical period hypothesis. Taken together, the findings suggest that experience is important in the development of taste preferences. However, because all of these data are cross-sectional, cohort effects, maturational effects, and genetic differences among the cohorts, all of which are correlated with age, cannot be eliminated as possible explanations for the observed age-related differences. Although the results of research cited above suggest that critical or sensitive periods may exist during childhood in the formation of food preferences, research utilizing longitudinal, within-subjects designs that do not rely on retrospective report, is needed in order to establish definitively the role of early experience in the formation of food preferences.

In a recent experiment employing a within-subjects design to investigate the effects of a short-term experience with food on food preference, Birch (1979b) used a procedure developed to assess preschool children's preferences directly. Preference data for a set of fruits were obtained from 37 preschool children. In the direct assessment procedure, the child is presented with samples of all the foods in question and asked to taste each one and to place it in front of one of three faces, corresponding to the child's reaction to the food. One face was designed to depict someone who had just eaten something that tasted good; a second face depicted someone who had just eaten something that tasted bad; the third face had a neutral expression. After the child tasted each food and placed it in front of the face corresponding to his or her response to the food, the child then rank ordered the foods within each category. To accomplish this rank ordering, the child was asked to indicate the most preferred food in the set. As an item was designated by the child, it was removed from the set. This process was repeated until the foods in the set were rank ordered according to the child's preference.

The preference data were analyzed using multidimensional scaling procedures. Based on information obtained from food histories completed by the children's parents and from the children's ability to name the foods correctly (e.g., all the children named bananas correctly, but only 7 out of 37 could supply the correct name for dates), the first dimension of food preference was labelled familiarity. It is the first dimension because it accounts for the largest percentage of the variance in the data (29%). The second dimension, accounting for an additional 26% of the variance, was labelled sweetness. When the data from three subsequent preference assessments of the same children, obtained over a period of approximately 6 months, were analyzed, the same two dimensions consistently emerged.

Familiarity is, of course, a function of experience and exposure, and its consistent emergence as a salient dimension underlying preference attests to the importance of experience in the establishment of children's food preferences. Zajonc (1968) stated a general hypothesis relating the effects of experimental exposure to preference in the following way: "Mere repeated exposure of the individual to a stimulus is a sufficient condition for the enhancement of [the individual's] attitude toward it." Presumably, "mere repeated exposure" leads to increased familiarity and produces increased preference. The mere exposure hypothesis has received support from research with adult subjects using a variety of stimuli, including Chinese characters (Zajonc, 1968), paintings (Maslow, 1937), and human faces (Zajonc, 1968); a study by Kail (1974) with school-age children using visual stimuli similar to those used by Zajonc (1968) also produced results consistent with the exposure hypothesis. However, there is only one study in the literature that investigated the effects of exposure on preference using foods as stimuli. In that study, Peryam (1963) presented novel foods to American soldiers four times at monthly intervals. Preference for the foods was initially low and no positive shift in preference was noted with repeated exposure. The failure to note an exposure effect may have been due to the low levels of exposure his subjects received.

In the Birch (1979b) study, an initially unfamiliar food, dates, was repeatedly presented to the children. Dates were selected based on the results of the multidimensional scaling analysis, food history data, and the children's ability to name the foods. If mere repeated exposure increases familiarity, then the location of dates on the familiarity dimension was expected to shift toward the familiar pole of the dimension when preferences were reassessed following repeated exposure. A comparison of the preference orders from the pre- and post-exposure assessments would indicate whether this increased experience with the food increased preference.

The children were exposed to dates each day for seven consecutive days of the preschool program. The food was presented in the context of the lunch program, and the children received the initially unfamiliar item in addition to the other foods on the menu. The resulting preference data indicated that at the end of the experimental period, dates were ranked as more familiar than before, consonant with the expected direction of change. However, although familiarity was increased, no positive shift in preference occurred as a function of the additional exposure.

A closer look at the data from the ten children who initially ranked dates last in their preference order provides some information on the failure to note consistent support for the exposure hypothesis. Half of these ten children showed increased preference, and all of them were 3-year-olds. Two of these children indicated that dates were now their favorite fruit and the other three children ranked dates in the middle of their preference order. The food histories of these five children indicated that for four of them, dates had never been served at home and were unfamiliar. Results of the multidimensional scaling analysis indicated that familiarity was weighted heavily by these 3-year-olds. In contrast, the other five children showed no change in preference. All of them were 4-year-olds. The food histories of these children indicated that dates had been served to all of these children at home and were, therefore, familiar to the children at the beginning of the exposure procedure. Food histories also indicated that four of these five children consistently refused dates when they were served. Results of the multidimensional scaling analysis showed that sweetness was more heavily weighted by these children than familiarity and that they tended to prefer the more sour fruits, such as grapefruit and pineapple, to the sweeter ones. The information indicating that a change in preference occurred in children for whom dates were initially unfamiliar is consistent with the generalization that the exposure effect is noted only when stimuli are unfamiliar initially (Zajonc, 1968). When the total sample was divided into 3- and 4-year-old groups, and the data for the two groups analyzed separately, familiarity was found to be the first dimension for the 3-year-olds and sweetness the first dimension for the 4-year-olds, reflecting the age difference in the salience of the two dimensions noted for the subsample of ten children.

The importance of familiarity as the major dimension of preference for the youngest children suggests that early exposure and experience with foods is very important in the formation of food preferences. Children tended to like the familiar and dislike the unfamiliar foods. The relatively rapid shift from familiarity to sweetness as the primary dimension underlying preference from 3 to 4 years is consistent with the data cited previously suggesting the existence of sensitive periods in the formation of food preferences, with items that are exposed during the period while familiarity is particularly salient tending to become preferred.

Notwithstanding the preceding discussion of the effects of "mere repeated exposure," experience does not take place in a vacuum, and the context in which exposure occurs can be expected to make important contributions to the formation of food preferences. Because of the importance of these context effects, they will be discussed as a separate topic in a later section of this paper.

In contrast to research suggesting that experience plays an important role in the formation of preferences for foods, there are data indicating that experience does not figure centrally in the formation of preferences for the four basic tastes (sweet, sour, salty, and bitter). For example, when Desor, Maller, and Turner (1973) studied the responses of newborns to plain and sweetened water, the neonates indicated a preference for sweet solutions over plain water and increased their consumption of the sugar solutions at higher concentrations. When they compared the responses of the neonates to those of older infants (5 to 11 weeks and 20 to 28 weeks) using the same preparations, all groups showed the same relative pattern of consumption: More of the sugar solutions than of the water was consumed, and consumption increased at higher sugar concentrations. Desor, Maller, and Greene (1977) also reported a comparison of the infant data cited above with adult data obtained by Stellar (1967) and noted that the two sets of results were strikingly similar. They concluded that, despite the extensive dietary experience adults have had, they continue to exhibit the same ingestive responses to sweet that they had at birth and that experience contributes little to the etiology of the taste preference for sweet.

With respect to the question of whether early preferences and aversions persist throughout life, the only evidence available from human subjects appears in the retrospective reports of Garb and Stunkard (1974). People frequently reported that food aversions formed in childhood persisted into adulthood, some for as long as fifty years. The authors did not attempt to determine whether foods that were preferred early in life were still preferred in adulthood. However, there is some evidence from nonhuman species suggesting that early preferences persist later in life. For example, Capretta and Rawls (1974) demonstrated that rats who were exposed to a garlic flavor during nursing and after weaning showed a greater preference for the flavor than did controls later in life. Although the retrospective data of Garb and Stunkard (1974) suggest that preferences may persist throughout life, longitudinal data are needed in order to trace the course of food preferences through the life span.

DESCRIPTIVE STUDIES OF CHILDREN'S FOOD PREFERENCES AND CONSUMPTION PATTERNS

During the past 50 years there have been numerous descriptive studies of children's consumption patterns and food preferences. Studies of consumption patterns are cited in this discussion because consumption data have frequently formed the basis for inferences regarding preferences. In some cases, consumption data were obtained through direct observation (Davis, 1928; Dunshee, 1932; Harrill, Smith, & Gangever, 1972; Lamb & Ling, 1946), and in others, maternal reports of children's consumption have formed the basis of inferences about children's food preferences (Bryan & Lowenberg, 1958; Dierks & Morse, 1965; Eppright, Fox, Fryer, Lamkin, Vivian, & Fuller, 1972; McCarthy, 1935; Sanjur & Scoma, 1971).

When consumption measures are used as the basis of statements regarding food preferences, the implicit assumption made is that the more an individual eats of something, the more highly preferred that something is. This assumption can be criticized on the grounds that factors other than preference affect consumption patterns. For example, foods differ in satiety value: The fact that an individual consumes more lettuce than chocolate fudge does not necessarily indicate that lettuce is preferred to chocolate fudge. Furthermore, when data are obtained by presenting foods on different days, and relative consumption of those foods is used as a measure of preference, the observed differences in consumption may be a function of day-to-day differences in the physiological state of the individual, rather than reflecting differences in food preference.

Investigators have relied rather heavily on maternal report in obtaining information on children's consumption patterns and preferences. Their rationale for the use of maternal report has been that children are unreliable sources of information and cannot provide data regarding their own food preferences (Bryan & Lowenberg, 1958). Unfortunately, mothers are also unreliable sources of data regarding their children's behavior, and with respect to food preferences,

Glaser (1964) noted considerable variation in the parents' and the children's reports of the children's food preferences. For example, although parents stated that 31 percent of their children disliked broccoli, only 10 percent of the children indicated a dislike for broccoli. Further evidence on the inaccuracy of maternal report comes from a study by Birch (1980b) in which maternal reports of children's preferences were compared and correlated with children's preferences obtained using the direct assessment procedure described earlier. Based on 76 mother-child pairs, the median correlation (tau) between these two measures of children's food preferences was only .29 (the tau value corresponding to the $p < .05$ level of significance is .60), and the correlations were significant in only 20 percent of the mother-child pairs. Furthermore, observations made in our laboratory fail to confirm Bryan and Lowenberg's contention that children cannot provide reliable information regarding their own preferences; children as young as 2½ years do not hesitate to communicate their likes and dislikes about foods presented to them, and the data obtained using the direct assessment procedure have demonstrated that the preference data are reliable (Birch, 1979b) and valid predictors of consumption (Birch, 1979c).

Because consumption patterns are determined by factors other than preference (e.g., satiety value, availability, physiological state of the individual, cost, caloric content), it is not appropriate to use consumption measures as the basis of inferences regarding food preference. However, because preference is an important determinant of consumption patterns, knowledge about food preference should be useful in predicting consumption patterns. Birch (1979c) established that preference data were effective predictors of children's consumption in a self-selection setting. Independent measures of preschoolers' preferences and consumption patterns were obtained during snack periods for four consecutive days. Snacks were eight different kinds of small, open-faced sandwiches with different types of spreads. Preference assessment procedures were the same as those described previously. To obtain the consumption data, four groups of four preschoolers participated in a "special snack" period each day for four consecutive days. An array of serving plates, each with a different type of sandwich on it, was presented to the children, who were given small plates and told that they could take the sandwiches they wanted to eat and that they could return for more if they liked. An observer recorded each child's consumption. The order of preference assessment and consumption was counterbalanced over days. The obtained correlation between the measures of preference and consumption was .80 for the total sample, higher than correlations of preference and consumption reported by Pilgrim (1961) for adult subjects, which ranged from .50 to .70. It is possible to speculate that the relationship between preference and consumption is stronger for children than for adults because cultural factors that come to play an influential role in the food choices of adults (e.g., nutritive value, caloric content, cost, prestige value) have not yet become relevant for young children, whose preferences and consumption patterns are primarily a function of input from their direct experience with foods.

An example of a carefully conducted study of consumption patterns in very early childhood is the early work of Davis (1928), whose results are widely quoted and frequently misinterpreted. She observed the consumption patterns of three newly weaned infants in a setting where they were allowed to self-select their diets. She did not draw inferences regarding preferences. The infants were presented with a large variety of foods, simply prepared, with no added seasonings or salt. Salt was available at mealtime for seasoning but sugar was not. The foods offered included selections from the following categories: Muscle meats, organ meats, seafoods, cereals, bone products, eggs, milk, fruits, and vegetables. Davis concluded that, given this set of alternatives, the infants were able to select a nutritionally adequate diet. This work is frequently cited as evidence that children can select a nutritious diet from among the alternatives available to them. The fallacy of the interpretation has been pointed out by Gussow (1972): Given the set of alternatives available to the children in the study, it would have been difficult for them to select a diet that was *in*adequate. The experimental situation bears little resemblance to the alternatives typically presented to children in our contemporary society, who are frequently pre-sented with arrays of highly sugared and processed foods and who are the targets of media campaigns designed to sell highly sugared cereals, soft drinks, snack foods, and candy.

CONTRIBUTIONS TO THE FORMATION OF FOOD PREFERENCES IN THE YOUNG CHILD: INTRINSIC DIMENSIONS OF FOODS, CHARACTERISTICS OF THE INDIVIDUAL, AND CONTEXT

Young (1968) has maintained that, in man, the pleasantness or unpleasantness of contact with food determines acceptance, rejection, and preference. Aspects of three elements of the contact situation can potentially contribute to the formation of food preferences: The food, the person, and the context.

Intrinsic Dimensions of Foods

Foods are very complex, multidimensional stimuli. Despite the numerous descriptive studies of children's consumption patterns and preferences, very little is known about the relative salience for young children of the dimensions of food, e.g., texture, temperature, aspects of taste and aroma, and visual charac-teristics. Are some of these dimensions more important than others in determin-ing preferences? Are there individual differences and/or age differences in the relative contributions of these dimensions to preferences?

A major objective of the study by Birch (1979b), discussed above, was to begin to obtain information on these questions. The method used in this research to assess children's preferences has already been described. Two dimensions consistently emerged throughout a series of four assessments: Familiarity and sweetness. Although other dimensions in addition to these may have been used by the children in making preference judgments, these two dimensions consistently accounted for approximately 60% of the variance in the preference data. The implications of the existence of a familiarity dimension were discussed in a previous section of this paper. The emergence of a sweetness dimension is not surprising in light of the data indicating that the preference for the sweet taste is innate and changes little with experience (Desor, Maller, & Greene, 1977). Results of other studies (Birch, 1979a, 1979c) have also shown sweetness to be a salient dimension in preschool children's preference judgments for foods in addition to fruits, including sandwiches and snack foods.

Physiological Characteristics and Bodily States of the Individual

The effects of disruption of homeostasis on taste preference have been studied in adult humans and in other organisms, but there is no evidence regarding the effects of deprivation and satiation states on children's preferences for foods. Grinker (1977) did report that no difference was found in children's taste preferences for simple sucrose solutions when the solutions were tasted before and after lunch. These findings are consistent with the results of work by Moskowitz, Kumaraiah, Sharma, Jacobs, and Sharma (1975), who reported no differences in the pleasantness ratings for citric acid and quinine sulfate solutions when they were tasted before breakfast and after lunch. In contrast, Cabanac (1971) and Moskowitz, Kumaraiah, Sharma, Jacobs, and Sharma (1976) noted that after a satiating glucose load, adults' taste and aroma preferences shifted from liking toward disliking, and Cabanac has maintained that pleasure serves the physiological function of helping to maintain homeostasis. The conflicting results noted in the two sets of studies may be due to differences in procedures used to manipulate metabolic state. In the research reporting differences in preference as a function of metabolic state, satiety was defined by ingestion of a glucose load. In contrast, in studies providing no support for differences in preference as a function of metabolic state, satiation was defined as "after lunch." The view that homeostatic needs affect palatability and preference for foods agrees with common sense; water "tastes better" when you are thirsty than when you are not; a steak "tastes better" when you are hungry than after a large meal (Young, 1977). Despite intuitive appeal, generalizations from results of research on the effects of physiological state on taste preferences to their effects on food preferences must be made with caution.

Obesity, a more stable characteristic of the individual, has been shown to be related to preference. Obese adults show different preference functions for sweet than do normals (Grinker & Hirsch, 1972). Whereas normal weight adults tend to show increasing preference for increasing concentrations of sugar solutions until a breakpoint in preference is reached, obese individuals found the same series of increasing sucrose concentrations increasingly unpleasant. Grinker (1977) reported that when taste preference data were obtained from normal weight and obese school age children from 8 to 10 years old, the obese children showed preference functions remarkably similar to those described for obese adults: The more concentrated the solution, the less frequently it was preferred. The normal children performed more like the normal adults, preferring the more concentrated solutions over less concentrated ones.

The sensory capacity of the individual can be expected to influence taste and food preferences. It has been reported that humans have a wider distribution and greater number of taste buds during infancy and early childhood than at any time later in life (Arey, Tremaine, & Monzingo, 1935), and there is reason to believe that the form of the functions relating the concentration of preparations to perceived intensity and preference may change with development. Although there has been speculation on this point, very little evidence exists. Feeney, Dodds, and Lowenberg (1966) explored age differences in sensory thresholds using preschool children and their parents as subjects. Parents and children were presented with distilled water and asked to compare it with low concentration sucrose solutions and to indicate when the two solutions tasted differently. These data were used to determine sensory thresholds for the two age groups. No age differences were noted; children and their parents showed equivalent sensitivity in discriminating between distilled water and the sucrose solutions. However, the absence of age differences in thresholds does not provide information on whether the forms of the functions relating concentration to perceived intensity and preference differ with age.

In a study discussed previously, Desor, Greene, and Maller (1975) compared the taste preferences of children and adults and indicated that children tended to prefer higher concentrations of sugar solutions than did adult subjects. If children are more sensitive than adults, then this age difference is not in the predicted direction unless the form of the function relating perceived intensity and preference is very different for the two age groups. Unfortunately, data on the perceived intensity of the solutions were not reported, so it is not possible to determine whether the differences in preference are mediated by differences in perceived intensity.

There has been a good deal of research on the taste sensitivity of neonates. Investigators have noted, for example, that sweet is discriminated from nonsweet at birth (Desor, Maller, & Turner, 1973; Engen, Lipsitt, & Peck, 1974; Nisbitt & Gurwitz, 1970), and, as previously noted, that newborns will ingest increasing amounts of sweet solutions at increasing concentrations. These data, which suggest that the preference for sweet is present at birth, are consistent with LeMagnin's (1977) statement that the sweet taste acts as an unconditioned stimulus for eating and drinking in many species—apparently including humans.

Probably the most extensive literature on the influence of the physiological state of the organism on preference is that on conditioned aversions.

It has been shown repeatedly that an initially preferred food can be made aversive after only a single association with illness which follows ingestion (Garcia, Hankins, & Rusinak, 1974; Garcia, Kimeldorf, & Koelling, 1955). In a related phenomenon, positive shifts in preference are noted in cases where ingestion of a foodstuff is followed by positive effects such as recovery from thiamine deficiency (Garcia, Ervin, Yorke, & Koelling, 1967; Rozin, 1965). Although the research elucidating the nature of conditioned aversions and the mechanisms involved in their acquisition has employed nonhuman species, Garb and Stunkard's (1974) work showed that conditioned aversions frequently occur in humans as well.

The laws of learning apply to the formation of affective processes and preference (Young, 1968), and Garcia et al. (1974) pointed out that it is possible to operationally describe the acquisition of taste aversions in classical conditioning terms. However, they also point out that in the case of conditioned aversions (and perhaps in the acquisition of preferences), the animal does not appear to have acquired an if-then relationship which describes what is generally learned in classical conditioning, e.g., "if bell, then food," but, rather, a change in the preference for the food occurs. A bit of introspection suggests that this is also the case in humans. For example, if you had once become ill after eating chocolate ice cream, your subsequent response to chocolate ice cream would probably not be, "If I eat this ice cream, (then) I'll get sick," but rather one of revulsion and nausea reflecting your aversion and leading to the rejection of chocolate ice cream. As a result of the pairing of the food with illness, a negative shift in preference has occurred rather than the acquisition of a new contingency relationship.

Context

Within the limits set by innate taste preferences and characteristics of the individual on the range of food preference, the social-affective context in which foods are presented influences the acquisition of food preferences. Context functions in a number of ways to influence the formation of food preferences. Children's preferences are influenced by the food choices and eating behaviors of others present (Birch, 1980a; Duncker, 1938; Harper & Sanders, 1975; Marinho, 1942), by the behavioral consequences of eating (Ireton & Guthrie, 1972), and by the social affective context in which foods are presented (Birch, 1979a; Birch, Zimmerman, & Hind, 1980). Although a discussion of the effects of television advertising on children is beyond the scope of this paper, concern with the effects of television advertising on the acquisition and modification of children's food preferences has been voiced recently in hearings held by the Federal Trade Commission on the topic of television advertising directed at children, and there is evidence that such advertising does influence children's food preferences as well as the purchasing patterns of parents (Galst and White, 1976; Goldberg, Gorn, & Gibson, 1978; Reiss, 1977).

Harper and Sanders (1975) investigated young children's willingness to sample novel food when mothers and strangers modeled the eating of the food. The mothers were more influential than the strangers, although modeling produced effects on the children's eating behavior in both cases. Younger children were more affected by the procedures than were older children. Results also indicated that children were more likely to eat a novel food if the adult modeled eating than if the adult merely offered food to the child. No preference data were obtained from the children so it is not possible to ascertain whether modeling also produced increased preference for the foods.

In a study of social influence on children's food preferences, Duncker (1938) employed two different social contexts in an attempt to modify preschool children's food preferences, including the use of a story in which the hero showed a strong preference for a bad tasting food over one with a more pleasant taste. As a result, the children's preferences showed a temporary shift to the food preferred by the story's hero. The second procedure involved exposing children to other children with different preferences. After observing other children choosing foods to eat, each child was asked about his or her own preferences in the presence of the other children. When these preferences were compared with those obtained from the children prior to social influence, results indicated that the children who were exposed to others' choices showed a high percentage of choices of the peers' preferred foods. Age differences in the effects of social influence appeared: When the child who was the object of influence was younger than the others, more change in preference was noted than when the child was older than the peer model. Duncker did not obtain adequate data on the children's preference in the absence of other children in order to determine whether the children's choices were a function of conformity or whether the changed choices reflected a shift in preference. Marinho (1942), in a subsequent study of the effects of social influence on food preference, noted that success in modifying the children's preferences was a function of how well established the initial preference was and that modification of preference occurred more readily in younger children, who presumably have less well-established preferences.

In an attempt to modify existing food preferences, Birch (1980a) investigated, in a natural setting, the influence of peer models' food selections and eating behaviors on preschoolers' (3- and 4-year-olds) food preferences and food choices and eating behaviors during lunch. Based on assessed preferences for vegetables, a "target" child who preferred vegetable A to vegetable B was seated at lunch with three or four peers with the opposite preference pattern. The children were then presented with their preferred and nonpreferred vegetable pairs and asked to choose one. Choices were made in a specified order. On the first day, the target child chose first, while on days 2, 3, and 4 of the procedures the peers made their selections first. Seventeen situations of this type were arranged. The target children showed a significant shift from choosing their preferred vegetable on day 1 to choosing their nonpreferred vegetable on day 4. When the target children's preferences were reassessed at intervals up to several weeks following the conclusion of the luncheon procedures, the target children still showed a significant positive shift in preference for their initially nonpreferred vegetable. Because this later preference assessment was performed in the absence of peers, conformity cannot account for the shift in preference. Consumption data also indicated a significant increase in the amount of the nonpreferred food that the target children consumed over days. Thus, exposing children to peers with different preferences who selected and ate the target children's nonpreferred foods was sufficient to change both preference and consumption patterns. Age differences also appeared in the data, with more younger children than older children showing positive preference shifts. These results indicate that modeling appears to have both immediate and more lasting effects on food preferences. The consistent emergence of age differences in the effects of modeling on food preferences noted in the studies presented above is again suggestive of the existence of a sensitive period during the early preschool years for the formation of food preferences.

The success of the social influence procedures in producing changes in food preferences suggests that if children were routinely exposed to other children with food preferences differing from their own, they would begin to broaden the set of foods acceptable to them. This is particularly important in light of the findings of Eppright et al. (1972), who reported that one of the central concerns of the mothers they interviewed was the limited number of foods their preschool children would accept.

Ireton and Guthrie (1972) looked at the effects of operant conditioning procedures on children's consumption patterns. In an attempt to increase vegetable consumption, the children were given tokens and verbal reinforcement contingent upon their consumption of premeasured servings of vegetables. Results indicated that this procedure produced significant increases in consumption but no data are reported to indicate whether positive shifts in preference for the vegetables may also have occurred as a result of the operant conditioning procedures.

Recent works by Birch (1979a) and Birch, Zimmerman, and Hind (1980) indicate that positive shifts in preference can be obtained by manipulating the social-affective context in which foods are presented. Participants in this study were 3- to 5-year-old preschoolers whose preferences for a set of eight snack foods were assessed at the beginning of the experiment. Based on these assessed preferences, a "neutral" food was selected for presentation to each child in one of four contexts: As a reward; noncontingently, paired with adult attention; in a nonsocial context; or at snacktime, in addition to the other seven snack foods. Presentations were made twice per day on 21 days over a period of six four-day preschool program weeks; 16 children participated in each condition. Preferences were reassessed during the presentation procedures at four and six weeks (following 30 and 42 presentations), and again six weeks after the conclusion of the procedures. The results of this research are presented in Figure 1. It is clear that the social-effective context in which foods are presented influences food preferences. Both presenting foods as rewards and presenting them noncontingently paired with adult attention produced significant increases in preference. The effects were not transitory, but persisted for at least six weeks after the termination of the procedure. Familiarity cannot account for the effects because in each condition, the other foods in the set were presented to the child at snacktime on each day of the classroom presentation procedures, ensuring approximately equivalent exposure to all the snack foods. Half of the children in each presentation condition received a sweet food and half a nonsweet food. No differences in the effects of context were noted as a function of whether the presented food was sweet or nonsweet.

It is common practice for adults in many cultures to use sweet foods as rewards to control children's behavior or as treats or pacifiers; sweet foods are also consistently presented in other positive contexts, including holiday celebrations and parties. Evidence on the pervasiveness of these practices in the United States comes from the work of Eppright et al. (1972), who interviewed 2,000 mothers of preschool children in the North Central region of the United States regarding their food habits and nutritional practices. Sixty-two percent of the sample indicated that they used sweet foods as rewards, treats, pacifiers, or that they withheld sweets as punishment (in the same interview, 21% of the mothers were concerned that their children were consuming too many sweets).

The results of the research by Birch (1979a) and Birch, Zimmerman, and

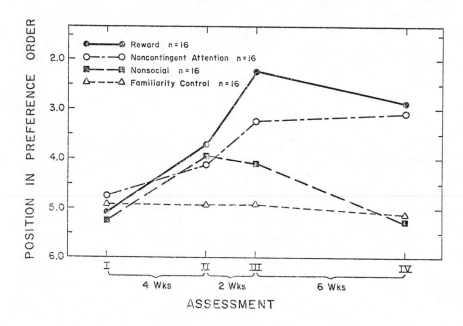

Figure 1.

Hind (1980) have shown that the practices reported by the mothers in the Eppright et al. (1972) research, including presenting foods as rewards or treats in positive contexts, produce enhanced preferences for those foods, and the findings take on particular importance in light of current concern with per capita consumption of refined and processed sugar that is reflected in the revised Dietary Goals for the United States (1977): Consumption of refined and processed sugars should be reduced by nearly half (45%). One way to help curb our "sweet tooth" would be to make individuals who interact with young children aware that using sweet foods in positive contexts enhances preference for those foods, and to urge the use of alternative practices. The results have also demonstrated that positive social-affective contexts can increase preferences for nonsweet foods as well. This suggests that positive contexts could be used to produce positive shifts in preference for foods relatively low in refined and processed sugar and therefore more desirable from a nutritional standpoint.

CONCLUSIONS AND IMPLICATIONS

1. It is clear that early life experiences influence the formation of food preferences in the young child. However, evidence consistent with the assumption that the effects of early experience persist throughout the life span is lacking, and longitudinal data are needed to resolve this issue.

2. Our knowledge regarding how developmental changes in the sensory systems of taste and olfaction might influence the development of food perception and preference is extremely limited. In contrast to the simple solutions typically used in studies of taste preference, foods are complex, multidimensional stimuli. Generalizations to food preferences from work on taste preferences must be made with caution.

3. Despite many normative-descriptive studies of children's consumption patterns and food preferences, our understanding of the relative salience of the many intrinsic dimensions of food in determining food preference is far from complete.

4. Although innate taste preferences and cultural factors appear to set limits on the range of food preference, transitory and relatively stable states of the individual, the context in which foods are presented, and dimensions of the foods can influence the formation of food preferences.

5. Learning and experience are very important in the formation and modification of food preferences, and evidence from several diverse sources suggests that early childhood may be a particularly sensitive period in the formation of food preferences and aversions. Additional data obtained from human subjects are necessary to resolve this point.

6. Whether or not the data provide support for the existence of sensitive periods during early childhood, it is clear that young children's food preferences are modified by exposure to peer models who have different preferences and by the social-affective context in which foods are presented. These findings have implications for child rearing practices. The range of foods acceptable to children could be expanded by systematically exposing children to others with different preferences, and day-care settings should be particularly amenable to such efforts. It should also be possible to minimize the enhancement of the preference for sweet foods by avoiding practices involving the presentation of sweet foods in positive contexts. Positive social-affective contexts could also be used to enhance preference for foods lower in sugar content and higher in nutritional value that are not initially highly preferred by young children.

REFERENCES

Arey, L., Tremaine, M., & Monzingo, F. The numerical and topological relations of taste buds to human circmuiallate papillae throughout the lifespan. *Anatomical Record,* 1935, *64,* 9-25.

Beauchamp, G. K., & Maller, O. The development of flavor preferences in humans: A review. In M.R. Kail & O. Maller (Eds.), *The chemical senses and nutrition.* New York: Academic Press, 1977.

Birch, L. L. Using foods as rewards: Effects on food preference. Paper presented at the biennial meeting of the Society for Research in Child Development, San Francisco, 1979. (a)

Birch, L. L. Dimensions of preschool children's food preferences. *Journal of Nutrition Education,* 1979, *11,* 77-80. (b)

Birch, L. L. Preschool children's food preferences and consumption patterns. *Journal of Nutrition Education,* 1979, *11,* 189-192. (c)

Birch, L. L. Effects of peer models' food choices and eating behaviors on preschooler's food preferences. *Child Development,* 1980, *51,* 489-496. (a)

Birch, L. L. The relationship between children's food preferences and those of their parents. *Journal of Nutrition Education,* 1980, *12,* 14-18. (b)

Birch, L. L., Zimmerman, S., & Hind, H. The influence of social-affective context on the development of children's food preferences. *Child Development,* 1980, *51.*

Bryan, M. S., & Lowenberg, M. E. The father's influence on young children's food preferences. *Journal of the American Dietetic Association,* 1958, *34,* 30-35.

Burghardt, G. M., & Hess, E. H. Food imprinting in the snapping turtle, Chelydra Serpentina. *Science,* 1966, *151,* 108-109.

Cabanac, M. Physiological role of pleasure. *Science,* 1971, *173,* 1103-1107.

Capretta, P. J., & Rawls, L. H., III. Establishment of a flavor preference in rats: Importance of nursing and weaning experience. *Journal of Comparative and Physiological Psychology,* 1974, *86,* 670-673.

Carroll, J. D., & Chang, J. J. Analysis of individual differences in multidimensional scaling via an n-way generalization of Eckhart-Young decomposition. *Psychometrika,* 1970, *35,* 283-319.

Davis, C. Self-selection of diets by newly-weaned infants. *American Journal of Diseases of Children,* 1928, *36,* 651-679.

Desor, J., Greene, L., & Maller, O. Preferences for sweet and salty in 9- to 15-year-old and adult humans. *Science,* 1975, *190,* 686-687.

Desor, J., Maller, O., & Greene, L. Preference for sweet in humans: Infants, children and adults. In J.M. Weiffenback (Ed.), *Taste and development: The genesis of sweet preference.* Bethesda, Maryland: United States Department of Health, Education and Welfare, 1977.

Desor, J., Maller, O., & Turner, R. Taste acceptance of sugars by human infants. *Journal of Comparative and Physiological Psychology,* 1973, *84,* 496-501.

Dierks, E. C., & Morse, L. M. Food habits and nutrient intakes of preschool children. *Journal of the American Dietetic Association,* 1965, *47,* 292-296.

Duncker, K. Experimental modification of children's food preferences through social suggestion. *Journal of Abnormal and Social Psychology,* 1938, *33,* 489-507.

Dunshee, M. E. A study of factors affecting the amount and kind of food eaten by nursery school children. *Child Development,* 1932, *2,* 163-181.

Engen, T., Lipsitt, L. P., & Peck, M. B. Ability of newborn infants to discriminate sapid substances. *Developmental Psychology,* 1974, *10,* 741-744.

Eppright, E. S., Fox, H. M., Fryer, B. H., Lamkin, G. H., Vivian, V. M., & Fuller, E. S. Nutrition of infants and preschool children in the North Central region of the United States of America. *World Review of Nutrition and Dietetics,* 1972, *14,* 269-332.

Feeney, M. C., Dodds, M. L., & Lowenberg, M. E. The sense of taste of preschool children and their parents. *Journal of the American Dietetic Association,* 1966, *48,* 399-403.

Galst, J. P., & White, M. H. The unhealthy persuader: The reinforcing value of television and children's purchase-influencing attempts at the supermarket. *Child Development,* 1976, *47,* 1089-1096.

Garb, J. L., & Stunkard, A. J. Taste aversions in man. *American Journal of Psychiatry,* 1974, *131,* 1204-1207.

Garcia, J., Ervin, F. R., Yorke, C. H., & Koelling, R. A. Conditioning with delayed vitamin injections. *Science,* 1967, *155,* 716-718.

Garcia, J., Hankins, W. G., & Rusinak, K. W. Behavioral regulation of the milieu interne in man and rat. *Science,* 1974, *185,* 824-831.

Garcia, J., Kimeldorf, D., & Koelling, R. A. A conditioned aversion towards saccharin resulting from exposure to gamma radiation. *Science,* 1955, *122,* 157-159.

Glaser, H. Nursery school can influence food acceptance. *Journal of Home Economics,* 1964, *56,* 680-683.

Goldberg, M. E., Gorn, G. J., & Gibson, W. TV messages for snack and breakfast foods: Do they influence children's preferences? *Journal of Consumer Research,* 1978, *5,* 73-81.

Greene, L., Desor, J., & Maller, O. Heredity and experience: Their relative importance in the development of taste preference in man. *Journal of Comparative and Physiological Psychology,* 1975, *89,* 279-284.

Grinker, J. A. Effects of metabolic state on taste parameters and intake: Comparisons of human and animal obesity. In J.M. Weiffenback (Ed.), *Taste and development the genesis of sweet preference.* Bethesda, Maryland: United States Department of Health, Education and Welfare, 1977.

Grinker, J., & Hirsch, J. Metabolic and behavioral correlates of obesity. In J. Knight (Ed.), *Physiology, emotion and psychosomatic illness.* Amsterdam: CIBA Foundation Symposium, 1972.

Gussow, J. Counternutritional messages of TV ads aimed at children. *Journal of Nutrition Education,* 1972, *4,* 58-52.

Harper, L. V., & Sanders, K. M. The effect of adults' eating on young children's acceptance of unfamiliar foods. *Journal of Experimental Child Psychology,* 1975, *20,* 206-214.

Harrill, I., Smith, C., & Gangever, J. H. Food acceptance and nutrient intake of preschool children. *Journal of Nutrition Education,* 1972, *4,* 103-106.

Ireton, C. L., & Guthrie, H. A. Modification of vegetable-eating behavior in preschool children. *Journal of Nutrition Education,* 1972, *4,* 100-103.

Kail, R. V. Familiarity and attraction to stimuli: Developmental change or methodological artifact. *Journal of Experimental Child Psychology*, 1974, *18*, 504-511.

Lamb, M. W., & Ling, B. C. Analysis of food consumption and preferences of nursery school children. *Child Development*, 1946, *17*, 186-217.

LeMagnin, J. Sweet preference and the sensory control of caloric intake. In J.M. Weiffenback (Ed.), *Taste and development the genesis of sweet preference*. Bethesda, Maryland: United States Department of Health, Education and Welfare, 1977.

McCarthy, D. Children's feeding problems in relation to the food aversions of the family. *Child Development*, 1935, *6*, 277-284.

Marinho, H. Social influence in the formation of enduring preferences. *Journal of Abnormal and Social Psychology*, 1942, *37*, 448-468.

Maslow, S. H. The influence of familiarization on preference. *Journal of Experimental Psychology*, 1937, *21*, 162-180.

Moskowitz, H. W., Kumaraiah, V., Sharma, K. N., Jacobs, H. L., & Sharma, S. D. Cross cultural differences in simple taste preferences. *Science*, 1975, *190*, 1217-1218.

Moskowitz, H. R., Kumaraiah, V., Sharma, K. N., Jacobs, H. L., & Sharma, S. D. Effects of hunger, satiety, and glucose load upon taste intensity and taste hedonics. *Physiology and Behavior*, 1976, *16*, 471-475.

Nisbitt, R., & Gurwitz, S. Weight, sex and eating behavior of newborns. *Jornal of Comparative and Physiological Psychology*, 1970, *73*, 245-253.

Peryam, P. R. The acceptance of novel foods. *Food Technology*, 1963, *17*, 33-39.

Pilgrim, F. What foods do people accept or reject? *Journal of the American Dietetic Association*, 1961, *38*, 439-443.

Reiss, E. S. Advertising and product development. *Food Technology*, 1977, *31*, 75-77.

Rozin, P. Specific hunger for thiamine: Recovery from deficiency and thiamine preference. *Journal of Comparative and Physiological Psychology*, 1965, *59*, 98-101.

Sanjur, D., & Scoma, A. D. Food habits of low-income children in northern New York. *Journal of Nutrition Education*, 1971, *3*, 85-94.

Senate Select Committee on Nutrition and Human Needs. *Dietary Goals for the United States* (2nd ed.). Washington, D.C.: United States Government Printing Office, 1977.

Stellar, E. Hunger in man. *American Psychologist*, 1967, *22*, 105-117.

Young, P. T. Evaluation and preference in behavioral development. *Psychological Review*, 1968, *75*, 222-241.

Young, P. T. Hedonic processes in the development of sweet taste preferences. In J.M. Weiffenback (Ed.), *Taste and development the genesis of sweet preference*. Bethesda, Maryland: United States Department of Health, Education and Welfare, 1977.

Zajonc, R. B. Attitudinal effects of mere exposure. *Journal of Personality and Social Psychology Monograph Supplement*, 1968, *9*, 1-27.

4

Mothering and Teaching— Some Significant Distinctions

Lilian G. Katz, Ph.D.
University of Illinois at Urbana-Champaign

Among the outcomes of research on young children is the welcome acknowledgement that parents' behavior plays a central role in the intellectual development of their children. The influence of parents on their children's personalities has long been recognized, if not exaggerated, but recent research findings, exemplified by the well-known work of White et al. (1979), Levenstein (1970), Schaefer (1979), and others are now reflected in such catch phrases as "parents are the child's first teacher" or even "best teacher." As a result, while traditionally teachers have been said to stand *in loco parentis,* recent slogans seem to be putting pressure on parents to stand *in loco magisteris,* i.e., in place of teachers.

The new optimism about the potential educational role of parents has given rise to numerous programs designed to help parents become more effective teachers of their young children. The objectives of many of these programs go beyond strengthening the so-called "parenting" skills to include training in tutorial and instructional skills as well.

Alongside current enthusiasm for parent training and parent involvement in schooling is increasing pressure on teachers in day care centers, preschools, and primary classes to respond to the apparent needs of children assumed to be unmet by their busy, working, and, in many cases, single mothers. In an article entitled "When the School Is the Second Parent" (Mittenthal, 1979), Joseph Featherstone is reported to have said that the boundaries between parents and teachers are "nowhere as clear as they used to be." The article goes on to illustrate ways in which the stresses experienced by single and working mothers impinge upon the work of their children's teachers, who seem to feel obliged to assume responsibility for some of the nurturing and comforting parental functions thought to be neglected at home.

In summary, pressures seem to increase on mothers[1] to instruct their children in ways that will render them more responsive to schooling, perhaps in part due to a lack of confidence in teachers and schools. On the other hand, it is not uncommon to hear teachers of young children complain that they must supply the nurturance and affection children seem to need before they can be instructed. Whereas mothers often believe that their children might better attain academic success if teachers were more responsive, teachers often believe that their own efforts would be more successful if only mothers attended properly to their children's psychological needs. So long as such recriminatory attitudes persist, parent-teacher relationships cannot be focused, as they should be, on mutual support.

The purpose of this essay is to examine distinctions between the roles of mothers and teachers, and from these distinctions to draw some implications for mothers, for teachers, for programs, and for research.

DIMENSIONS OF DISTINCTION

It is obvious that teachers do many of the same things with young children that mothers do, and vice versa. It is in the nature of young children that from time to time they will require of their teachers at school some of the same tending, caring, and guiding given them by their mothers at home. Similarly, mothers are helping their children to acquire knowledge and skills that teachers consider important. In their total interactions with children, it is likely that mothers and teachers engage in many of the same behaviors. However, in this discussion, my emphasis is on the *distinctions* rather than on the similarities in the two roles.

Although the behaviors of the two role-takers are likely to overlap on each of the seven dimensions discussed below, their central tendencies can be expected to yield the distinctions indicated in Figure 1. In the service of exploration the role distinctions are somewhat overstated. No role-takers occur in the pure types described in this essay. Furthermore, it should be understood that although the dimensions on which the two role-takers are distinguished interact with each other, they are enumerated separately in order to highlight potential problems arising from confusion between the two roles.

---

[1]The teacher-parent distinction discussed here may apply to fathers as well as to mothers. There appears to be no biological or other *a priori* reason why the behaviors attributed to mothers in this essay could not also be ascribed to fathers. Current research indicates that fathers do have a powerful impact upon their young children's development; however, though equally important, the father's influence is different from the mother's (see Zigler & Cascione, in press).

Role Dimension	Mothering	Teaching
1. Scope of Functions	Diffuse and Limitless	Specific and Limited
2. Intensity of Affect	High	Low
3. Attachment	Optimum Attachment	Optimum Detachment
4. Rationality	Optimum Irrationality	Optimum Rationality
5. Spontaneity	Optimum Spontaneity	Optimum Intentionality
6. Partiality	Partial	Impartial
7. Scope of Responsibility	Individual	Whole Group

Figure 1. Distinctions between mothering and teaching
in their central tendencies on seven dimensions.

Scope of Functions

In a discussion of some of the discontinuities between families and schools, Getzels (1974) points out that the two institutions are discontinuous in at least two ways, namely the scope and the affectivity characterizing the relationships in the two settings.

Under the rubric of scope, Getzels points out that the functions to be fulfilled by the family are diffuse and limitless, in contradistinction to those of the school, which are specific and limited. The all-encompassing scope of the responsibilities, duties, and potential content of the relationships within families is "taken for granted." There is, according to Getzels, nothing about the young child that is not the parents' business. Thus it is unnecessary to prove that any aspect of the child's life is within the purview of the family.

However, in the case of the school, relationships between teachers and children are specific in scope, function, and content in that the legitimate area of interaction "is limited to a particular technically-defined sphere, and what is not conceded to the school because of its special competence remains the private affair of the participants" (Getzels, 1974, p. 48).

Similarly, the Newsons (Newson & Newson, 1976) point out that the responsibility society "enjoins on parents to their young children is quite different from that which it expects from teachers, nurses and other professionals . . . for one thing it has no fixed hours . . . parents of preschool children never go off duty . . ." (p. 400).

The distinctions in scope of functions proposed by Getzels and the Newsons appear to become greater and sharper with increasing age of the pupil. To teachers of preschool and primary children, the distinctions are problematic precisely because of the age of the child: The younger the child, the wider the range of functioning for which adults must assume responsibility. Thus age and the level of maturity associated with it, in and of themselves, give rise to confusion between the two roles. To expect day care, preschool and primary school teachers to accept as wide a scope of functions as mothers do serves to exacerbate the long-standing problems of unclear role boundaries.

Getzels' formulation of the discontinuities between families and schools also raises the question, "What is the nature of the 'technically-defined sphere,' 'special competence,' or nonmaternal functions of the teacher in day care, preschool, and kindergarten classes?" In the case of the elementary school teacher, the technical and specific competence resides in managing of instruction in specific academic skills and content and in fostering the life of the instructional-unit group. Indeed, departmentalization of schooling increases with the grade level, reflecting increasing specialization of teachers and their responsibilities. In day care and preschool education, specific competences related to *instruction* are typically eschewed. Furthermore, the success of the parent cooperative nursery schools and preschool playgroups (in North America, the United Kingdom, Australia, and New Zealand), operated by untrained and volunteer mothers, casts some doubt upon the necessity for specific technical competencies for teachers of young children (see Haystead et al., 1980). In addition, the frequent assertion that "children learn through play" adds to the difficulties of defining just what special skills early childhood educators do and should have. As long as only the "insiders" understand and/or recognize the special functions and competencies required of teachers of young children, and as long as the unique attributes of mothers in relation to their children are underappreciated by teachers, effective collaboration between the two groups of role-takers will be difficult to achieve and maintain.

Intensity of Affect

It seems reasonable to assume that both the *intensity* of affect (of all kinds) and the *frequency* with which behavior is marked by intense affect would also distinguish the two sets of role-takers. That is to say that on the average, when the central tendencies of mothers are compared to those of teachers, we should find more frequent and greater affective intensity in the behavior of mothers than of teachers. As Rubenstein and Howes have pointed out, the role of day care teachers is "both more specified and limited than the role of mother at home . . . the mother's emotional investment may enhance the likelihood of high-intensity affective responses" (Rubenstein & Howes, 1979). The Newsons address this dimension by calling it "involvement" and point out that "parents' deep involvement with their own children is precisely the quality which makes parents different from other more 'professional' caretakers" (Newson & Newson, 1976, p. 371). They point out also that the parent-child relationship often becomes "violent and stormy because it is so deep." On the other hand, the teacher-child relationship is "less intimate, more formal and much less permanent":

> . . . A good parent-child relationship is in fact very unlike a good teacher-child relationship; yet because the roles have certain *ingredients* in common, though in different proportions (nurturance, discipline, information-giving, for example), they are sometimes confused by the participants themselves, to the misunderstanding of all concerned . . . (p. 401-402, italics theirs)

Pressure on parents to take on more instructional-type functions can lead to a variety of difficulties, one of which is exemplified in the case of a mother of a child with so-called learning disabilities. The mother reported that she and her child were enrolled in a special "home intervention" program designed to teach mothers to give their "learning disabled" children regular rigorous instruction and skill training at home. Although unintended by the program leaders, the mother reported that she became so anxious about being able to get her son to meet the specified learning objectives set for them both that their relationship deteriorated. With each lesson in which he fell behind, she became disappointed and tense, and the child became nervous and recalcitrant, which increased her own disappointment and tension, and so forth until, as she reported, she realized "the boy had no mother." She stopped the lessons and asked the professionals to continue to teach him while she supported his struggle to learn by being the soft, understanding and relatively nondemanding adult in his life. In some ways her story reminds us of common problems encountered when trying to teach a close friend or relative to drive a car. We become aware of how much easier it is to be patient and understanding of a stranger than of someone close to us. Very often the stress encountered in trying to teach someone close to us places heavy burdens on the relationship.

In sum, one would expect the average level of affective intensity of the two role-takers to be distinguished from each other as indicated in Figure 1. The affectivity dimension is closely related to the attachment dimension discussed below.

Attachment

Although the term *attachment* is widely used in professional as well as popular literature on child development and child rearing, it is a difficult one to define. In the literature on infant development, attachment refers to an underlying variable inferred from infants' reactions to strangers and to separations and reunions with primary caretakers (Cohen, 1974). Rutter (1979) indicates that attachment is a construct involving several features and should be distinguished from *bonding* to adults. The available definitions focus almost exclusively on the attachment of the child to the adults. What is required for this discussion is a way of defining the attachment of the adults to their children. Ramey and Farran offer a broad definition of adult-child attachment using the term *functional maternal attachment* to mean "simply those caregiving functions that must be performed for infants to sustain a normal development" (Ramey & Farran, 1978, p. 2). The set of functions includes "at a minimum a refrain from physical and verbal abuse, the provision of information and affection, and direct personal involvement with the infant."

Research on the reciprocity and rhythmicity which characterize normal mother-infant relationships brings us closer to a way of defining attachment so that the adults' attachment to the child is included. For the purposes of this essay the term attachment is defined as *the capacity to be aroused to a wide range of behaviors and intense feelings by the status and behavior of the other.* If the attachment is a mutual one, then one would expect the behavior and feelings of either member of the pair to activate strong feelings and/or reactions in the other. This definition is intended to include such feelings as anxiety, alarm, fear, anger, and rage, as well as the proverbial pride and joy and other tender loving and caring emotions, and the behaviors that express them. Common usage of the term *attachment* tends to refer primarily to the nurturant side of the spectrum of feelings and behaviors of adults, and to overlook the point that intense rage or terror in the face of impending danger to the child are also manifestations of what we call attachment. The definition proposed here implies that the opposite of attachment is not rejection or anger, but indifference.

In Figure 1 the entry "optimum attachment" is intended to reflect the notion that whereas development could be jeopardized by mother-child attachment that is too weak (minimal), it could also be undermined by excessive attachment, commonly called "smother-love."[2]

The optimum attachment recommended here as an ideal feature of mother-child relationships is distinguished from the *optimum* detachment which should mark teacher-child relationships. The latter is often referred to as "detached concern" (Maslach & Pines, 1977). The term detachment is used not only in order to characterize the distinctions in the functions of the two role-takers, but to suggest also that it is appropriate for professionals to make self-conscious or deliberate efforts to distance themselves (optimally) from their clients. As Maslach and Pines (1977) have suggested, people who work intensively and intimately with people for extended periods of time inevitably suffer stresses associated with strong emotional arousal. As they point out, one of the ways of coping with such potential stress is to adopt techniques of detachment, which vary in their effectiveness as well as in their relationship to the conduct of work: "By treating one's clients or patients in a more objective detached way, it becomes easier to perform the necessary interviews, tests, or operations without suffering from strong psychological discomfort" (Maslach & Pines, 1977, p. 100). The authors go on to suggest that "detached concern" is a term which conveys "the difficult (and almost paradoxical) position of having to distance oneself from people in order to cure them" (Maslach & Pines, 1977, p. 100).

Teachers who are unable to detach themselves optimally from their pupils and become too close to them are likely to suffer emotional "burn-out" which is typically accompanied by loss of capacity to feel anything at all for the

---

[2]What constitutes an *optimum* degree of attachment for any given mother-child pair would be difficult to predict or pre-specify since we only know whether the attachment is optimum if the child is observed to be thriving; however, failure to thrive may not always be attributable to disturbances in attachment. This "endless regress" definitional problem appears to be inescapable. (See Bronowski, 1977.)

clients. Certainly those who are extremely detached at the other extreme, for whatever reason, are unlikely to be effective in their work with children because such extreme detachment is also accompanied by low responsiveness to client needs and demands.

One of the advantages mothers have over teachers in dealing with the stresses of attachment, as well as intense affect, is the tacit knowledge that their child's psychological and physical dependency upon them will slowly but surely be outgrown. Teachers of day care, preschool, and kindergarten children, on the other hand, must continually cope with dependent children, year in and year out. They must protect themselves from potential "burn-out" by developing an optimal level of detached concern—optimal in terms of their own emotional stability and effective functioning.

It should be noted also that teachers who are suspected of cultivating close attachments to their pupils in order to "meet their own personal needs," as the saying goes, are subject to substantial criticism or derision from co-workers and other professionals. Occasionally such teachers come to perceive themselves as protecting children from their own parents, and occasionally the child's responsiveness to such teacher closeness gives rise to parental jealousy. As Anna Freud pointed out long ago, a teacher "is neither mother nor therapist." A teacher with "objective attitudes can respond warmly enough to satisfy children without getting herself involved to a dangerous extent . . ." (Freud, 1952, p. 232). She adds that a teacher must not think of herself as a "mother-substitute." If, as teachers, "we play the part of a mother, we get from the child the reactions which are appropriate for the mother-child relationship" (p. 231). All of this could result in "rivalry with mothers" and other undesirable consequences, making teacher-mother mutual support and complementarity difficult to develop.

Optimum detachment is also desirable for teachers because it can free them to make realistic evaluations of their pupils' development and learning, which is a major component of their work. Mothers, on the other hand, may not have to make realistic or so-called "objective" evaluations of their children's growth very often, although their lack of realism is a frequent source of frustration to teachers! In the long run, a mother's optimism about her child's progress, even if it seems excessive, is probably in the child's best interest. Such optimism in and of itself may contribute to the child's growth and development. Maternal pessimism, on the other hand, may be more damaging than any teacher's realism. Many children seem to think that mother, being omniscient and knowing the child more fully and completely than the teacher, is in possession of the "real" truth, and that when there is a discrepancy between the mother's and the teacher's evaluation, the former is more accurate. Experience suggests that individuals caught between their mother's pessimism concerning their potential for achievement and a teacher's optimism devote considerable energy to the problem of how to keep "the real truth" from the teacher—having no choice but to accept mother's view as the "true" one. Such discrepancies may account for some cases of lifelong doubts about one's true abilities.

Differences in the assessments of the two role-takers may be related to the differences in the base-lines to which the child in question is being compared. They may also be due to dramatic differences in the child's behavior in the home and at school. It is not uncommon to hear both mothers and teachers comment on how strikingly different the child seems in the "other" setting. Frequently, a mother will report that the teacher's description of her child was difficult to reconcile with her own experiences with the child. Studies of this phenomenon and the ways children cope with discrepant evaluations have not been found.

Another consideration leading to the recommendation of optimum detachment for teachers is the importance of minimizing the likelihood of incidents we might call "invasions of privacy" or other forms of encroachment upon aspects of children's socialization which are the legitimate domain of the family. Similarly, optimum detachment is recommended in order to help teachers with the ever-present temptation to engage in favoritism. Since it is unlikely that one can be strongly attached to more than one or two pupils, the risk of favoritism increases with increasing closeness to any one pupil. The detachment approach should help to reduce those dangers.

Many early childhood workers reject the value of optimum detachment because of their deep concern for children's need to feel closeness and attachment to adults. It is not clear how the proposed detachment would affect such "needy" children. But it is useful to keep in mind that whereas the relationships between adults and children in day care, preschool, and primary classes are reciprocal, they are not necessarily symmetrical. In particular, it may be possible for young children to feel very attached to their teachers, even to worship and adore them, without the teachers' responding at the same level of intensity. Such "unrequited love" during the early years may help the child to gratify needs for cathexis without placing severe emotional burdens on teachers. Research on such asymmetrical attachment might help to clarify the potential effects on such children of the detachment of their teachers.

Rationality

It is hypothesized here that effective mothering is associated at least in part, with *optimum* irrationality, and that the two extremes may both be damaging to the growing child. On the one hand, extreme rationality in a mother might be perceived by the child as cool, calculating unresponsiveness that could lead to a variety of emotional disturbances. Extreme irrationality, on the other hand, may present the growing child with a range of problems stemming from insufficient predictability of the interpersonal environment.

By using the term "optimum irrationality" I do not intend to propose chaotic, scatterbrained mindlessness! Rather, the emphasis is upon the depth and strength of what we sometimes call "ego-involvement"—similar in nature to attachment as defined above.

The irrationality suggested here is, in a sense, a matter of the mind, or the rational aspects of functioning, employed "in the service of the heart," so to speak. On the other hand much literature is prepared for and presented to teachers to remind them to bring their hearts to bear upon their professional minds.

The element of "ego-involvement" is also illustrated by the notion that if a mother perceives herself as a failure at mothering she is likely to experience painful guilt, strong feelings of inadequacy, and deep regret, perhaps for a lifetime. If on the other hand a teacher perceives herself to have failed at teaching she/he can leave the occupation in a fairly orderly fashion (e.g., at the end of an academic year), and residual emotions like guilt, feelings of failure, regret, and defeat are likely to subside and disappear within a few months.

Newson and Newson point out that parents can show their flexibility because their relationships with the children are both permanent and intimate, and that although it is often suggested that parents "ought to strive after consistency at all times: fortunately most are human enough to fail in this unusual aim" (1976, p. 402).

A different aspect of this dimension is captured in the expression, "No one in her right mind would be a mother!" As Bronfenbrenner has put it, "in order to develop, a child needs the enduring, irrational involvement of one or more adults," by which he means, "Somebody has to be crazy about that kid!" (Bronfenbrenner, 1978, pp. 773-774). However, for modern, well educated mothers this may appear to be something of an overstatement.

A rational analysis of the pros and cons of motherhood would be unlikely to lead to a decision to undertake it. Indeed, it is difficult to find "reasons" for having children today. Offspring are not "useful" as a hedge against economic dependency in old age. Rather than being considered potential members of the family labor force and contributors to the family income, they are expected to become substantial drains on the family finances. Thus, even more than their forebears, modern parents have children just because they "have to"—irrationally, so to speak. Truly rational analyses of parenthood, at this time, would probably provide more counterindicators than not!

Teachers on the other hand should be optimally rational, in that they should bring to bear upon their work careful reasoning concerning what is to be done or not done. Teaching calls for rational analysis of how to proceed in the education of young children on the basis of accumulated knowledge of how children develop and learn, and of what is appropriate pedagogy for children of a given age range and experiential background. Presumably the value of teacher training is precisely that it equips the future teacher with information and knowledge from the relevant "supply" disciplines and from pedagogy, all of which become available for proceeding rationally in the work of teaching. It seems reasonable to assume that teachers' possession of relevant knowledge would serve to increase their confidence in their own behavior and in their general role competence. However, increased knowledge for mothers may have the opposite effect, and may serve to undermine what is often rather fragile confidence when facing "experts" who may appear comparatively cool and confident in their own advice and procedures.

Spontaneity

Along very similar lines, parents should strive to be optimally spontaneous in dealing with their children. Many programs of parent education run the risk of encouraging parents to become excessively cerebral and self-conscious in responding to their children. Extreme pressure to modify their behavior may lead parents to a condition called "analysis paralysis," or inability to act with confidence, which could be damaging to the mother-child relationship. The resolve to respond to one's child according to certain steps and procedures arrived at cerebrally—intellectually, as it were—may work well on the first or even second occasion; but very often, even the strongest resolutions break down under the weight of what is (and should be) an emotionally loaded relationship. Such "break-downs" are related to the fact that the child's behavior/ status *really matters* to the parent, which comes with "attachment" as defined above. The cool, calculating, ever reasoning or reasonable parent might be perceived by the child as indifferent.

Another aspect of spontaneity is that it is precisely what gives a mother's day-to-day behavior at home the variation and contrast which the growing child can use as a basis for hypothesis formulation and testing in the quest to make sense of experience. Indeed, it may well be that what gives *play* its reputed high value in children's learning derives from the spontaneous, casual and often random variations produced in many types of play (Newson & Newson, 1979). These variations provide information which the child operates on and transforms into meaningful contents of the mind. The opportunity to observe such spontaneous variations, and to obtain parental help in making logical inferences from them, may be the very thing the slogans such as "mother is the best teacher" refer to. As the Newsons state:

> . . . it must surely be within the circle of the family that the child must learn to adjust to and cope with living among other people in all their inconsistency and moodiness . . . Moodiness, understanding and failure are all part of the ordinary human condition, and parents' role is to present and interpret these things to the child within a permanent loving relationship which offers plenty of time for mistakes to be made and to be forgiven on both sides. (Newson & Newson, 1976, p. 402)

By contrast, instruction can be defined as nonrandom prespecified sets of stimuli or information *intended* to cause specific constructs and skills to be acquired. This contrast between play and instruction may also help to account for some of the dissention in the ranks concerning appropriate programming for infant day care. On the one hand there is pressure to rise above the custodial functions of day care and to provide "developmental" programs. On the other hand, formal lessons, instruction, or "structured" activities are thought to be inappropriate for the young. If the staff must await spontaneous "teachable moments," they may feel as though they are not earning their keep, not really "working," and role ambiguity may intensify.

Whereas mothers should be optimally *spontaneous* with their children, teachers should strive to be optimally *intentional* about their work. Their activities should be largely predetermined, premeditated in terms of some aims, goals, and broad objectives which are more or less explicit and are responsive to parents (the primary clients) as well as to pupils. With training and experience teachers' intentional behavior takes on a spontaneous quality as well.

Perhaps it is this very degree of *intentionality* which most clearly distinguishes mothering from teaching and child-rearing from education. That is not to say that parents have no intentions! It is likely, however, that parental intentions are less explicit to parents themselves as well as to others, and all less formal, more global, and more personalized in that they are held for their own individual offspring. Research on the degree and specificity of intentions among the two sets of role-takers might help to sharpen understanding of these role distinctions.

Early childhood educators often speak appreciatively of the great amounts children learn from the hidden curriculum, from incidental learning or from unintended or unplanned events. However, by definition, such unintended learning cannot be intended—one cannot intend something to happen unintentionally! Presumably the purpose of training in pedagogy is to bring the consequences of one's pedagogical methods into closer and closer agreement with the intentions underlying one's pedagogy. Similarly, the virtue of instruction would seem to lie in the deliberate minimization of spontaneous or random variations in activities and responses, maximizing the likelihood that specific stimuli will be presented to the learner, and intended or predicted learning outcomes will most likely be assured.

Spontaneity of the mother is important also in that it may contribute to the widest possible variations in behavior, which in turn give rise to the widest possible range of information becoming potentially available to the child. The availability of a wide range of information increases the probability that children will be able to locate information that matches adequately or optimally what they are ready to operate upon and/or to assimilate. Furthermore, if the child's location of appropriate information is followed by mother's focusing on the selected events or information, then the child's environment becomes a highly informative and responsive one. In studies of mother-infant interaction it has been suggested that adults exaggerate their facial and vocal expressions in order to provide "behavioral contrasts" in response to infants' "limited information processing capacities" (Tronick et al., 1980, p. 20). Thus the spontaneous variations in behavior ideally serve to increase the likelihood that matches between the child's readiness to process information and the adult's provision of it will be maximized.

As suggested above, instruction and pedagogy are concerned with narrowing the variations presented to the child so that specific information and child operations upon it can be maximized. However, if the narrow range of information presented by the pedagogue misses the mark for a particular child the child's alternatives are fewer than they might be at home and the result may be a sense of failure or inadequacy, which in turn, may have deleterious effects upon the child's education.

Questions concerning what sets of variations, stimuli or information should be made available to young children in preschool classes have occupied curriculum developers for many years and definitive answers have not yet been formulated.

Partiality

Along lines very similar to those discussed above, mother-child relationships are not only charged with highly intense emotions, but "children in the family are treated as special persons . . .," and in school they are "necessarily treated as members of categories" (Lightfoot, 1978, p. 22). It is thus in the nature of things that parents are partial toward their own children, biased in their favor, champions of their children's needs, and exaggerators of their virtues, gifts and assets. This so-called particularism stands in sharp contrast to the *universalism* expected of teachers. Thus it is appropriate for parents to ask teachers to make special allowances and provisions for their own children, and that is precisely what a teacher often cannot do, since the teacher must treat the children impartially. Teacher impartiality means that whatever skills, knowledge, insights, techniques, etc., the teacher has at his or her disposal, they are made equally available to every child *as needed,* whether the child is liked or not. Indeed, it is the very capacity to make all of one's pedagogical know-how available to the child one does not especially like which marks the teacher as a genuine professional.

Scope of Responsibility

The great emphasis placed by early childhood educators on the importance of meeting the "individual needs" of their pupils may have obscured yet another distinction between the roles of mothering and teaching, namely, that mothers are typically concerned about the welfare of one rather than all of the teacher's pupils. Consequently, a mother may make demands on the teacher which might place the welfare of the whole group of pupils at risk. Parents have a right to protect their own child's cultural/ethnic uniqueness and to ask of the teacher that special consideration, as appropriate, be made for their child. But mothers are often unaware of the pressures from other mothers, as well as from institutional sources, that the teacher is attempting to respond to. The teacher is responsible not only for every individual in the group, she is also responsible for the life of the group as a unit that is more than the sum of the lives of the individual members. The teacher has to balance the importance of responding to unique individual "needs" against the responsibility to establish and maintain the ethos of the group through which the norms of behavior, expected levels of achievement, and even many feelings are learned.

SUMMARY

The seven dimensions outlined above probably reflect some kind of common underlying variable which is difficult to name. As Lightfoot put it:

> The universalistic relationship encouraged by teachers is supportive of a more rational, predictable, and stable social system with visible and explicit criteria for achievement and failure. It does not suffer the chaotic fluctuation of emotions, indulgence, and impulsiveness that are found in the intimate association of parents and children . . . Even the teachers who speak of "loving" their children do not really mean the boundless, all-encompassing love of mothers and fathers but rather a very measured and time-limited love that allows for withdrawal. (Lightfoot, 1978, p. 23)

The Newsons, in a study of 700 elementary school children and their relationships to their families and schools, also underscore this point:

> Parents have an involvement with their own children which nobody else can simulate . . . The crucial characteristic of the parental role is its partiality for the individual child . . .. The best that community care can offer is impartiality—to be fair to every child in its care. But a developing personality needs more than that: it needs to know that to someone it matters more than other children; that someone will go to *unreasonable* lengths, not just reasonable ones, for its sake. (Newson & Newson, 1976, p. 406, italics theirs)

Our understanding of the potential problems arising from confusing the two roles might be helped by studies of those women who are simultaneous occupants of both roles. Casual observation and experience suggest that teachers who are also mothers of young children may have elevated expectations of their own children as well as of themselves. It has been reported that such mothers are sometimes ashamed and embarrassed by their emotionality with their own children, expecting themselves to be as level-headed at home as they are in the classroom. Similarly, some expect their own children to exemplify perfection to enhance their credibility as teachers.

To the extent that such role fusion does occur and produces these kinds of expectations, clarification of the distinction between the two roles suggested in this paper may help to alleviate some of the strains for those who occupy both at the same time. In addition, some research on the ways such dual role-takers define the two roles and what sources of role fusion, confusion, and strain they identify would be helpful.

Implications for Parent Education

One of the major functions of parent education programs should be to help parents think through their own goals for their own children, to develop and clarify what kind of lifestyle they want to construct with the family, and to identify what they themselves perceive to be the major issues deserving attention. The program should offer parents insights and various kinds of information while encouraging them to accept only what makes sense and what is consistent with their own preferences.

Parent education programs should also encourage and support parents' confidence in their own impulses and in their own competence. It is hypothesized that, in the long run, efforts to support impulses already in place and available to the mother will result in greater change and improvement in parental functioning than efforts to change or replace those impulses directly. This hypothesis rests on the assumption that parental confidence, in and of itself, leads to greater effectiveness (particularly in matters relating to the assertion of authority in parent-child interaction) and that greater effectiveness, in and of itself, leads to greater confidence. This "looping" or "circularity" in which effects become the causes of effects would seem to be especially powerful in relationships marked by high intensity of affect, i.e., in which effects really matter to the actors. The hypothesis is also related to the assumption that greater parental confidence is more likely to promote greater advice seeking and greater openness to new information than is parental embarrassment, shame, or low self-confidence.

As indicated earlier in this discussion, parent education that is excessively technique based or technique oriented may yield positive effects in the *short run* and greater feelings of failure and/or guilt in the *long run*. This hypothesis is based on the assumption that parenting is not primarily technical but is more dispositional and ideally largely unselfconscious. A related point here is that children respond not so much to the specific behavior of the parents as to the meanings they assign to that behavior. But the meanings they attribute to any given episode are a function of the larger pattern of which *they* perceive that episode to be a part. Children may have difficulty giving the meanings their mothers intended to technique-bound episodes. Thus, for example, parental reliance on specific techniques, phrases, or other maneuvers may confound the problems issuing from faulty patterns of behavior or from characteristic parental dispositions. The latter take time to change and to reshape, and may perhaps be more effectively modified in parents who have more, rather than less, confidence.

Parent educators often report that the spontaneous impulses of some of the parents they work with put the children in jeopardy, usually in relation to their psychosocial rather than their academic development. To what extent such judgments are matters of taste, preference, and/or value differences between parent educators and their clients is not yet clear. In fact, it may be in the nature of things that parent educators have to work in the absence of sufficient certainty concerning the potential benefit or damage of a given maternal pattern. One way to cope with such uncertainty is to scrutinize as carefully as possible each case of potential jeopardy with regard to the certainty of risk or danger to the child. When—in the educator's best judgment at a given time—the potential for danger seems reasonably clear, then referral to specialized agencies should be made. However, when examination of the available information raises doubts about the potential danger to the child, then the next appropriate step seems to be to encourage and support the mother's own pattern of responding to the child. Differences in taste, philosophical positions, and/or values probably underlie many of the judgments that educators make concerning the mother's need to change her behavior. However, it is useful to remember that parent educators as well as teachers of young children are bound to take firm stands on their beliefs and philosophical positions, since the latter serve to give teachers the kind of certainty required for action in complex situations in which reliable data cannot serve as a basis for decision making (see Katz, 1977).

Powell (in press) suggests that when parents are given new information or are pressed into changing their patterns of behavior in ways that are discrepant with their own values, they minimize the discrepant stimuli and reduce their influence. Powell's analyses of the various parental strategies for coping with the pressures placed upon them to change serve to remind us that education in parenting is not an easy matter. It may be that trying to get mothers to instruct their children in preacademic tasks is easier than helping them with deeper and more complex aspects of development (e.g., self-reliance, moral development, social skills, motivation, etc.).

Implications for Teachers of Young Children

The analyses presented above seem to suggest a number of points which may help teachers in their encounters with mothers as well as in coping with the day-to-day problems of working with young children.

It seems obvious, even without detailed analyses of the two roles, that the special contributions of each role taker to the ultimate socialization of the young child should be underscored, accepted, and respected by each of them. Parent educators as well as those who write in the popular press for parents might help by acknowledging the complementarity of these functions, rather than engaging in trying to fix blame on one or the other for whatever social disaster is capturing popular attention at a given moment. Expressions like

"Parents are the child's best teacher" seem to suggest that teachers are, if not the worst, then certainly a distant second best. The comparison itself is inappropriate: What should be emphasized are the functions and characteristics of each role and how the efforts of each role taker might be supported by the other.

Another implication of the analyses attempted in this essay is that teachers should take time periodically to consider whether they have achieved an optimal level of involvement or detachment in their relationships with children. The risk of teacher "burn-out" is a real one, especially when the work is with children whose families are under stress. Teachers who work together as members of a teaching team might also help each other by developing a system for giving each other relief on those moments when the emotional load feels too heavy to cope with.

Teachers may also be helped by focusing on those aspects of the child's functioning they actually do control. A teacher cannot change the family into which a child is born or with whom he is living; nor can the teacher generally change very much of the mother's behavior. But a teacher can take responsibility for the time a child is actually directly in his or her care, and focus on making that time as supportive, enriching, and educative as possible. The latter is a sufficiently big task by itself, without adding to it the need to make up for the child's alleged missing mothering!

Teachers may also find it helpful in their relations with mothers to acknowledge and accept the mother's advocacy for and partiality toward her own child as natural components of motherhood. Similarly, as mothers approach teachers to request special dispensations for their own children, teachers' acknowledgement of the "naturalness" of such demands may help them to respond more patiently and less defensively than they seem typically to do. Teachers might be mindful on such occasions that although they may practice impartiality within their own classroom, they champion their own classes when representing them as a group in comparison with other teachers' classes! On such occasions teachers also ask for special dispensations and also describe their own classes as having special or unique needs, gifts, and strengths—much the way mothers do for their individual children. Recognition of this phenomenon may help teachers respond to parents with greater respect and understanding.

CONCLUSION

Much of the discussion presented above is speculative, based on informal observations and reports of the experiences of teachers, parents, and parent educators. Research that would verify the accuracy of these speculations would be helpful. Of all the potential research efforts on matters referred to in this essay, those should have high priority which would advance our understanding of the stresses and coping skills of teachers and day care workers. Present social and economic developments suggest that more and more children and their parents will come to depend upon professional child care workers and preschool teachers, and more parents will stand to benefit from well-designed parent education programs. Much is yet to be learned about how such professional activities should be conducted, and what kinds of working conditions are desirable. Certainly, mutual support of the persons involved should help each to cope more effectively with the stresses encountered when living and working with young children every day.

REFERENCES

Bronfenbrenner, V. Who needs parent education? *Teachers College Record,* Vol. 79, No. 4, May, 1978, 767-787.

Bronowski, J. *A sense of the future.* Cambridge, Mass.: MIT Press, 1977.

Cohen, Leslie J. The operational definition of human attachment. *Psychological Bulletin,* Vol. 81, No. 4, April 1974, 207-217.

Freud, A. The role of the teacher. *Harvard Educational Review,* Vol. 22, No. 4, Fall, 1952, 229-243.

Getzels, J. W. Socialization and education: A note on discontinuities. In H. Leicher (Ed.), *The family as educator.* Teachers College Press, 1974.

Haystead, J., Howarth, V., & Strachan, A. *Pre-school education and care.* Edinburgh, Scotland: Scottish Council for Research in Education, 1980.

Katz, L. G. *Talks with teachers.* Washington, D.C.: National Association for the Education of Young Children, 1977.

Levenstein, P. Cognitive growth in preschoolers through verbal interaction with mothers. *American Journal of Orthopsychiatry,* 1970, *40,* 426-432.

Lightfoot, S. L. *Worlds apart; relationships between families and schools.* New York: Basic Books, 1978.

Maslach, C., & Pines, A. The burn out syndrome in the day care setting. *Child Care Quarterly,* Vol. 6, No. 2, Summer, 1977, 100-113.

Mittenthal, J. When the school is the second parent. *New York Times,* May 3, 1979.

Newson, J., & Newson, E. *Seven years old in the home environment.* Halsted Press, 1976.

Newson, J., & Newson, E. *Toys and playthings.* Middlesex, U.K.: Penguin Books, 1979.

Powell, D. R. Toward a socio-ecological perspective of relationships between parents and child care programs. In S. Kilmer (Ed.), *Advances in early education and day care, Volume 1.* Greenwich, Conn.: JAI Press, in press.

Ramey, C. T., & Farran, D. C. The functional attachments of mothers and their infants. A paper presented to the Annual Meeting of the American Psychological Association, Toronto, Canada, August, 1978.

Rubenstein, J., & Howes, C. Caregiving and infant behavior in day care and in homes. *Developmental Psychology,* 1979, *15,* 1-24.

Rutter, M. Maternal deprivation, 1972-1978: New findings, new concepts, new approaches. *Child Development,* 1979, *50,* 283-305.

Schaefer, E. Perspective on the Family. *Professionals and Parents, Moving Toward Partnership.* Conference Proceedings. Richmond, Virginia: Virginia Commonwealth University, 1979.

Tronick, E., Als, H., & Brazelton, T. B. Monadic phases: A structural descriptive analysis of infant-mother face to face interaction. *Merrill-Palmer Quarterly,* 1980, *26,* 3-24.

White, B., Kaban, B. T., & Attanucci, J. *The origins of human competence: The final report of the Harvard preschool project.* Lexington, Mass.: Lexington Books, 1979.

Zigler, E., & Cascione, R. On being a parent. In *Memphis Papers on Parenting,* ERIC/ EECE. Urbana, Ill.: College of Education, University of Illinois, in preparation.

5

Contemporary Single Mothers*

Bernice T. Eiduson
University of California at Los Angeles

The single mother, an appellation which once designated young women who became pregnant out of wedlock without the option of abortion, now also embraces women who have elected to have a child and to become a household head without a man in the picture. Many of these women had been identified with the Women's Movement and have seen themselves as pioneers in developing a new family style. As a group, however, these single mothers have often been overlooked because the census combines them with divorced or widowed women in reported statistics of the rapidly growing number of single parent households. (Such households are increasing nineteen times as rapidly as dual parent ones, with a 73 percent increase in the number of women heading single parent households since 1970.)

In order to see how and to what extent contemporary, elective single mothers reinterpret traditional roles and responsibilities and restructure their lives, we began to study a group of these mothers in 1973. Our subjects were

*Preparation of this paper was supported in part by the National Institute of Mental Health Research Scientist Career Award No. 2 K05 70541-07 to Bernice T. Eiduson, Ph.D., and by the United States Public Health Services Grant 5 R01 MH24947-06 and Carnegie Corporation Grant B-3970-06. The research findings on alternative families draws upon data produced in the project, Child Development in Alternative Family Styles, at UCLA. Senior investigators directing the longitudinal endeavor on 200 children and families are Bernice T. Eiduson and Thomas S. Weisner, project co-investigators; and Jannette Alexander, Field Director, Max R. Mickey, Biostatistician, and Irla Lee Zimmerman, Psychologist.

The paper was presented in part at the symposium chaired by J. Brooks-Gunn, The Changing American Parent: Implications for Child Development, at the meeting of the Society for Research in Child Development, San Francisco, March 1979.

fifty Caucasian, never-married single mothers, aged 18-30, who had opted to keep their babies. These women were studied longitudinally, from the last trimester of pregnancy through the first three years of their children's lives. Their values, attitudes, aspirations for their children, child rearing practices, family organization, and activities were documented through naturalistic home observations, detailed interviews and questionnaires, and self reports of daily routines. When these data were first analyzed, there emerged not a composite profile of "the" elective single mother, but rather a picture of three different types of single mothers, each with fairly distinct attitudes, expectations and experiences. Further analyses were made to compare these three subgroups of the single mother sample.

The single mother population was one of four family lifestyle groups being studied simultaneously. The study included fifty mothers in traditional nuclear families (two married parents living together with a child) and a total of 150 mothers in alternative arrangements: fifty in living groups or communities, the contemporary extended families; fifty in "social contract" relationships (two unmarried parents living together with a child), and the fifty single parent families under discussion here.

Finally, the development of offspring of these single mothers was assessed periodically through structured and semi-structured tests, so that aspects of cognitive, physical, and socio-emotional growth could be monitored (Eiduson, 1978; Eiduson & Alexander, 1978; Eiduson & Weisner, 1978).

From our extensive data on the single-mother family I shall try to summarize the picture of this parent who has been little studied or acknowledged to date. After describing her background, I shall focus on her roles as a parent, her values, attitudes, and behaviors, and the issues that warrant our attention as she rears an infant and preschool child.

BACKGROUND CHARACTERISTICS

First, a glimpse into her background: The elective single mother in our sample averaged 25 ± 4.5 years of age and came from a middle-class or stable working class background. She averaged approximately 13.9 years of schooling; only 14 percent of the fifty women lacked a high school diploma and 25 percent had a college degree. In these demographic features, single mothers were comparable to mothers in the other alternative groups (the social contract and extended family arrangements). In regard to size of their own family of origin (i.e., the mothers' own parents and siblings), place in the family, and other such background characteristics, these women also appeared to be similar to women in all the other groups studied (Cohen & Eiduson, 1975). There were, however, three differences between the families of origin of the alternative women in general and those of the traditionally married. Alternative women's families made a significantly greater number of residential moves during the women's childhood, and had a significantly greater number of remarriages than the families of the traditionally married. Also, in general, alternative mothers perceived their relations with their own parents in childhood more negatively than did the traditional married population; however, among the alternatives, the single mothers reported having been closest to parents.

TYPOLOGY

When entering the study, most single mothers had glibly spoken of their desire and right to have a baby even though they were single and their family style from the outset did not conform to norm. However, more intense study of their attitudes at pregnancy, their aspirations and expectations for the child, and their affiliation with the alternative philosophy led some members of our project group (Kornfein, Weisner, & Martin, 1977) to recognize the within-group variability among the single mothers and to suggest the following typology which identify the subsets:

1. *Nest-builders:* This group (one-fourth of the whole) had consciously planned to become pregnant and frequently selected (with some thought) the man who might be a suitable father. Nest-builders were distinguishable from other single mothers in being more highly educated (two Ph.D.s in the sample), the most vocationally competent and experienced, and the most career-oriented. They lived by themselves, had the highest incomes, and were the most economically, socially and psychologically self-sufficient.
2. *Post Hoc Adapters:* These women had not intended to become pregnant; however, once pregnant, they did not avail themselves of abortion because they felt happy about their situation and felt able to adapt to and enjoy the circumstances. These women lived alone, or with other female friends in rooms or an apartment, or with relatives, such as siblings or aunts. Work experience had been primarily in administrative, business, clerical, or skilled jobs. Education was more limited than in the case of the Nest-builders, and vocational goals were less specific.
3. *Unwed Mothers:* The backgrounds and attitudes of these women regarding their "fate" had such a strong resemblance to those of the unwed teenage pregnant girl, about whom so much has been written, that the label "unwed mother" seemed most apt. These women had the lowest competencies of all the elective single mothers. Work prior to pregnancy had been clerical, skilled, or semi-skilled, and annual income was at least $1,000.00 lower than that of the *Post Hoc* group. Some *Unwed Mothers* still resided with their own parents. They anticipated pregnancy unhappily, but they did not choose abortion because, as Luker (1977) has suggested in regard to another single mother population, the benefits of having a child seemed to outweigh the benefits of not having one. The benefits they perceived seemed both financial (expected Aid to Dependent Children) and psychological.

This typology proved heuristically interesting, as the values, belief systems, and perspectives of the contemporary single mother were studied (Rocheford, Cohen, & Weisner, 1978). We had hypothesized a strong anti-conventional thrust in the single mothers as a group because of their anti-mainstream behavior in regard to having a baby. Analysis of data, however, showed a significant range in the single mother population. The most salient finding in regard to the single mother sample was, first, the close alignment of these mothers' values with some of the values espoused by traditional married parents, and, second, the split of the group and their value identification: at times being like the alternatives; at other times, like the traditionals.

For example, single mothers placed high values on the conventional rewards of achievement—money, status, and advancement—as did the traditional marrieds. Their similarity to traditional marrieds was also evident in their educational and vocational aspirations. For example, when asked during pregnancy how far they would like their child to go in school, 35 percent of single mothers suggested college, a figure significantly closer to the 48 percent of traditional marrieds than to the 15 percent range of the other two alternative groups. Similarly, a significantly higher percentage of single mothers and traditional mothers desired their child in professional or artistic careers, as compared with the more alternative groups who wanted to leave vocational choice exclusively to the child. But swinging toward the alternative perspective, the single mothers were much less concerned with materialism; and, like the social contract and living group mothers, they were strongly drawn to sensory and intuitive means of apprehension, seeing these as valuable modes for problem solving to supplement or supplant scientific and rational ways of thinking.

Further, the within-group variability among single mothers played a role in their value affiliations. Their attitudes regarding sex equality, which might generally be assumed to be favored by the elective single mother, provide a case in point. In ratings of sex equality, the scores of *Nest-builders* were indeed high, but scores of *Post Hoc Adapters* were in the middle of those of the total population, and scores of *Unwed Mothers* (like those of the traditional marrieds) were low. The same direction of within-group differences was found in regard to the extent to which planning for the future was part of the family philosophy.

PREGNANCY AND PARENTING IN THE FIRST YEAR

Attitudes and behavior in anticipation of parenthood showed a vacillation of single mothers between traditional and alternative perspectives. During pregnancy all sought prenatal care, became conscious of nutritional intake, and reduced their drug use, as did all the alternatives in general. In addition, the single mother had hospital deliveries almost exclusively (94 percent had a doctor in attendance and 74 percent used anesthetics in their deliveries). This is the same pattern of behavior during birth as found in the traditional mothers' group, a pattern significantly different from that of the other alternative populations. During her child's infancy, the single mother was the main or almost exclusive caretaker for the child. This pattern dominated the other three groups as well; however, it was not in accord with attitudes expressed during the anticipatory period. At that time the other alternative populations, the women in social contract and living groups, had expected to be full-time caretakers for their children, whereas the single mothers and the traditionals had not. Among single mothers, 83 percent breast-fed their babies and 7 percent were still breastfeeding when the child turned two. This pattern at year two resembled that of the alternatives more than the traditionals. Furthermore, the children of single mothers slept in the mother's room in 45 percent of the cases at year one and in 25 percent of the cases at year two; this is a pattern more like that of the alternatives than the traditionals, for in the latter group 85 percent of children had their own rooms by one year.

In feelings about parenthood, single mothers as a group were not different from other groups. About 40 percent of them found parenting more difficult than anticipated; they felt ignorant about child-rearing, and to a lesser extent became sensitive to how much of their own time was invested in the child and how much this curtailed other interests. The single mother group was the only group that showed a preference for a female child prior to birth: That preference was in fact granted, for 60 percent of them had girls, as compared to 52 percent of the total population studied. In contrast, the traditional marrieds had significantly more boys than girls, although they had not expressed such a preference.

On the Newborn Neurological Examination (Parmalee & Michaelis, 1971), single mother babies scored lower, but not significantly lower, than other groups. Their scores were close to the mean and standard deviation for the total group, which was in the normal range, and 11 percent of the scores were one standard deviation or more below average. Scores on the mothers' condition during birth, as obtained on the Obstetrical Complication Scale (Parmalee & Littman, 1977), also were slightly lower for single mothers, but, again, not significantly so. Although neither of these measures predicted the child's score on the Bayley at 8 months or 1 year, these data suggest possible factors that may have made child caretaking during infancy a bit more difficult for the single mother group than for others (Eiduson, Zimmerman, & Bernstein, 1977).

On the Ainsworth Strange Situation Test, administered at one year, the stranger was approached by single parent children significantly more often ($p = .002$) than by other children, both when the mother was in the room and when she left. It must be noted, however, that the single mother children showed more advanced motor development than other youngsters, so that this behavior was obviously easier for them than for any of the others. On the same test, the patterns summarized in the "ABC" patterning showed no significant difference as a function of parent's lifestyle on the children's distress reaction to separation from the mother. However, a discriminant analysis, in which more refined patterns are elucidated, separated the children of the *Nest-builders, Post Hoc Adapters,* and *Unwed Mothers* more than any other factor among the one-year data. The *Unwed Mothers* had more A children—children who seem to deny any separation anxiety, a stance described by Ainsworth as the child's response to rejection (p. 316)—than any other group.

Child-parent interaction scores sampled such characteristics as initiation of contacts by the mother, caretaker response to child-initiated contacts, affect changes, etc., in a single three-hour noon feeding period. Here the single mother appeared different from other mothers only in summary scores of intensity and variability of social and nonsocial stimulation. As a group, the single mothers, especially those with a second child, scored low on these dimensions. Differences were not significant in attentiveness during caretaking. Also, children of single mothers had the same number and variety of toys as did children in other families.

To describe the ecological niche that the single mother creates for herself and the child during the first year, a large number of adjectival ratings made by observers at the six-month period were summarized, intercorrelated and then factored (Weisner & Weibel, in preparation). The four factors which emerged to characterize the mothers' homes were disorderliness or "funkiness"; intellectuality, particularly as indicated by the presence of books or intellectual objects; child-orientation and warmth; and decorative complexity. Homes of single parent families were not particularly strong on any single factor. A sizable percentage of single mothers' homes were rated disproportionately (compared to other groups) at both low and high ends of the warmth/child orientation factor. They also ranked low on decorative complexity and on disorderliness.

SATISFACTION AND MOBILITY

After one year the single mothers, of all the mothers, were the least satisfied with their fate (Kornfein, 1978). Twenty-one (42 percent) expressed ambivalence toward their lifestyle and ten (20 percent) were openly negative. These figures were significantly greater than for any other family groups. Single mothers expressed a desire for marriage and companionship for themselves. They were significantly more often concerned about how their child was developing, especially in regard to emotional and nutritional growth.

One explanation for their dissatisfactions may be that the income and earnings of single mothers, during the period studied, proved to be the lowest of all the groups, with the mean of approximately $5,500 consisting of welfare, and, for one-third of the group, some part-time work. At the time of the child's infancy, only 10 percent of the single mothers were in the high SES groups;

36 percent were in the middle; and over 50 percent were in the lowest SES groups. Their downward mobility comes out unequivocally through comparison with the SES they enjoyed in their families of origin, for 30 percent of the single mothers are down "one or two steps," and only about one-third of them are ranked in the SES in which they grew up. Their educational level is also lower than that of their parents.

A further indication of dissatisfaction is evident in changes from the single mother unit into another family style. By the time children were 1 year old, thirteen, or 26 percent, of the single mothers had left single motherhood, a trend that was continued at the eighteen-month period, when seventeen, or 34 percent, were in other family styles. Of this group, seven had become traditional marrieds, seven were cohabiting with a male mate, and three women had gone into a living group. By the time children were 18 months old, only 56 percent of the elective single mothers were in the same residential situation (i.e., sharing a home with the same people) as they had been when their child was born: The majority were still living in a small family situation, but 14 percent were at that point with grandparents; 6 percent were with other members of their family of origin, siblings, or aunts; 8 percent were with roommates; and 6 percent were in collectives. In their rate and direction of change in family style, both in legal marital status and residential situation, they were like the other alternative groups, all of whom sharply contrasted with the traditional marrieds, 91 percent of whom had experienced no change.

The *Post Hoc Adapters* made many more changes than did the other single mothers. About half the *Post Hoc Adapters* changed their family style before their child's first birthday, compared to 30 percent of the *Unwed Mothers* and 15 percent of the *Nest-builders*. This pattern is consistent with our typology in which the *Nest-builders* are more settled, so to speak, and the *Post Hoc Adapters* are most likely to experiment with different relationships. Also, the *Post Hoc Adapters* moved much more frequently than did the *Nest-builders* or the *Unwed Mothers*. When looking at the total number of household member changes *and* geographic moves, the *Post Hoc Adapters* still made the most changes. This is again consistent with our typology in which the *Nest-builders* had the motivation and ability to build a firm foundation for single parenthood, whereas the *Unwed Mothers* in their dependent status had fewer options and the *Post Hoc Adapters,* in adapting to necessity, moved from situation to situation.

This factor of mobility is an important variable in understanding the elective single mother. It reflects her seeking of new options when dissatisfactions occur and her search for change *in* change, as well as the experimental flair that probably led to her decision to have and keep a baby initially. In this regard the single mothers' behaviors may help tell us what the contemporary "here-and-now" perspective of young people is about.

PARENTING THE TODDLER AND PRESCHOOLER

Parenting behavior of the single mother after eighteen months of motherhood is distinguished by a number of characteristics. First, in home observations at the dinner hour, the single mother children showed the lowest number of child-initiated, as opposed to parent-initiated, interactions. Yet children were seldom ignored. When responses of mothers to child-initiated interactions were quantified, it appeared that the single mothers, like the traditional marrieds, tended to be extremely tuned in to their children, responding readily to requests for interaction. Whereas this behavior was characteristic of single mothers and traditional marrieds, it was not prevalent in social contract households or living groups. Second, the percentage of children who were observed moving out of visual sight of the single mother was about half as great as the percentage who moved out of sight of the mother in other families. The majority of single mother children moved back and forth in the mother's vicinity throughout the period (Jenkins, 1978). These data reflect both the smallness of the single parent abode, which is actually smaller in space than other family dwellings, and the importance of the parent to the child.

Another facet of the parent-child relationship worth noting is that at the eighteen-month period, the single mother group showed the least encouragement of independence of the child (reacting to or countering the child's strivings?) (Eiduson, 1978). This came out both in interviews and in home observational data. More parents in this group admitted ambivalence about the child's growing independence, or openly sought dependence. Relevant to this finding were the responses of single mother children on the Ainsworth Strange Situation Test, discussed above with other data from year one. Also in point are data suggesting that the single mothers were spending slightly (but not significantly) more time with the child alone than were mothers in other groups. At the two-year period, children of single mothers had more limited exposure to women other than their mothers than did children in other groups: The average child in the other three groups saw one or two women other than the mother per week, but only 25 percent of the single mother children saw this many other women per week. Also, the single mother's child was exposed to men significantly less often than were children of other families.

After two years, 39 percent of the single mothers were occupied at home exclusively on a full time basis, while 12 percent worked part time with the child in day care or in some informal care, and 49 percent worked full time with children in day care. By four years, 47 percent of this group's children were in nursery schools, 2 percent in informal arrangements, and 49 percent at home all day—the last a figure which is the highest for any family group.

Eleven single mothers were in school on a full-time basis and ten attended school on a part-time basis, thus comprising a group where attendance was significantly higher than for mothers in other life styles. This trend continued at the 2-year, 9-months period.

Caretaking supports for the working single mother were primarily grand-parents, and, secondarily, friends—at both the 18-month and 2-year periods. It was these persons to whom she turned for support when she was ill or away overnight. The single mother group also used babysitters significantly more often to supplement child care by the mother. This is in contrast to the other groups, where friends and the father played larger roles. These data are suggestive of a particularly strong tie between mother and child, perhaps even a longer than usual period of mutual dependency. In this regard, preliminary data point to overweight, depression, and a need for outside psychological help for the single mothers, data which do suggest some unusual dependency in this group of women.

This hypothesis is being pursued. It must be considered together with evidence of the extent to which these ties result from economic and ecological realities, or represent the socio-psychological needs of the parent, for, in fact, the child defines the mother's social role. In her identity, the child is the major element. Whereas the role of a single parent had a highly desirable and valued social status in the early 1970s, especially among the mother's peers, one wonders if it continues to arouse such interest and sense of challenge today.

SUMMARY

The picture of the elective single mother that emerges from our intensive longi-tudinal studies thus far is as follows:

1. In background and demographic characteristics single mothers were indis-tinguishable from young mothers who sought a traditional marriage, except that they came from homes in which signs of instability (remarriages, geo-graphic moves) seemed to be more frequent than in the homes of the conven-tional mothers.
2. Their values vacillated or distributed bimodally between those of young mothers in other alternative life styles (social contract relationships, living groups) and those of young mothers in conventional marriages. In some of the characteristics deemed particularly relevant to the development and learning experiences of the child (e.g., achievement motivation, educational aspirations for children, pride in maturation and development), they tended to identify with conventional values.
3. The single mothers differed from each other as a function of their education and vocational competence, their age, and their economic self sufficiency.
4. Despite some alternative leanings, loneliness and needs for support and affection made most single mothers regard marriage as very desirable after a short time (one to two years) as household head.
5. Single mothers' lives were marked by residential and life style changes so that they were recreating their own family lives from their childhood in this respect.

6. Beginning between the child's second and third birthdays, they worked and returned to school in greater numbers than did women in other family groups.

7. Their needs for support stem from economic and psychological caretaking pressures, and perhaps from their own psychology, which may make them perpetuate a dependency in the child that gratifies both the child and themselves.

POLICY IMPLICATIONS

What are the policy and planning implications of these findings? The primary goals for the service provider and policy maker are to strengthen the effectiveness of the single mother unit and reduce its vulnerabilities so that a child is not handicapped. This means recognizing and attacking the problems confronting single mothers. First and foremost, since the economic limitations of many one-parent families put a large percentage of them in the poverty class, the provision of dollars for basic necessities is the most important concern. Associated with economic problems are downward social mobility and frequent residential moves, generally into high-stress neighborhoods; these factors can inhibit and depress parents' activities and foster a sense of instability and rootlessness in the child. Second, programs must be concerned with the negative attitudes toward the one-parent family that are prevalent in our society, oriented as it is toward seeing any unit other than the two-parent nuclear family as deficient. This bias makes the family feel it has a low status in the immediate and extended community, and actually imposes a degree of social isolation on both mother and child. Third, the single mother unit needs legal, health, educational, and child care services, not only for the direct assistance they provide but also for the opportunities they create to integrate mother and child into the community.

To ascertain the specific kinds of services that might be most responsive to need, it may be worthwhile to examine the kinds of self-help efforts that elective single mothers have developed or in which they have sought participation. Examination of these activities provides information on:

1. The ways and extent to which elective mothers involve themselves;
2. The motivation for participation and the rewards they reap; as well as
3. The lacks or gaps in the more institutionalized interventions.

Our studies show that some of the most effective programs, regardless of their level of skill or sophistication, are multi-purpose. This is because there are differences in the women embraced by the "single mother" rubric. The programs that flourish are those that are sufficiently flexible to permit women to have options—to avail themselves of services appropriate to their needs and desired involvement level. Services have to be able to withstand change in contact persons, organizational structure, high attrition rates, cycling- in and out, and resistance to appointments and scheduling.

Professional contact people must be seen as providing social and informational resources for parents. Many single mothers are likely to be more anxious than they admit, especially around sensitive issues such as:

Whose needs (mother's or child's) have priority when they conflict?
How does the parent get the necessary "r and r" without denying her responsibility to the child?
Who can provide approbation for her parenting efforts, rather than merely help or criticism?
How should problems of housing, work, and companionship best be handled in the light of the limitations that child care imposes?

Single mothers' need for training opportunities is self-evident. Our data show that educational and vocational competence are salient variables in attitudes about self and satisfaction with lifestyle as well as in opportunities available. In this regard, attention must be given to some of the problems of motivating the parent toward seeking to improve her own life in ways appropriate to her new family framework.

Another goal of programs and policies should be to orient the single mother toward establishing her identity and sense of self based on other multifaceted roles she plays—not solely on her single mother status. This seems to be especially urgent in order that the child's experiences and growth toward maturity not be hampered by the mother's own need for dependency. The aim of such psychological redirection necessitates some sophistication in services, but it is not new in the services field. It is certainly an aspect of services and programs that might be most acceptable, and even exciting, to the contemporary elective single mother. Such an orientation would be congruent with the attitudes of some of the most forward-looking women today, women who would be excellent role models for her.

REFERENCES

Ainsworth, M. D. S., Blehar, M. D., Waters, E., & Wall, S. *Patterns of attachment.* Hillsdale, N.J.: Lawrence Erlbaum Associates, 1978.

Cohen, J., & Eiduson, B. T. Changing patterns of child rearing in alternative lifestyles: Implications for development. In A. Davids (Ed.), *Child personality and psychopathology: Current topics.* (Vol. 3) New York: Wiley, 1975.

Eiduson, B. T. Emergent families of the 1970's: Values, practices, & impact on children. In D. Reiss & H. Hoffman (Eds.), *The family: Dying or developing.* New York: Plenum Press, 1978.

Eiduson, B. T. *Alternative families: Implications for policy.* Paper commissioned by the National Forum for Children, Youth, & Families. Cornell University & the National Parent-Teachers Association, Chicago, August 1979.

Eiduson, B. T. Changing sex roles in alternative family styles: Implications for young parents. In E.J. Anthony (Ed.), *Changing sex roles of parents and children,* in press. Also presented at the T. Stapleton (Chair), Changing roles of parents and children. Plenary Session, Congress of International Psychiatry and Allied Disciplines, Melbourne, Australia, August 1978.

Eiduson, B. T., & Alexander, J. The role of children in alternative family styles. *Journal of Social Issues,* 1978, *34,* 149-167.

Eiduson, B. T., & Weisner, T. S. Alternative socialization settings for infants and young children. In J. Stevens & M. Mathews (Eds.), *Mother/child, father/child relationships.* Washington, D.C.: National Association for the Education of Young Children, 1978, 197-221.

Eiduson, B. T., Zimmerman, I. L., & Bernstein, M. M. *Single vs. multiple parenting: Implications for infancy.* Paper presented at the meeting of the American Psychological Association, San Francisco, August 1977.

Jenkins, J. Selected variables relating to mother-child interaction observed at 18-month home visits. In J. Alexander (Chair), *Characteristics of alternative families and their children: Implications for mental health.* Symposium presented at the meeting of the American Orthopsychiatric Association, San Francisco, March 1978.

Kornfein, M. Motives, satisfactions and lifestyle stability in alternative families. In J. Alexander (Chair), *Characteristics of alternative families and their children: Implications for mental health.* Symposium presented at the meeting of the American Orthopsychiatric Association, San Francisco, March 1978.

Kornfein, M., Weisner, T. S., & Martin, J. C. Women into mothers: Experimental family lifestyles. In J.R. Chapman & M.J. Gates (Eds.), *Women into wives.* Sage annual of women's policy studies (Vol. 2). Beverly Hills, California: Sage Publications, 1976.

Luker, K. Contraceptive risk taking and abortion: Results and implications of a San Francisco Bay Area study. *Studies in Family Planning,* 1977, *8,* 190-196.

Parmalee, A. H., & Littman, R. Obstetrical complications scale. University of California at Los Angeles, 1977. (Mimeo).

Parmalee, A. H., & Michaelis, R. Neurological examination of the newborn. In J. Hellmuth (Ed.), *Exceptional infant studies in abnormality.* (Vol. 2), New York: Brunner/Mazel, 1971.

Rochford, B., Cohen, J., & Weisner, T. S. Family values in traditional and alternative lifestyles. In J. Alexander (Chair), *Characteristics of alternative families and their children: Implications for mental health.* Symposium presented at the meeting of the American Orthopsychiatric Association, San Francisco, March 1978.

Weisner, T. S., & Weibel, J. Home environments in conventional and non-conventional families (in preparation).

6

Human Ecology and Television in Early Childhood Education

Klaus Schleicher, Ph.D.
University of Hamburg, West Germany

I. HUMAN ECOLOGY

If adults have difficulty coping with the accelerating changes of modern life, children in their sensitive stages of development and psycho-physical vulnerability are all the more threatened by technological developments, social mobility and environmental disintegration. The hazards of social mobility are related to constant insecurity and lack of identity due to dissolved relationships and changing value patterns. Environmental threats range from the physical dangers of chemical poisons and urban living conditions to the stresses produced by the media and broken families. In addition to these well-recognized problems, children suffer:

— because parents and educators have lost their pedagogical self-confidence (due to the diversity of competing strategies in education);
— because researchers have not really developed integrated educational concepts nor adequately considered long-term and side effects of their curricula (due to a high degree of specialization and the pressure for instant success of programs); and
— because educational policy is strongly geared toward functional abilities needed in society (e.g., modern math) and toward adult perceptions of the world (e.g., the need for income equality), but not toward the child as such.

As a result of this, preschool education has had to struggle with numerous problems. For example, because the expansion of preschool education was heavily influenced by social unrest, most attention was paid to improving the external life conditions of the child (e.g., a depriving environment and inadequate incentives for learning). Furthermore, preschools were set up with particular learning theories in mind, so that children were observed against linear standards of development (e.g., the testing ideology). Finally, preschool education was strongly aligned with school, so that an emphasis on academic preparation (e.g., reading and writing programs) was the consequence. Comparatively less attention was paid to the comprehensiveness of the child's individual experience (although it defines what is learned), to the inner structure and transformation of personality (i.e., to the capacity for absorbing and transferring educational stimuli) (Kornwachs et al., 1978; Möhlenbrock, 1979), and to inconstancies, discontinuities, and bi-modal developments (e.g., what follows from conflicts of motivations) (see Sameroff, 1976; Tinbergen, 1972). As a result, preschool education served to a certain extent only a feeder function, with long-term and side effects not sufficiently taken into account and with paradigms of research rendered inappropriate (Clarke et al., 1976).

Already in the 1960s there was substantial criticism of the schools, accusing them of perpetuating the cycle of deprivation (Holt, 1964; Plowden, 1973). As one remedy, the enrichment of children's environments before school entrance was advocated. Supplements and alternatives to the earlier preschool concept were tested (Kinderläden, preschool play groups, Home Start programs). These developments demonstrated that effective early childhood education must begin with the parents (Bronfenbrenner, 1974; Gordon, 1971, 1972), that it has to be understood as a continuous process extending from birth through school (White et al., 1973), and that it needs comprehensive activities combining social welfare and health services, as well as media, with education (Appalachian Educational Laboratory, 1977; Appalachian Regional Commission, 1975; Organization for Economic Cooperation and Development, 1977).

In Europe an important movement arose from the community-based and parent-oriented play groups in England (Crowe, 1973) and from decentralized day-care centers or parent-child groups organized as part of family education in the Netherlands and West Germany (cf. Niehuis, 1976). Predominantly, these were mixed-age groups. Their emphasis was on the development of the child's own capacities as an individual and not on curricula; and they provided self-educating measures for parents through participation in the program (Schleicher, 1975b). One of the major achievements of this movement was that the emphasis of early childhood education in the preschool shifted from academic preparation to child development. Generally, there is still a tendency to educate children more to cope with the environment than to develop their own personalities.

One of the more challenging concepts related to personality development can be found in the Rudolf Steiner approach to education. This philosophy, applied in "Waldorf education," strives for the comprehensive development of the child; the integration of imagination, will power, social behavior and other learning capacities by means of playful self actualization; and imitative learning (because one learns to be human only through humanity). The aim here is to establish personal stability rather than to develop particular skills (Kügelgen, 1973; Lievegoed, 1976).

From the point of view of human ecology, it seems advisable for early childhood educators to consider research results and social conditions, to avoid the alienation inherent in curricular systems (as may be learned from the play group movement) (Parlett, 1970), and to strive for a mutual activation of the child's areas of experience (Dewey, 1969; Petersen, 1953). In general, the feeder function of preschool education should be clearly limited, and personal development of the individual child should be fostered.

After all, children and even embryos are not only in a stage of becoming human beings; they are already human beings (Blechschmidt, 1968). Therefore preschool education cannot be planned in retrospect—that is, exclusively from the adult's state of development. Furthermore, children urgently need help to master their "inner world" as well as their environment, because the lability of the vegetative, cerebral, and endocrine systems continuously increases (Ehrhardt, 1975), while children are faced with more and more environmental restrictions to organic, creative and practical experiences.

However, child development is burdened not only by the feeder function of preschool education but by research paradigms as well. Some characteristics of these paradigms are that only those aspects of life which can be tested are considered to be real and that the development of the child is viewed as a continuous process of improvement. These accepted views of continuity and improvement (strongly molded by Protestantism, biological determinism, nativistic theories of development, retrospective research approaches, etc.) easily overlook processes of transformation that may be marginal (Isnard et al., 1975; Zeeman, 1973). Furthermore, unidimensional modes of explanation are not sufficient to explain biological and ecological processes (Parke et al., 1975). At least until now, deviant behavior has not been sufficiently well predicted through structures which have been revealed in retrospect (Sameroff et al., 1975); qualitative aspects of developmental processes can hardly be accounted for by a theory of continuity; and possibilities for educational action may be more concealed than revealed if the assumptions of continuity and linear cause-effect improvement go unchallenged.

A similar consequence emerges from a strong alignment toward "normalcy." This orientation is a consequence of several factors, including empirical thinking, pragmatic decision making, and the "cult of normalcy" (Benne, 1969). An uncritical orientation toward normalcy easily leads to decisive reductions of the child's complexity as well as the ecological complexity. In addition, this orientation encourages an exposure of children to pressures of adaptation; it fosters uncritical attitudes toward the Zeitgeist in early childhood education; and it supports the creation of educational fads.

Even if preschool educators accept such views of normalcy and continuity, they must take into account the following research results:

- In the long run kindergartens seem to have the same and not a smaller effect than special preschool programs on children's cognitive and social development (Projektgruppe Kleinkindforschung, 1976; Moskal, 1976);
- There seems to be no curriculum which enhances the overal cognitive development of children in an outstanding way, but the relationship between the educator and the child seems to be most important for success (Smith, 1973; Weikart, 1975). Furthermore, there has been no adequate analysis of the value judgments inherent in different approaches to curriculum development, nor has there been adequate research on the socializing side effects and consequences of the implicit value judgments (Schleicher, 1977a);
- According to international comparisons of achievement in different subject areas (e.g., math and language), early admission to school has no marked effect (Postlethwaite, 1974a; Noonan et al., 1976; Postlethwaite, 1974b).

Thus, it is still pertinent to ask, as Robert Kennedy did in 1968 (Lewis, 1970), where an optimal investment in preschool education should be placed. At least it can be said that one-dimensional training programs have little meaning to the children and only minor long-term effects in education, that curricula are far less important in early childhood education than was expected (Bronfenbrenner, 1976), and that the feeder function of preschool education is rather problematic. Therefore, it appears almost self-evident from a human-ecological perspective that educators should favor preschool programs which are strongly child centered, care for children as individuals, pay attention to marginal transformations of their development, use a comprehensive and integrative approach, and above all attempt to support personal stability and open-mindedness of children. Obviously such a child-centered orientation is not without consequences for preschool television.

II. TELEVISION

Rapid changes in the visual, auditory, and tangible environments, and the quick mutations of individuals' habits and attitudes, are greatly affected by the development of communication technologies—mainly computers and television. We are not yet aware of all the long-term and side effects of these media. Nevertheless, the enormous impact of television is obvious—if one bears in mind the increase in television viewing during the last twenty years as well as the appointment of political and expert committees for the appraisal of its social implications (Report of the Surgeon General, 1972; Sloan Commission, 1971). An additional influence on society is, of course, the development of computer technology (Brown, 1970) which is more and more interrelated with television. Because most of the media, originally developed for mastering the outer world, are meanwhile somehow dominated by their own dynamics, it is hardly surprising that they are at the same time important educating and alienating forces. On the one hand TV is highly recommended for education of all ages; on the other hand it has remarkably changed the life style of the family and it challenges children in a powerful way. Preschool children have been growing up with television since the late fifties, and they increasingly participate in media viewing, even at night. Hence, the medium is a strong socializing influence (Schleicher, 1973; Schleicher, 1977b).

In the face of this situation the broadcasting corporations in a variety of countries have reacted quite differently. In Great Britain a special program for small children was developed as early as 1953 ("Watch with Mother," later "Play School"). In West Germany, on the other hand, it was officially recommended that young children should not watch TV at all. Furthermore, the minimum age for viewing was repeatedly raised (up to 8 years of age in 1958), and no preschool series were developed until the mid sixties (Programmbeirat für das Deutsche Fernsehen, 1960). In the U.S., young children became the most dedicated TV watchers in society, and their entertainment programs were heavily loaded with commercials and "bash, bang, and burn" elements (Schleicher, 1972).

Educational aspects of early childhood television did not receive much attention until there existed some examples from educational programs for schools, a strong drive for an expansion of early childhood education to safeguard equal educational opportunity, and a sufficient amount of feedback from compensatory programs (like Head Start) to demonstrate that supplementary encouragement in the home was desirable. The most important push for the development of preschool television programs came in response to "Sesame Street," in the late sixties. On the one hand, the compensatory concept, the clear objectives, the thorough planning and evaluation schemes, the endeavor to provide additional learning material, and the sometimes overpowering selling strategy resulted in an international demand for and supply of preschool television programs. On the other hand, it is precisely because of "Sesame Street's" too narrow and formal objectives, because of its psychedelic methods, and because of its very limited compensatory effect (if there is any at all) that more and more important questions were raised. These questions include:

— whether training in formal skills really leads to new perceptions or perhaps prevents them;
— how short-term interests of children (encouraged by TV) can be extended, and how the child's own activity can be stimulated;
— whether or not children's ways of coping with their environment calls for a clear separation of realistic, fantasy, and trick elements in television programs; and
— what long-term side effects result from TV viewing by children.

Probably it is no mere coincidence that the side effects—if not the dangers —of the "plug in drug" are now perceived especially in the U.S., following ten years of "Sesame Street" (Winn, 1979). Attention is now being paid to mental and behavioral changes in children who are heavily geared toward TV, and there is a demand for more supervision of children's TV viewing. Some writers have even recommended that children be kept away from the "tube" whenever possible (Kügelgen, 1975; Petitjean, 1978). This viewpoint (though on a different level of experience and discussion) is almost identical to that of the West German counseling committee's recommendation to TV stations in 1960.

In sum, over the last ten years there have been two patterns in the development of preschool TV in different countries. In countries with little previous experience, such as the U.S., Japan, or West Germany, large-scale programs came suddenly on the market. They had been designed to use the capacities of the media and to further the aims of educational policy rather than with respect to the developmental capacities and personal needs of children. In contrast, countries with longer experience in the area of preschool television, such as Great Britain and Switzerland, did not have very high expectations with regard to televised education and were not ready to concentrate on cognitive training. Instead they used approaches similar to kindergarten to stimulate the child's own activity (Craft, 1971; Dölker-Tobler, 1979; Sims, 1971).

Within the last ten years these concepts and strategies have had an impact on preschool TV in European countries. After an initially strong orientation toward the technical "know how" of "Sesame Street," the half hour dramatized show as well as the magazine-style program prevailed. The resulting European programs entertained in an amusing way, offered factual information closer to children's own experiences, and tried to promote children's understanding of interaction problems. There was little commercial-like animation and little training in preparatory skills for school but more continual endeavor to stimulate and "orient" the child's experience. The overall situation of preschool television in Europe is to a certain extent in line with recommendations of the *Television Guidelines for Early Childhood* (Mukerji, 1969) and with television series like "Ripples," "Around the Bend," or "Mr. Rogers' Neighborhood."

Altogether, the preschool television programs in Europe are more homogeneous today than they were ten years ago, and they are better adjusted to children's experience in kindergarten than in the past. Nevertheless, certain national preferences persist: e.g., the child's own activity is strongly promoted in Switzerland, England and Finland, whereas training in the cognitive domain is favored in France. In addition, it is still unclear in what ways the activities of television and kindergarten should be interrelated. Finally it must be stressed that most day care centers and preschools do not integrate TV programs into their work, and that many teachers, sponsors, and national representatives are not quite convinced that preschool television programs support children's educations or are really beneficial to children (Council of Europe, 1977; Schleicher, 1973).

The general importance of TV for preschool children is still up for debate. It cannot be properly assessed if one takes into account only the overall amount of TV viewing and the effects of preschool television programs. The child's mastering of the mediation effect of TV has to be considered too, along with the fact that the media are only part of a complex environment and a related socialization process. But, since the majority of children in Europe and the U.S. watch TV (in Europe about 1½ to 2 hours per day; in the U.S. more than 4½ hours), it clearly seems to be necessary to create specific TV shows at the preschool level.

There is of course controversy over how and to what extent children assimilate the content offered by TV. Here, evaluative studies seem to indicate that in the short run TV may be an effective medium through which simple skills and concepts in the cognitive domain could be taught, though the data are not beyond question (Cook et al., 1975; Schleicher, 1972). What still must be clarified is the long-term importance of cognitive skills for the child's intellectual curiosity and capacity and, furthermore, what happens if the child's conceptual comprehension through primary experience is replaced by an assimilation of mediated concepts (Dölker, 1979).

Besides producing some "gains" in the cognitive area, the exposure to pro-social programs has been said to result "in increased pro-social interpersonal behavior" (Coates et al., 1976; Liebert et al., 1973; Marencic, 1976; Stein et al., 1972). But until now, only limited and responsive behavior modifications have been observed. Even then, neither the social viewpoint of the communicator nor the recipient's purposeful action based on the recipient's identity has been sufficiently taken into account. In addition, the importance of complementary social and environmental influences has hardly been considered (Teichert, 1972).

Finally, the contradictory finding that children appear to be influenced by pro-social segments and not by segments showing brutal content needs to be clarified (see Report to the Surgeon General, 1973). Ever since the mid 1970s, when the supposed cognitive and pro-social effects of preschool television were tested (primarily in one-dimensional studies), it has been emphasized that television effects could be evaluated only as an element within a more complex socialization process. At least there were a few attempts to analyze whether television messages reinforced, contradicted, or were irrelevant to messages from other sources (Anderson et al., 1976; Schramm et al., 1961).

Until now, only a few basic observations have been pointed out in European studies:

— that parents, preschool educators, and teachers differ in their attitudes toward preschool television (Bredow Institute, 1975);
— that the more parents watch TV, the more their children watch too (Emnid, 1971; Feilitzen, 1975);
— that there is a stronger tendency to communicate during preschool telecasts

if viewing is done at home rather than in day care centers (Bredow-Institut, 1973);
— that selection of preschool programs is substantially influenced by parents (especially the mother) (Frank, 1974; Hess et al., 1962; Horn, 1976);
— that there is a marked influence on children's learning from TV if adults join them in watching (Grewe-Partsch, 1975; Leifer et al., 1975).

So far, studies have concentrated mainly on the intervening effects of television programs. Researchers have paid less attention to the change of interaction patterns of the socializing agents with the children and with one another. Hardly any consideration has been given to the long-term psychological consequences of unintegrated and competing influences from television and the environment. After all, aside from comments on the teaching capacity of television and its meaning as an interacting socialization factor, there are some clues which show that the mediation effect of television—the effect of the medium as a medium, so to speak—should be of some concern. Although research is in the initial stages, it appears likely that the medium has some strong affective and emotional side effects which have been underestimated. According to memory curves, apprehended knowledge decreases rather quickly, whereas it takes much longer for emotional impressions to fade. Consequently, emotional impressions which have been provoked through media tend to gain a certain autonomy and disconnect themselves from the overall comprehension (Allouche-Benayoun, 1975; Huth, 1978; Sturm et al., 1972; Sturm, 1973). However, the psychic consequences of this disconnected emotional excitement have not been analyzed at all, although hints of Lorenz might stir up speculations (see Lorenz, 1972).

Some further concerns exist about the emotional repercussions of television viewing. Some studies indicate that the preschool child who passes through a period of high activity and experimentation is forced into increasing passivity—if not lethargy—through extensive television viewing. In that case, television not only reduces the child's inclination toward play (Firnkes et al., 1972) and limits the child's social and environmental first-hand experiences, but it may also reduce the basic learning drive and self-guidance of the child. On occasion, it might even provoke symptoms similar to a drug-induced state of mind (Kügelgen, 1975; Winn, 1977).

Although not much is yet known about psychological effects of media viewing (disregarding content), it would be irresponsible to ignore the possible effects of TV on mental health. Consequently, the overall importance of preschool TV should not be assessed only in terms of cognitive gains and the development of pro-social attitudes. The psycho-physical side effects of TV viewing and the role of TV in the child's socialization should also be considered. From the perspective of human ecology, it can be stated that the impact of media on children is far more intensive than the impact on adults, since the children's emotional, intellectual, and volitional capacities have not yet been developed through primary experiences (Brudny, 1974). Furthermore, the inner strata of the child's mind are not sufficiently protected against interference because children meet with television "as an object and subject of interaction" (Likhachew, 1975; Zieris, 1960) and sufficiently understand neither the content nor the methods of the media (Sturm, H., et al., 1977). This suggests that early childhood educators and parents should guarantee: (1) that small children watch far less TV than adults; and (2) that children are not left to face all the media options without guidance or to cope with raw impressions unassisted.

Altogether, the development of preschool television programs seems to be desirable, since such programs are geared far more toward the needs of children than are competing programs. However, preschool programs should not be rated primarily on the number of viewers they attract or the extent to which they further specific aims of educational policy. Above all, preschool programs should be conceptualized as a contribution to the advancement of children's personal stability. As far as the content of preschool TV is concerned, there should be less preparation (for school abilities) because such programs tend to incorporate reality into ready-made answers and may easily contradict the child's own experience. In contrast, there is a need for programs which activate children's experiences with their environment and among themselves, because such programs could strengthen the motivation to master different stimuli, and they are more likely to promote the individual identity of children. To prevent the mediation effects of television from undermining such an experience-oriented concept, it is necessary to concentrate on half-hour dramatized shows and to develop multi-media components. The dramatized shows at least allow for emotional continuity and guide the children's attention in a concentric way (see the concept of "Pusteblume"). In addition, the multi-media components offer a chance for children to get rid of some irration, to pick up some television impulses, and to work on them in their own environment. Whenever possible the multi-media concept should be expanded by "compound measures." The simplest form of a compound system already exists, if parents join the TV set. Certainly it would be advantageous if there were more integrated family programs (White House Conference, 1971) or complex multimedia systems (Liikanen, 1974).

Whereas it is clear that there are many problems (e.g., the *amount* of time children spend watching TV) that cannot be solved even by the most thoroughly planned TV programs, it is possible for parents and educators to use television in a child-centered rather than a media-centered way. Because we can expect an expansion in the development of audio-visual media in the coming years and an accompanying increase in children's TV viewing, it is important that educators consider television in setting their goals. Previous goals have focused on social problems (e.g., inequality of income) or educational fads (e.g., reading drill, modern math), rather than on the child's own right for developmental particularity or the ontogenesis of the human personality. Now it is time for a new orientation in early childhood education, one that focuses instead on human ecology.

REFERENCES

Allouche-Benayoun, B. Der EingluB des bewegten Bildes auf Kinder und Jugendliche. Französische Forschungen von 1970-1975. *Fernsehen und Bilding. Internationale Zeitschrift für Medienpraxis.* 1975, *2-3*, pp. 229-249.

Anderson, K., Comstock, G., & Dennis, N. Recommendations for priorities; Research on television and the young. *Journal of Communication,* 1976, *26* (2) 98ff.

Appalachia Educational Laboratory. 1966-1976: Ten years of service to education through research and development. *Annual Report,* 1976, Charleston, 1977.

Appalachian Regional Commission. Subcommittee on health and child development. *Final Report,* 1975.

Benne, K. D. The soul of post-contemporary man. Boston, Mass.: 1969.

Blechschmidt, E. Vom Ei zum Embryo. Stuttgart, 1968.

Bredow-Institut für Rundfunk und Fernsehen: Begleituntersuchung zur Fernsehserie 'SesamstraBe.' Aufbau der Untersuchung und erste Ergebnisse. Hamburg, 1973.

Bredow-Institute für Rundfunk und Fernsehen: Begleituntersuchung zur Fernsehserie 'SesamstraBe.' Ausgewählte Ergebnisse des Gesamtprojekts. Hamburg, 1975.

Bronfenbrenner, U. Ökologische Sozialisationsforschung (K. Luscher, Ed.). Stuttgart, 1976.

Brown, G. N. Towards an education for the 21st century: A world perspective. In G.N. Brown & S.J. Egglestone (Eds.), *Towards an education for the 21st century.* University of Keele, 1970.

Brudny, M. Audio-Visual media in Kindergarten. *Educational Media International,* 1974, *4,* 23ff.

Clarke, A. M., & Clarke, A. D. B. The formative years? In A.M. Clarke & A.D.B. Clarke (Eds.), *Early experience: Myth and evidence.* New York: Free Press, 1977.

Coates, B., Pusser, H. E., & Goodman, J. The influence of "Sesame Street" and "Mister Rogers' Neighborhood" on children's social behavior in the preschool. *Child Development,* 1976, *47* (1), 138ff.

Cook, T. D., Appleton, H., Conner, R. T., Shaffer, A., Tamkin, G., & Weber, St. J. 'Sesame Street' Revisited. New York: Russell Sage Foundation, 1975.

Council of Europe. Pre-School education for children living in sparsely populated areas. Doc. CCC/EGT (77) 43. Strasbourg, 1977.

Craft, R. Play school play ideas. London: 1971.

Crowe, B. The playground movement. London: 1973.

Dewey, J. The child and the curriculum. Chicago, Ill.: University of Chicago Press, 1969.

Dölker-Tobler, V. Medienkundliche und medienkritische Sendungen im Fernsehprogramm für Kinder und Jugendliche. In G. Wodraschke (Ed.), *Medienpädogogik und Kommunikationslehre.* München, 1979a.

Dölker, C. 'Wirklichkeit' in den Medien. Stuttgart/Zürich, 1979b.

Ehrhardt, H. E. Aggressivitat, Dissozialität, Psychohugiene. Bern, 1975.

Emnid-Institute. Siedlungsverband Ruhrkohlenberzirk: Freizeit im Ruhrgebiet. Bielefeld, 1971.

Feilitzen, D.v. Ergebnisse skandinavischer Forschungen zum Thema: Kind und Fernsehen im SozialisationsprozeB. *Fernsehen und Bildung. Internationale Zeitschrift für Medienpraxis,* 1975, *2-3,* pp. 143ff.

Firnkes, M., Keilhacker, M., & Vogg, G. Das Fernsehen im Vorschulalter. Empirische Studie über Funktion und Wirkung des Fernsehens bei Kindern im Vorschulalter. München, 1972.

Frank, B. Kinder vor dem Bildschirm—Sehgewohnheiten und Sehinteressen. In A.-L. Heygster & D. Stolte (Eds.), *Fernsehkritik, Kinder vor dem Bildschirm,* Mainz, 1974.

Gordon, I. J. Parent involvement in compensatory education. Urbana, Ill.: 1971.

Gordon, I. J. What is success? Paper presented at the National Association for the Education of Young Children Conference (ED 071 767), Atlanta, 1972.

Grewe-Partsch, M. Fernsehen und Sozialisationsprozesse in der Familie. Ergebnisse des Prix Jeunesse Seminars 1975. *Fernsehen und Bildung,* 1975, *9* (1), pp. 70-79.

Hess, R. D. & Goldman, H. Parents' view of the effect of television on their children. *Child Development,* 1962, *33,* 411ff.

Holt, J. How Children Fail. New York: 1964.

Horn, J. Kinder und Fernsehen. Neuere Untersuchungsergebnisse zum Fernsehverhalten von 3-9 jährigen. *Media Perspektiven,* 1976, *8,* 357ff.

Huth, S. Emotionale Wirkungen von Film und Fernsehen. Ergebnisse aus der empirischen Forschung. *Fernsehen und Bildung,* 1978, *3,* 235ff.

Isnard, C. A. & Zeeman, E.C. Some models from catastrophe theory in the social sciences. In L. Collins (Ed.), *Use of models in the social sciences.* London: 1975.

Kornwachs, K. & Lucadou, W.v. Funktionelle Komplexität und Lernprozesse. *Grundlagenstudien aus Kybernetik und Geisteswissenschaft,* 1978, *19* (1), 1-10.

Kügelgen, H.v. Plan und Praxis des Waldorfkindergartens. Stuttgart, 1973.

Kügelgen, H.v. Fernseh-geschädigt. Begründete Literatur zu einem Aufruf, die kleinen Kinder vor dem Bildschirm zu schützen. Studienheft 7, Internationale Vereinigung der Waldorfkindergärten. Stuttgart, 1975.

Leifer, A. D., Gordon, N. J., & Graves, S. B. Kind und Fernsehen—Aktionsplan für künftige Forschungen. *Fernsehen und Bildung. Internationale Zeitschrift für Medienpraxis,* 1975, *1,* 9ff.

Lewis, A. Preschool breakthrough: What works in early childhood education. Washington, D.C. 1970, ED 054 846.

Liebert, R. M., Neale, J. N., & Davidson, E. S. The early window: Effects of television on children and youth. Elmsford, N.Y.: Pergamon Press, 1973.

Lievegoed, B. C. Entwicklungsphasen des Kindes. Stuttgart, 1976.

Liikanen, P. The use of TV-programmes and other materials in the Finnish kindergarten. *Educational Media International,* 1974, *4,* 3ff.

Likhachew, B. Television, art, and children. *Soviet Education,* 1975, *17,* 56ff.

Lorenz, K. Die acht Todsünden der zivilisierten Menschheit. München, 1972.

Marencic, H. Soziales Lernen mit 'SesamstraBe': Konfliktverhalten. In J. Kob et al. (Eds.), SesamstraBe-Vorschule im Fernsehen. Bredow Justitut, Hamburg, 1976.

Möhlenbrock, R. Modellbildung und didaktische Transformation. Grundzüge und exemplarische Anwendung eines modelltheoretisch-orientierten Transformationkonzeptes. Ph.D. Hamburg, 1979.

Moskal, E. Probleme des Übergangs zur Schule aus der Sicht des Kindergartens. Unsere Jugend, 1976, *1,* 12-19.

Mukerji, R. Television guidelines for early childhood education (Prepared for National Instructional Television), Bloomington, Ind., 1969.

Niehuis, E. Dezentraler Kindergarten. Elternmitwirkung und Elternbildung. (Ed. by Paritätisches Bildungswerk, Landesverband Niedersachsen e.V.), Hannover, 1976.

Noonan, R. & Wold, H. Nipals path modelling with latent variables. Stockholm, 1976.

Organization for Economic Cooperation and Development, Centre for Educational Research and Innovation: Early Childhood Education. Integration between the educational sector and the health and welfare sector within the framework of early childhood. Report by B. Sandgren, Memeo, CERI/ECE, 77.4 (c.f.: OECD, CERI/ECE, 77.2-77.7).

Organization for Economic Cooperation and Development, Centre for Educational Research and Innovation: Early Childhood Education. Report by M. Rein and S. White. Mimeo. CERI/ECE, 77.8.

Park, R. D. & Collmer, C. W. Child Abuse: An interdisciplinary analysis. In M.E. Hetherington, et al. (Eds.), *Review of Child development research,* Vol. 5, 1975.

Parlett, M. R. The syllabus-bound student. In L. Hudson (Ed.), *The ecology of Human intelligence.* London, 1970.

Petersen, P. Führungslehre des Unterrichts. Hamburg, 1953[4].

Petitjean, A. L'>overdose<televisee. In Le Monde, September 15, 1978.

Plowden, B. Presidential Address to be given at the Annual Conference of the Preschool Playgroups Association, Edinburgh, April 7, 1973 (Mimeo).

Postlethwaite, N. T. A Selection from the overall findings of the IEA study in science, reading comprehension, literature, French as a foreign language, English as a foreign language and civic education. IIEP Occasional paper, 1974, *33. (a)*

Postlethwaite, N. T. Cognitive results based on different ages of entry to school. A comparative study. *Journal of Educational Psychology,* 1974, *66* (6). *(b)*

Programmbeirat für das Deutsche Fernsehen: Empfehlungen für ein Nachmittagsprogramm. *Fernseh-Rundschau,* 1960, *6.*

Projektgruppe Kleinkindforschung an der Pädagogischen Hochschule Rheinland/Abt. Köln: Überschau über die Ergebnisse der Vergleichsuntersuchung der Projektgruppe 'Kleinkindforschung' im Modellversuch 'Kindergarten und Vorklasse' des Landes Nordrhein-Westfalen, Köln 1976.

Report to the Surgeon General: *Television and growing up: The impact of televised violence.* Washington, D.C.: U.S. Government Printing Office, 1972.

Sameroff, A. J. & Chandler, M. J. Productive risk and the continuum of caretaking casualty. In F.D. Horowitz (Ed.), *Review of child development research, Vol. 4.* Chicago/ London: University of Chicago Press, 1975.

Sameroff, A. J. Early influences in development: Fact or fancy? In S. Chess & A. Thomas (Eds.), *Annual progress in child psychiatry and child development, Vol. 9, 1976.* New York: Brunner/Mazel, Inc., 1977.

Schleicher, K. Sesame Street für Deutschland? Notwendigkeit einer vergeleichenden Mediendidaktik, Düsseldorf, 1972.

Schleicher, K. Erziehung im Elementarbereich. Erziehungs-ufgaben und Kooperationsprobleme von Elternhaus, Kindergarten und vorschulischem Fernsehen. In K. Schleicher (Ed.), *Elternmitsprache und Elternbildung.* Düsseldorf, 1973.

Schleicher, K. Elternmitwirkung in der Eingangsstufe des Primarbereichs. In Deutscher Bildungsrat, Gutachten und Studien der Bildungskommission (Ed.), *Die Eingangsstufe des Primarbereichs, Vol. 3, Perspektiven und Modelle.* Stuttgart, 1975.

Schleicher, K. Die Notwendigkeit einer anthropologisch-ökologischen Dimension in der Curriculumentwicklung. In *International Review of Education,* 1977a, *1,* pp. 79-95.

Schleicher, K. The use of television in preschool education in sparsely populated areas. Council of Europe, Doc. CCC/EGT (77) 26-E, StraBbourg 1977b.

Schramm, W., Lyle, J., & Parker, E. B. *Television in the lives of our children.* Stanford, Cal.: Stanford University Press, 1961.

Sims, M. L. BBC Television children's programs. *EBU Review,* 1971, *3.*

Sloan Commission. On the cable. The television of abundance, New York, 1971.

Smith, M. S. Short-term cognitive effects of eleven preschool models. A summary of the evaluation of the second year of Head Start Planned Variations. Paper prepared for the proceedings of the 1973 biannual meeting of the International Society for the Study of Behavioral Development. Mimeo 1973.

Stein, A. H., Friedrich, L. K., & Vondracek, F. Television content and young children's behaviour. In J.P. Murray, E.A. Rubinstein, & G.A. Comstock (Eds.), *Television and social behaviour. Reports and papers, Vol. 3.* Washington: 1972.

Sturm, H., Haeber, R., & Gelmreich, R.v. Medienspezifische Lerneffekte. Eine empirische Studie zu Wirkungen von Fernsehen und Rundfunk. München, 1972.

Sturm, H. Das verschwundene Objekt. In Deutsche Schule, 1973, *1*, pp. 22ff.

Sturm, H. & Grewe-Partsch, M. Wirkungen des Fernsehens: Forderungen und Defizite. Ansätze zu einer Medienpädogogik. *Fernsehen und Bildung,* 1977, *3*, pp. 172ff.

Tinbergen, N. Instinktlehre. Vergleichende Erforschung angeborenen Verhaltens. Berlin/ Hamburg, 1972[5].

Teichert, W. >Fernsehen< als soziales Handeln. Zur Situation der Rezipientenforschung: Ansätze und Kiritk. *Rundfunk und Fernsehen,* 1972, *4,* pp. 421ff.

Weikart, D. P. Über die Mirksamkeit vorschulischer Erziehung. *Zeitschrift fur Pädagogik,* 1975, *21* (4), pp. 489-511.

White, B. & Watts, J. C. *Experience and environment: Major influences on the development of the young child.* Englewood Cliffs, N.J.: Prentice-Hall, 1973.

White House Conference on Children 1970. Report to the President, Washington, D.C. 1971.

Winn, M. Die Droge im Wohnzimmer, Reinbek bei Hamburg 1979 (The Plug-in-Drug, N.Y. 1977).

Zeeman, E. C. Applications of catastrophe theory. 1973 (Mimeo).

Zieris, F. Die Bedeutung des Fernsehens, für Kinder und Jugendliche, Ph.D. München, 1960.

7

Children's Behavior in Preschool Settings— A Review of Research Concerning the Influence of the Physical Environment

Elizabeth Phyfe-Perkins
University of Massachusetts at Amherst

INTRODUCTION

Whether they take the position that early interaction with a stimulating environment is crucial for development (Bloom, 1964; Deutsch, 1966; Hunt, 1961) or the more pragmatic approach that environmental design helps manage behavior (Dodge, 1978; Kritchevsky & Prescott, 1969), early childhood educators tend to be interested in the physical aspects of classroom organization. The purpose of this paper is to summarize the literature that focuses on the relationship between the physical environment and children's behavior in educational settings.

Hunt (1961, 1969) stressed the role of early interaction with the environment in determining the rate and nature of development—both mental and physical. By formulating "the problem of the match" in early childhood education, Hunt called upon educators to develop programs that would provide children with a variety of experiences that were sufficiently incongruous with their previous learning. The correct match, according to Hunt, should be neither too strange nor too familiar, thereby stimulating an optimal interaction between child and environment.

In a more recent exploration of the relationships between environment and development Kagan et al. (1978) spent two years studying children raised in a day care center and in their own homes. These authors concluded that there is little evidence to support the *prediction* of future characteristics from behavior measured during the first two years. Kagan et al. continue to affirm

*The author wishes to thank Dr. Paul Gump for his assistance in providing her with various articles and references.

the influence of environment but with the following caveat: If one supports the idea of development as an interactive process, then it is sensible to expect instability of traits over time as the child interacts with more, and more varied, settings. "We are led to suggest, therefore, that if a psychological structure established in early childhood is to be maintained for a long period of time, and some are, it must be supported by the current environment" (Kagan et al., 1978, p. 144).

If we can provide for an optimum level of child-environment interaction in the preschool years but cannot control future environments, what prognosis can we make concerning children's future development? This is a crucial question for early childhood educators as well as for the significance of the studies reviewed in this paper. Kurt Lewin (1931) offers a rationale for our attention to the immediate environment of young children. He asserts that, although situational effects cease when the child goes out of the field or setting, the influence of that environment remains because there have been changes in the individual as he or she interacted with the setting. Thus the environment ". . . changes the 'basis of reaction' to all later situations" (Lewin, 1931, p. 123).

Foreshadowing the work of the ecological psychologists such as Barker and the environmental psychologists such as Proshansky, Ittleson, and Rivlin (1970), Lewin speaks of the valences or coercive forces of the environment.

> Objects are not neutral to the child but have an immediate psychological effect on its behavior: many things *attract* the child to eating, to climbing, to grasping, to manipulating, to sucking, to raging at them, etc. These imperative environmental facts—we shall call them valences—determine the direction of behavior. Particularly from the standpoint of dynamics the valences, their kind (sign), strength, and distribution must be regarded as the most important properties of the environment. (Lewin, 1931, 101)

The valence of an object is positively correlated with the needs of the child at the moment. It derives its strength and positive or negative sign from the fact that the object either satisfies the child, is a means to such satisfaction, blocks the child, or is rivaled by other forces in the field. Valences change with the age and developmental level of the child as well as with the psychological state of the child. Behavior is seen as a function of the interaction between the person and the environment: $B = f(P\,E)$ (Lewin, 1931).

Thus, the concern of this paper with environment in early childhood education is based on an interactionist theory of development and a pragmatic interest in the influence of the environment on behavior. Although most educators accept the premise that development is a function of child-environment interaction, there is less acceptance among practitioners that today's classroom behavior can be analyzed in terms of the children's interaction with their immediate environment. In particular, three aspects of the physical environment will be considered. The first is the fixed and semi-fixed features of the environment, ranging from doors and windows to colors and textures; the second is the amount, variety, type, and display of movable objects or materials. The third is activity settings, which may include both objects and physical space. Research findings in each of these areas are summarized in order to discover significant principles underlying the influence of the physical environment on child behavior in preschool settings.

FIXED AND SEMI-FIXED FEATURE SPACE

Exploration of the effect of the physical environment on behavior involves the conceptualization of various dimensions of physical space. Fixed and semi-fixed feature space are two categories utilized by Hall (1966) in his study of physical effects called *proxemics*. Fixed features include doors, windows, room size, and other permanent aspects together with our human expectations regarding their permanence. Semi-fixed features include furniture, rugs, and large pieces of equipment. This category was expanded by Weinstein (1975) to include color, warmth, and texture. Hall adopted the terminology of Osmond (1957) when he described two opposing configurations of semi-fixed feature space. Sociopetal space brings people together, as in the arrangement of tables and chairs in a French sidewalk cafe. Sociofugal space keeps people apart, as in the placement of long benches in a railway station waiting room. Hall's thesis is that people are affected by the dimensions of fixed and semi-fixed features and that one's perception of and attitudes toward spatial elements are culturally bound.

The research on fixed and semi-fixed features relevant to preschool settings is primarily concerned with crowding, the arrangement of equipment, and the division of space. Each of these factors is discussed below.

Crowding

There have been various studies of the effect of crowding on the social interaction of young children (Hutt & Vaizey, 1966; Loo, 1972; McGrew, 1972; Preiser, 1972; Smith, 1974; Smith & Connolly, 1972). With the exception of those of Loo, Preiser, and McGrew, the studies reveal that the level of social interaction, including aggressive acts, increases as space decreases. McGrew (1972) distinguished between two aspects of crowding: social density, increasing the number of persons in a space; and spatial density, decreasing the amount of space available to a constant number of people. Running behavior was decreased when the space was reduced regardless of the size of the group in the space. But when space was held constant and the number of children was increased, the incidence of running was not influenced. McGrew found that children moderated their social interaction when social density was increased, perhaps to avoid conflict situations. McGrew concluded that both the variables of space and number of children were significant in relation to preschool children's behavior. With a reduced density of children (space remaining constant), more solitary activity and fewer aggressive acts occurred. Where space was reduced and the number of children was retained, there was less running and more physical contact among children.

Preiser reduced the floor space of a preschool from 35 square feet per child to 22 square feet, keeping the amount of equipment and toys constant. The author did not find increases in social interaction or aggression. He did draw the following conclusions regarding the reduction of space:

> The differentiation of activity areas is blurred.
> Children tend to stand rather than sit or kneel.
> Some children decrease their levels of social interaction.
> Single person usage of objects tends to decrease.

Loo (1972) found significantly less aggression, less social interaction, and more interruption of activities in the high spatial density condition for four- and five-year-olds in groups of six. Loo kept movable object resources constant in both conditions. She compared 44 square feet per child to 15 square feet per child. Loo analyzed her findings in the following manner:

> The effect of spatial density on aggression may differ from that of social density. In a condition where space remains constant while people increase, the new members may be perceived as the cause for discomfort. On the other hand, when the number of people remain constant while space decreases, members do not see each other as causes of their discomfort; rather they may perceive they are all pawns to something greater than themselves, their physical environment. In such a condition, it is postulated that aggression between members would be significantly less. . . . Assuming that interaction with other children is conducive to maturity of social behavior, crowdedness over a long time span may retard the development of more mature social behavior in children. (Loo, 1972, pp. 379-380)

Peck and Goldman (1978), in a naturalistic study of children's play behavior with simple versus complex play structures, found that increased social density resulted in significant increases in imaginative play, the sharing of a common play theme and neutral or onlooker behavior. The authors speculate that the addition of more peers in the play structure area stimulated the positive aspects of play by providing more opportunity for sharing of themes and interaction among dramatic sequences. The increase in the onlooker category may be related both to a decrease in social interaction due to crowding (Loo, 1972; Preiser, 1972) and/or due to interest in watching the increasingly imaginitive sociodramatic play going on in the space. The number of square feet per child in the crowded and uncrowded conditions is not reported.

Smith and Connolly (1976), in presenting some of their recent research, propose a formula for identifying the parameters that have been manipulated in studies of crowding.

N = number of children in the group

R_s = spatial resources

R_p = play equipment resources

D_s = spatial density = $\dfrac{N}{R_s}$

D_p = play equipment density = $\dfrac{N}{R_p}$

They suggest that the major crowding studies have manipulated different aspects of the environment and, thus, have achieved conflicting results. Other problems with these studies include the lack of distinction between aggression and rough and tumble play, the confounding influence of novelty in some of the restricted space conditions, and the violation of the independence requirement of statistical analysis (such violation contributes to an overestimate of the size of the significance levels found).

Smith and Connolly carried out three successive studies in naturalistic settings. Group size was varied in each of three conditions in which equipment and space were expanded to keep the same ratio ($D_p + D_s$) constant. In other words, the number of children increased as the equipment (R_p) and spatial (R_s) resources increased. No significant main effects were found except for a decrease in rough and tumble play in the smallest group size/resources condition in one of the experimental groups. In the second experiment both spatial (R_s) and play equipment (R_p) resources were varied independently, with group size being held constant at twenty-four children. One, two, or three basic sets of play equipment were provided to the children at different times during each spatial density condition: 25, 50, or 75 square feet per child. As there were no significant interaction effects, only the results for spatial variation will be presented here. There were no significant effects for levels of children's cooperative play or aggression, but rough and tumble play decreased significantly ($p < .05$), in the highest spatial density condition (25 square feet per child).

The third experiment varied spatial density using 15 square feet or 60 square feet per child, maintaining a group size of ten in one group, thirty in another, and an equipment density (D_p) of one play set per ten children. There was a nonsignificant tendency for less group play in the higher spatial density condition and significantly more aggression ($p < .01$) for one group in the small space condition. Rough and tumble play decreased significantly as space decreased. The authors suggest a possible threshold effect of 25 square feet per child for aggressive behavior. Smith and Connolly conclude that increasing spatial density to 15 square feet per child results in more aggression. However, Price (1971) and Loo (1972) used spatial densities of 15 square feet per child and found a decrease in social interaction. Their findings of reduced aggression may be due to the inclusion of rough and tumble play (which decreased at 14 square feet per child) in the category of aggression (Smith & Green, 1975).

Pollowy (1974) found that as the floor area expanded (no dimensions presented), there was an increase in child-equipment interactions as well as an increase in the use of the floor for the unexpected use of equipment. Simultaneously, the appropriate use of tables and table top equipment decreased. As a plausible explanation of these results the author suggests that the increase in floor area increased the children's initiative in choosing activities.

Krantz and Risley (1972) varied the spatial density of a constant number of children in familiar nursery activity settings. When the children were crowded onto a 3 x 4 foot blanket listening to a teacher reading a story their level of attentiveness and lack of disruptive behavior fell to 60 percent from a mean of 87 percent when they were spaced in a semicircle 2 feet apart. During a teacher-led demonstration of materials, they were coded as attentive only 51 percent of the time in the crowded condition as opposed to 90 percent when they were seated around a table.

Fagot (1977), attempting to control for the spurious effect of *change* of density on children's behavior, observed children in five preschools that varied in density from 1.6 m per child to 10.46 m per child. She predicted that positive social interaction and task behavior would be lower in schools with higher densities. However, the Dutch children in the high density conditions spent almost half their time in positive social interaction, whereas American children in less crowded schools spent only 27 percent of their time that way. The author concludes that high density does not necessarily result in negative behavior among children but does have an effect on teacher behavior and classroom structure. Teachers in the crowded schools were more directive and had more specifically planned curricula.

In a study of the effect of spatial density on Head Start teachers' controlling behaviors, Perry (1977) found that teachers in classrooms with less than 30 square feet per child exhibited more controlling behavior toward children (46.7 percent) than did teachers who had over 49 square feet per child at their disposal (16.2 percent). In eight of the ten higher spatial density classrooms, free play consisted of playing with manipulative materials at tables as opposed to the use of blocks, wheel toys, and doll corner in the larger classrooms. Although the author does not record specific differences in resources within the two types of classrooms, one can infer from the description of free play that the smaller classrooms contained fewer and smaller items than the larger ones.

Shapiro (1975) observed children's behavior in seventeen preschool classrooms which varied in ratio from 29 to 52 square feet per child. She found that in the crowded classrooms (under 30 square feet per child) noninvolvement of children was the highest, occurring 26 percent of the time. This behavior category included deviant, onlooker and random behaviors. In classrooms measuring between 30 and 50 square feet per child, noninvolvement fell to 15 percent; and in large classrooms, over 50 square feet per child, noninvolvement rose 20 percent. The first finding, that of high noninvolvement in crowded classrooms, echoes the threshold effect suggested by Smith and Connolly (1976) that aggressive behavior increases below 25 square feet of space per child. Since Shapiro included deviant behavior in the category of noninvolved but did not report component scores, it may be that the incidence of deviancy contributed largely to the increase of noninvolvement in classrooms having less than 30 square feet per child.

It seems that broad generalizations are not warranted about space variation, per se, except for a possible bottom threshold of 25 to 15 square feet per child for increased aggression, lower social interaction, and increased noninvolvement. When social density increases and/or when the competition for equipment resources increase, then there are more apparent effects.

The Arrangement of Equipment and the Division of Space

Prescott, Jones, and Kritchevsky (1967) carried out a large study of fifty randomly selected day care facilities in Southern California. Among their findings was that average sized playgrounds, 2,000-4,000 square feet, were seven times more likely to be of "high yard quality" than small yards (less than 2,000 square feet). They also found that the shape of the yard was consistently related to its level of organization: the relationship between clear paths, yard boundaries, and amount of surface covered with equipment (Prescott et al., 1967). Square yards had consistently low levels of organization in that a large open "dead" space often occurred in the middle. Irregularly shaped and rectangular yards, using the same principle of placing objects around the perimeter, fared better because the middle area resembled a long path, channeling children along to other activities. The authors' definition of "high quality" space leads into an analysis of Hall's (1966) second category—that of semi-fixed features. All yards were rated according to the level of organization (defined above), special problems, and three equipment classifications (degree of complexity, variety, and amount).

Maximum crowding of yards was related to low yard quality.

> Space quality clearly predicts differences in teacher behavior and children's responses. High quality space is associated with sensitive and friendly teachers, interested and involved children, non-routine encouragement, and high numbers of lessons in consideration and creativity. Low space quality tends to have neutral and insensitive teachers, children who are less involved and less interested, increased guidance and restriction and lessons in rules of social living tend to be high. . . .

> We feel that our data have shown not only that space strongly influences behavior in day care centers, but also that space itself is subject to influence by other factors, and that by and large the staff has little or no awareness of either influence. (Prescott et al., 1967, pp. 330-331)

The organization of equipment within a fixed space has been the subject of various authors (Day & Sheehan, 1974; Dodge, 1978; Fitt, 1974; Irwin &

Bushnell, 1976; Kritchevsky & Prescott, 1969; Mangurian, 1975; Sheehan & Day, 1975). The size of play spaces within a room tends to regulate the size of the group and thus may draw children of varying social abilities and inclinations. Fitt (1974) found that a classroom arranged in several large areas contained groupings of from five to eight children often involved in noisy, boisterous activities, whereas a separate classroom arranged in small learning areas was typified by groups of two and three children engaged in quieter interactions. There was more large muscle movement in the former and more task involvement in the latter.

As Proshansky and Wolfe (1974) have noted, there are two major ways that the physical design affects the learning process in classrooms: (1) the physical arrangement communicates a symbolic message of what is expected to happen; and (2) there are functional consequences resulting from the arrangement of the furniture (e.g., several seats around a small table encourage conversation more than do rows of individual desks).

Although the design of semi-fixed features is often a concern of early childhood practitioners, there is little resource material relating the arrangement of equipment to children's behavior. Day and Sheehan (1974) related the integration of the physical space, arrangement of materials, and adult-child interactions in nurseries and day care settings to seven growth-producing categories of child and teacher behaviors. Positive elements of organization included the use of several small rooms, provision for privacy, accessibility of materials, high frequency of adult-child interactions, and compatibility of adjacent learning areas. However, no specific research was reported that related such environmental variables to frequencies of child behaviors. Dodge (1978) suggests that the design of semi-fixed feature space and the display of materials elicit various behaviors and feelings in children, but she does not report any research.

Sheehan and Day (1975) recommend the presence of both open and enclosed spatial areas to provide for the needs of children in day care. Open space does not allow children to escape noise and stimulation, whereas small spaces allow for privacy, introspection, and retreat. These authors noticed particular children wandering or in irritable and aggressive moods in day care centers that contained no private areas. To such a large open-space classroom known for its noisy, boisterous character, the authors added 6-foot dividers and low shelves for frequently used materials. They reported a subsequent drop in frantic behavior, an increase in cooperation, and a decrease in noise. Irwin and Bushnell (1976) suggest that interest areas be spread out on a noisy-quiet, active-passive continuum. They suggest that rooms be arranged so that the amount of waiting and readying behavior is diminished. Mangurian (1975) describes a "structured open plan" which makes use of strong visual cues that continue to organize the space when the movable partitions are withdrawn. Without the partitions a free-flowing open environment is available to all the children. Movable walls contain shelves and display areas. Structural steel beams support swings or divider curtains. He suggests that the children and teachers can control such an environment rather than be controlled by it.

In the interests of exploring children's preference for the arrangement of equipment, Pfluger and Zola (1974) arranged for a group of nursery school children to move their classroom equipment into an adjacent hall. The children then brought in and arranged the items they wished to play with. After several weeks most of the equipment was returned to the classroom, but with some notable differences. First, all the semi-fixed features were arranged against the walls, leaving a large open area in the center. Second, the piano and the tables and chairs were never returned to the room. The children enjoyed the freedom of the floor space for carrying out art and construction projects as well as for informalizing the snack procedure. Major foci of activity in the new arrangement were the trucks, blocks, and housekeeping areas. Children brought materials from various curriculum areas to form complex dramatic play settings such as a hospital or a space ship. Pfluger and Zola conclude that the children created a truly "child centered" room arrangement in which their activities were not constrained by an adult designed environment.

The importance of clarity and size of paths among activity centers has been emphasized by Kritchevsky and Prescott (1969) and Pollowy (1974). Pollowy found that an increase in the ease with which children could visually identify learning areas was accompanied by a concomitant increase in the number of child-equipment interactions. There is no further definition of what constituted the "easy identification of learning areas," but perhaps the guidelines of Kritchevsky provide an operationalization of the concept of clarity. Paths may be too narrow (thus inviting an inappropriate flow of activity), may be visually obstructed at the child's eye level, may awkwardly detour around a sandbox (thus encouraging children to take a "short cut"), may lead children to a "dead" space, or simply may be nonexistent. The authors describe the behavioral consequences of each. They advocate the formation of clear paths as an environmental means of channelling children's energy into appropriate activity and preventing disruptions of ongoing activity.

In terms of conclusive research on the arrangement of semi-fixed feature space, work has been done with adults in mental health institutions (Ittleson, Rivlin, & Proshansky, 1970; Osmond, 1957; Sommer, 1959). Following Osmond's (1957) work on the arrangement of furniture to encourage social interaction, Sommer (1959) found that people occupying seats at corner table spaces talked more than people seated alongside or more than 5 feet apart across from each other. Sommer's later work (1969) indicates that furniture arrangement is a potentially effective means of influencing social interaction among people. One implication of such research may be relevant to the common early childhood practice of arranging an entire class of children in a large circle for group discussion time. Sommer found that although participants preferred opposing seats rather than alongside seats for conversational purposes, they avoided opposing seats when more than 5 feet existed between them. Thus, a large circle of children 15 feet in diameter may not support the developmental goal of language development usually attributed to "circle time."

Norum, Russo, and Sommer (1967) investigated the seating preferences of pairs of preschool children when they were given variously a co-active, a cooperative, or a competitive task to complete. Pairs of children entered an adjacent room in the preschool where there was a 30- by 66-inch table with six chairs, two at each side and one at each end. Pairs completing the cooperative task tended to sit side by side. During the competitive task they sat next to each other around a corner, and in the co-active task they chose the most distant seating arrangement of one at each opposite corner. Very few children sat directly across from one another, but girls tended to sit side by side, the most intimate condition, significantly more often than boys did ($p < .05$). The authors conclude that the task-induced relationship between the children affects the proximity of their chosen seating patterns. Srivastava and Good (1968) found that interaction occurs more often in spaces that have a functional reason for people congregating there (e.g., a nursing station or a window that provides contact with the outside world). Eastman and Harper (1971) acknowledge the support or lack of it that the physical environment can offer for certain activities. They advocate that designers not only plan to support all the anticipated activities of potential users, thus maximizing behavioral freedom, but also plan the environment to channel behavior, thus encouraging some behaviors while limiting others. For preschool children these objectives for behavioral planning are most appropriate because children of this age need an environment that both protects them and allows them freedom to exercise new skills and interests.

An example of behavioral planning is evident in a comparison of two third-grade integrated day classrooms (Zifferblatt, 1972). In one class the dependent variables of task attention span and number of correct problems were higher and the incidence of nontask talking and nontask movement was lower. The organization of semi-fixed features supported the desired behaviors in the successful classroom. Desks were arranged in clusters of three or fewer in separate areas (vs. one cluster of twelve desks), thus reducing visual and verbal distractions and providing for small group interaction over tasks. There was a private cozy nook that children used for quiet study or personal retreat. There were comfortable areas set aside for chatting and socializing, thus channeling this behavior in an appropriate way and avoiding the "contamination" of work areas. The function of each of the environmental provisions is, of course, speculative (Zifferblatt, 1972), as no controlled research was carried out. However, this study suggests the importance of providing spaces for a full range of behavior.

Provision for privacy has been advocated by various educational authors (Day & Sheehan, 1974; Prescott, 1978; Proshansky & Wolfe, 1974). Sommer (1969) has explored the human need to regulate interaction with the world, and Zifferblatt (as noted above) cites the provision of a small cubby-like private space as one of several variables that promoted task involvement and higher educational achievement in one classroom. Prescott (1978), in a comparison of home day care and two types of center based day care, notes that the child may easily find private space in the home but not in the classroom. She associates the provision of private space with the presence of softness. Indicators of softness include:

child/adult cozy furniture: rockers, couches, large pillows, etc.
large rug or full carpeting
grass on which children can play
sand for children to play in
dirt for digging
animals to hold and fondle
single sling swings
play dough
water play opportunities
very messy materials such as mud, finger paint, clay, shaving cream
laps, adults holding children
(Prescott, 1978, p. 16)

In Prescott's study, homes had high softness ratings. Closed structure day care centers (in which teachers make most of the decisions) contained three or fewer of the above indicators. These centers also ranked lowest in provision for privacy. Although the observed child behaviors cannot be linked solely to the presence or absence of privacy and softness, it is of interest to note that closed structure settings registered much lower frequencies of children being physically active, giving orders, selecting and choosing, asking for help, giving opinions, and engaging in playful intrusions than did either open structure settings (medium) or home settings. Home care settings had the highest frequencies of the "thrusting behaviors" just listed, as well as the highest softness and privacy ratings. It seems self-evident that young children may need a chance to rest and to control or limit their interaction with the world when they feel the need—not just at nap time. However, there does not appear to be any research that isolates the provision for or lack of privacy in order to correlate that variable with behavioral consequences for preschoolers. Campbell (1979) reports that preschoolers did not choose to use private spaces for solitary activity. He notes that their attention span on such activities was longer if they could look up and see other children playing.

However, several authors—Kohl (1970), Mack (1976), and Gramza (1970)—have explored children's preference for privacy. Gramza manipulated the degree of encapsulation of "closedness" of play boxes from two sides up to five or six. Children preferred complete enclosure in varying sizes of boxes. In examining the attributes of closed space with one side open that might attract children, Gramza constructed 32-inch cubes of opaque, translucent, and clear plexiglass. Children consistently preferred the opaque and translucent boxes, lending support to the idea that the attraction of enclosed space includes a visual limitation as well as a physical boundary. Herbert Kohl (1970), in a discussion with elementary school students about how to improve the classroom environment, found that they wanted private work spaces where they could think, work, or have a private conversation.

Mack (1976) gave 9-, 10-, and 11-year-old children permission to create private space in the classroom. They used cardboard and paper to close off areas utilizing a large metal T.V. stand, a corner of the room, a closet, a storage cabinet, the area underneath tables, the tops of tables, and a large packing box. Children reported relief, increased ease of concentration, and the ability to complete assignments.

These informal reports are in accord with Canter and Kenny (1975), who suggest that privacy is the right to regulate the input and output of information to and from oneself. They see this attempt to regulate as the basis of all human behavior in relation to spatial features.

Other variables in the physical environment that have been associated with successful child care include the provision of sufficient workspace (Prescott, Jones, & Kritchevsky, 1972; Proshansky & Wolfe, 1974; Weinstein, 1977), an appropriate noise level (Day & Sheehan, 1974; Proshansky & Wolfe, 1974).; Cohen and Lezak explored the effect of noise on the perception of social cues in adults in a laboratory setting and found that high noise levels inhibited social but not task-related cues. Weinstein and Weinstein assessed the effect of naturally occurring background noise on the reading achievement scores of fourth graders in their own home rooms. The authors found no adverse effects of noise on achievement except that children tended to work more slowly in the noisy condition.

In an impressive attempt to measure preschool environments, Harms and Clifford (1978) prepared a "Day Care Environment Rating Scale." This scale was developed from work done on the Day Care Environment Inventory (Harms & Cross, 1977). There are seven major variables: personal care of children, furnishings and display for children, language/reasoning experiences, fine and gross motor activities, creative activities, social development, and adult needs. Although the scale includes more variables than just physical space in its definition of environment, and although formal research has not been carried out that relates the ratings for furnishings and spatial organization to children's behavior, the scale is one of the few attempts to *measure* environments for young children found in the literature.

Although much more research is needed to relate aspects of fixed and semi-fixed feature space to behavioral outcomes in preschool settings, the following design principles emerge from the available data:

Crowding of children which provides less than 25 square feet per child for an extended period of time should be avoided. It may increase aggressive behavior and inhibit social interaction and involvement.

If one must increase the number of children or decrease the amount of space, adequate equipment must be provided for the number of children present to promote positive social behavior.

Square yards are more difficult to organize well than are rectangular or irregularly shaped yards. However, all yards can be arranged well.

The level of organization of a play space can be measured by judging the clarity of paths (to children), the avoidance of dead space, the ratio of uncovered space to equipment-filled space, and the presence of clear boundaries around activity areas.

Clear paths may result in fewer disruptions and more goal-related behavior.

Arranging physical space in early childhood settings so that it provides for a wide range of children's behavior includes the following principles:

Privacy seems to be a normal need of children in full-day group situations and the provision for privacy may increase desired behaviors;

The provision for softness as in home care may allow children to snuggle and comfort themselves when adult laps are in short supply;

Low noise levels may allow attention to social as well as to task related cues in the environment;

Small enclosed areas encourage quiet activity and small group interaction;

Physically bounded small work spaces may reduce visual distraction and increase work-related behavior in classrooms;

Large spaces allow for active boisterous play, large group activities, and higher noise levels;

The arrangement of seating spaces can encourage conversation or inhibit it.

Juxtaposition of activity settings along a continuum from noisy to quiet and from active to subdued may help children avoid distracting each other.

Semi-fixed feature space may be arranged so that the functional consequences of the physical design support the behavioral goals set for the children.

THE AMOUNT, VARIETY, TYPE, AND DISPLAY OF MATERIALS

Nicholson's Theory of Loose Parts states:

In any environment both the degree of inventiveness, and the possibility of discovery, are directly proportional to the number and kinds of variables in it. (Nicholson, 1974)

Various studies have been carried out relating materials to young children's behavior. Some studies looked at children's preferences for toys (Bott, 1928; Bridges, 1927; Cockrell, 1935; Farwell, 1925; Herring & Koch, 1930;

Hulson, 1930; Majer & Grimer, 1955; Thomas, 1929) and the type of social interaction that occurs when certain toys are used (Green, 1933; Hulson, 1930; Kawin, 1934; Markey, 1938; Murphy, 1937; Quilitch & Risley, 1973; Updergraff & Herbst, 1933; Van Alstyne, 1932). The effect of the amount of play materials on children's behavior has been investigated by Johnson (1935), Smith and Connolly (1973), and Doke and Risley (1972). Access to play materials has been studied by Montes and Risley (1974) and Pollowy (1974). Shure (1963) found that children's behavior differed depending on the learning center in which they were located. On the practical side, Kritchevsky and Prescott (1969) analyzed materials according to the level of complexity and the "amount to do per child." These authors, Proshansky and Wolfe (1974) and Dodge (1978), call for easy access to materials by children and the opportunity for children to follow through on activities without disruptions or distractions.

Holding Power, Attention Span, and Social Value of Materials

Bridges (1927) observed 3-year-old children during free play with Montessori apparatus and found that graded cylinders, bricks, and color pairs were chosen most often, with bricks being used for the longest amount of time, followed by the cylinders. In her 1929 study of 4-year-olds, Bridges found that dressing games, cylinders, inset tracing, and wooden insets were most popular. She concluded that materials which were colorful, presented self-evident problems, and yet allowed for variation were chosen frequently and sustained the interest of the 4-year-olds. However, Bott (1928), observing fourteen 2-, 3-, and 4-year-old children in nursery school, found that raw materials (e.g., clay, sand, blocks) and locomotor toys had the greatest appeal to all the children. Pattern toys gain in appeal as a child grows older, while mechanical toys have little value at any age. Herring and Koch (1930) observed children alone in their homes with five toys and found that toys do vary in their power to attract children (average number of times toys used) and to hold their attention (average amount of time per child spent with a toy). A truck was most attractive, followed by a top, acorns, tinker toys, a box, and then a book. But the acorns had the highest holding power, followed by the tinker toys, the truck, and the book. Older children had longer attention spans. Children in Bridges' (1929) preschool setting maintained an average attention span of 5.3 to 6.5 minutes, as opposed to 1.5 to 2.5 minutes in the Herring and Koch restricted setting. Farwell (1925), after fourteen days of observing 271 children during 30 minutes of daily free choice, concluded that floor blocks, clay, watercolors, alabastine paint, and sewing were the most popular with kindergarten, first-, and second-graders. Drawing and paper construction proved not very interesting, although there was increased interest in them at each successive grade level.

Moyer and Gilmer (1955) attempted to maximize the attention span of children by providing them with specially designed toys in a nondistracting environment. Only one toy was provided to one child at a time. The authors concluded that toys must satisfy the developmental needs of the child at a particular age. One toy, the "people wagon," had a mean attention span of 15.6 minutes for 3-year-olds, which increased steadily to a mean of 31.9 minutes for 6-year-olds. However, two other toys, the "circus wagon" and the "chips and wagon," held the attention of 2-year-olds the longest, with average spans of 26.5 minutes and 34 minutes respectively. The authors claimed that their data showed "that there is no regular increase in attention spans of children from year to year for toys specifically designed for maximum holding power" (Moyer & Gilmer, 1955, p. 200). Kounin & Sherman (1979), in a naturalistic study of the ecology of the preschool environment, distinguished between the attention span of children and the "holding power" of activity settings furnished with distinct categories of materials and props. He found few significant correlations between the duration of involvement (i.e., attention span) of each youngster and the nature of the activity area in which the youngster was playing. However, he did find that particular areas had high holding power, in that children tended to remain in them. Art, roleplay, sand, and books held children's interest the longest. Clothing, displays, and vehicles involved children for the shortest amounts of time.

Several studies in the 1930s looked at behavior when children were playing with specific types of toys. Updegraff and Herbst (1933) compared the social interaction among 2- and 3-year-olds when they were provided with blocks and with clay in a laboratory situation. The combined sociability index and the frequency of cooperative behaviors were higher for clay. There were more instances of conversations unrelated to the material (clay) and more watching and imitating. For the 3-year-olds, block play was accompanied by more conflict but also more mutual activity related to the material. Markey (1938) found cooperative behavior high when children played with blocks.

Hulson (1930) observed children in a preschool over a one-year period and ranked eighteen kinds of play materials according to the number of times chosen, the number of minutes used, the duration of usage (the holding power of the item), and the social value (defined as the number of children playing together). Blocks and sand ranked first and second respectively on all counts. Watching others was the third most popular activity but had a low social value. McDowell (1937), studying 2- and 3-year-old children during their free choice period, found that materials that could be used in constructing other objects were used most frequently.

Van Alstyne (1932) observed 112 children in seven nursery and kindergarten classes as they played with twenty-five kinds of play materials. She assessed the popularity of the toys, their holding power, their social value, and their constructive vs. manipulative usage. The social value index included the amount of conversation that occurred; the amount of parallel, passive, and active cooperative play that occurred; and the number of children engaged in play with a particular material. Raw materials—those that are open ended and can be used in many ways—occupied children from 33 to 55 percent of the time. And within this category, blocks were used from one-third to one-half of the time that raw materials were coded, with clay, painting, and doll corner following in popularity. Raw materials elicited the longest attention spans.

There were definite social value differences among the materials. Dishes, hollow blocks, doll corner, big wagon, parallel bars, telephone, wooden blocks, colored cubes, ball, crayons, and clay all evoked conversation from children 30 to 48 percent of the time. Passive cooperation was associated with clay, crayons, scissors, painting, beads, puzzles, books, and balls. Active cooperation occurred most often on the parallel bars (for 2- and 3-year-olds only) and with the wagon, dishes, hollow blocks, wooden blocks, doll corner, colored cubes, and dump trucks. Throughout all age groups (3 to 5 years) there was little interest in pattern toys, indicating that usage of a toy can be determined by physical construction of the toy. Van Alstyne found a positive relationship between age and the length of attention span, amount of conversation, and amount of passive and active cooperation. Over 50 percent of the children of all ages tended to play by themselves when engaged with material. Ninety percent of the play of 2-year-olds and 70 percent of the play of 5-year-olds involved no active cooperation. There was a significant correlation between age and the constructive (vs. manipulative) use of materials. Between 3½ and 4½ years, there was a rapid rise in the constructive use of seven raw materials: blocks, clay, scissors, hollow blocks, crayons, and colored cubes. Van Alstyne found that children were engaged with materials for 98 percent of the time during which they were observed, lending credibility to the importance of the materials in early childhood programs. The author suggests that the following factors may influence play behavior: amount of adult stimulation, prominent placement of materials, the ratio of toys to the number of children, the amount of previous experience, and the length of the play period (60 minutes as opposed to 45-minute periods elicited a two-minute increase in the average attention span). Since there was such a wide range in children's preferences for a material (from 0 percent to 60 percent), and since attention spans varied from 1 to 45 minutes, the author suggests that a wide variety of materials be made available to satisfy a range of individual needs. Since younger children played with twice as many toys as five-year-olds, she concludes that 2- and 3-year-olds may need a greater variety of toys than do older children.

In similar but less extensive observational studies, Murphy (1937) reported that cooperative behavior was more frequent when children used swings, tricycles with a place for a rider, and wagons; and Green (1933) found that dramatic play materials in the doll corner elicited the most cooperative behavior among preschoolers.

More recently Rosenthal (in Kounin, 1979) found that various materials have significantly different potentials for social interaction. Children were found working alone more than 50 percent of the time when using puzzles, vehicles, or putting on clothing. In contrast, groups of six or more were found most often (although less than 25 percent of the time) in the art, large blocks, and music areas. Sand, science props, climbers, and books frequently involved children in groups of two or three. Rosenthal did not measure social interaction but rather took the population density of an area as an index of the potential for social interaction.

Most of these studies reinforce the idea that children interact with different materials in qualitatively and quantitatively different ways. They are attracted to some materials more frequently and they seem to stay with activities for longer periods of time. The social interaction among children appears to vary with the materials.

The Variety and Complexity of Materials
Related to an Overall Index of Space Quality

Different play materials have different potentials for play. Prescott et al. (1967) and Kritchevsky and Prescott (1969), in two related publications, have suggested an analysis of play equipment based on the level of complexity, the variety, and the amount to do per child. Simple materials (for example, swings and tricycles) have one obvious use and do not have subparts. Complex play units (e.g., play house with furniture, water table with equipment) have subparts or involve the juxtaposition of two different types of material, allowing the child to improvise and/or manipulate. Super complex units involve three or more types of materials (e.g., water and measuring equipment added to the sandbox, boxes and boards for use with the jungle gym). The more complex the unit, the more choices there are for the child to make in the course of play, and the more potential there is for group play. Complexity is seen as sustaining attention and fostering dramatic play and social interaction. Variety is the measure of the number of different kinds of things there are to do. Variety is seen as facilitating free choice in programs where children are expected to play on their own for some length of time each day. The amount to do per child is a calculation of the number of play spaces per child. This figure needs to be larger than one per child if children are expected to choose their own activities at their own speed. Other play spaces must be available to a child when he or she has finished an activity; otherwise adult direction is necessary to move children to and from the few available play spaces. Kritchevsky and Prescott suggest scheduling smaller groups of children or adding complex and super units as a means of increasing the number of available play spaces per child. The authors maintain that the variables of complexity, variety, and amount to do per child, as applied to an analysis of materials in early childhood settings, are related to children's behaviors such as attention span, group participation, dramatic play, nondisruptive free choice of activities, and goal-directed behavior.

Ellis (1974) reports a study in which one of two available 8-foot climbing structures was made more complex in two successive stages. The first alteration consisted of attaching footholds. Initially these stimulated more activity on the

structure, but soon the children returned to the simpler structure. Ellis speculates that the footholds actually reduced the number of climbing behaviors
possible and thus "simplified" the structure; he attributes the initial increased
activity to the novelty of the change. The second variation involved ropes,
platforms and ramps. These sustained the increased activity of the children
beyond the novelty period. Thus, stimulus complexity is seen as an important
parameter in analyzing the potential of materials to sustain children's play.

A figure representing yard quality (Prescott et al., 1967) was computed
by combining the following scores: level of organization (described earlier),
degree of complexity of equipment, variety of equipment, special problems,
and amount to do per child. This composite score for quality of physical space
was then related to children's behaviors and other variables. High quality scores
were positively related to high ratings of interest and involvement on the part of
children. In addition, there was a direct relationship between the percentages
of yards that were crowded, the lowness of their quality of space ratings, and a
lack of interest and involvement on the part of children. This finding is confirmed by Shapiro (1975), who found that crowded space (below 30 square
feet per child) was disorganized. Clear boundaries between activity areas dissolved, and children were "uninvolved" more than one-quarter of the time.

The Amount, Type and Display of Materials

In an experimental manipulation of materials, Quilitch and Risley (1973)
provided 7-year-old children alternatively with six social toys and six isolate
toys in a free choice situation. With the group size held constant, there were
dramatic differences in the amount of time children played together (social
play) or played alone (isolate play) in the two conditions. It was found that
social play occurred 16 percent of the time when the children were provided
with isolate toys and 78 percent of the time when they were given the social
toys. The social toys included Don't Cook Your Goose, Don't Break the Ice,
Don't Spill the Beans, Pick Up Stix, checkers, and playing cards. The six isolate
toys were gyroscope, crayons, Tinker Toys, jigsaw puzzle, Farmer Says, Talking
Book, and Play Doh. Thus, Quilitch and Risley demonstrated the influence of
the type of material furnished on the social behavior of children.

Another area that has been investigated is the effect of the amount of
materials on the behavior of children. Johnson (1935) observed three groups of
children on three different playgrounds before and after a modification in the
amount of toys and equipment. In the more extensively equipped condition
(e.g., 3-foot wide slide, rocking boat, six tricycles, six wagons, six kiddy cars,
twelve trucks, outdoor building blocks, two large boxes, saw horses, planks,
kegs, spades, and balls) children played more with materials, had more bodily
exercise, fewer social contacts, and less undesirable behavior (e.g., teasing,
crying, quarreling, hitting). A reduction in equipment resulted in less exercise,
more social contacts and more teasing, crying, and quarreling. Doke and Risley

(1972) found that children, when they were required to follow a rigid schedule of activities, maintained a high level of participation (e.g., using any of the materials in an appropriate manner or exhibiting any of seventeen designated behaviors) *only* if there was an abundance of materials in each required activity.

Smith and Connolly (1973, 1976) and Smith (1974) varied both the types and numbers of toys available to preschool children as well as the amount of space. Variation in the type of play resources produced some interesting findings. When children were provided with only apparatus (e.g., tables, chairs, Wendy house, baby carriages, climbing frame), they significantly increased their verbal and physical interaction. There was more cooperative and less parallel play. Smith (1974) was intrigued by the increased unusual use of equipment such as positioning the tables end to end as a platform for walking baby carriages and the lining up of chairs to form a pretend train. In a comparison of two experimental conditions, an apparatus-only situation resulted in more looking at other children, smiling, laughing, walking, pushing, pulling, sliding, climbing, and pedalling. In a toys-only condition, there was more watching adults, being in a large group with an adult, and more object manipulation. The toys-only condition contained beads, dolls, teddy bear, dress up clothes, tea set, drum, cymbals, bells, doll house, easel and paints, sand pit and toys, bookcase, books, blocks, telephone, twenty chairs, and three tables.

In a comparison of the control situation of both toys and apparatus with the toys-only condition, children in toys-only engaged in more object manipulation, less active physical play, less eye-rubbing, nose picking, hand fumbling, etc. The authors speculate that perhaps the toys-only condition represents a decrease in stress and indecision for the children and thus results in a decrease in stereotypic and automanipulative behaviors. It is interesting to note that the control situation revealed less aggressive behavior and thumb sucking than either experimental condition.

In an earlier study, when the authors had decreased the total *amount* of equipment (both toys and apparatus), the frequency of stress behaviors such as thumb sucking increased. In a more recent study (Smith & Connolly, 1976), a decrease in equipment led to an increase in aggression, a result which was similar to Johnson's (1935) findings. Moreover, there were no significant differences in the level of cooperative play, but rough and tumble play increased significantly in one group under the condition of fewer toys and apparatus. It seems that reducing the amount of toys per child does lead to increased aggression and that varying the type of equipment may affect social interaction among the children. An increase in the number of children (increased social density) does not increase aggression as long as the amount of equipment increases commensurately. Since most conflicts in preschools occur in relationship to materials (Smith & Green, 1975), it seems logical that a reduction should lead to increased aggression during free play situations when the most frequent activity is the use of toys and equipment.

The way in which materials are displayed has been considered an important factor in the behavior of preschool children (Brophy, Good, & Nedler, 1975; Dodge, 1978; Kritchevsky & Prescott, 1969; Montes & Risley, 1975). For example, Dodge asserts that messy and crowded displays of materials do not encourage constructive use or care of materials. She advocates simplicity, labeling of shelves, sparseness of display, and the organization of materials to teach concepts such as number, sequence, classification, or color. However, there is little research available to substantiate such intuitively reasonable guidelines for arranging materials. Pollowy (1974) found that equipment distribution or layout that restricts child access or activity increases the supervisory involvement of adults.

In a study by Montes and Risley (1975), the environment of a day care center was rearranged so that children had three weeks of "free" access and three weeks in which they were required to request the use of equipment from a teacher. The authors found that children engaged in more cooperative behavior, dramatic play, and complex language interactions during the limited access periods.

Ellis (1974) has replicated two findings concerning the color and location of materials in preschool settings. He cites the principle of centricity—that children prefer to play with an item that is centrally located. Thus the position and display of materials are important design parameters. He found that in a semicircular array of four piles of blocks, children tended to play with the outermost sets. However, he did not find a preference for one color of blocks over another.

The effects of materials provided to children in early childhood settings have been studied extensively. It seems appropriate to summarize the main findings at this point rather than to extract principles for the selection and presentation of materials. That the amount, type, and display of materials do influence children's behavior seems clear. Making decisions concerning which behaviors should be enhanced is, however, a question of educational philosophy and values. The studies covered in this section shed some light on the behavioral consequences of the presentation of materials in early childhood settings.

Choice of materials provided to children is important for holding children's attention, facilitating social interaction, and eliciting cognitive play modes. Raw materials (clay, sand, blocks) seem popular with preschoolers; sand and clay elicit solitary and parallel play as well as a functional cognitive level of play. Blocks can facilitate parallel-constructive or cooperative-dramatic play about equally.

Doll corner or house play elicits the most cooperative and dramatic play. Puzzles are characterized by solitary or parallel constructive play.

Tricycles, wagons, and swings appear to encourage cooperative behavior. The variety of materials may encourage purposeful activity, and a sufficient number of play spaces per child are necessary to enhance the flow of children from one activity to another during free choice periods.

Complex and super-complex play units can foster cooperative play as well as sustain the play activity of groups of children.

An abundance of materials facilitates positive behavior in children who are required to follow a rigid schedule of activities.

Changing the kind of materials can result in changes in social interaction, unusual use of equipment, amount of object manipulation, and level of cognitive play.

The presence of college and art materials may tend to inhibit dramatic and symbolic play.

Alterations in storage areas, work spaces, size of areas, and the inclusion of private space can result in changes in children's behavior in an educational setting.

Accessibility and display of materials may influence the degree of adult supervision and the amount of waiting and disruptive behavior of children.

Children's preferences for materials vary with age.

ECOLOGICAL STUDIES OF MATERIALS
AND ACTIVITY SETTINGS

Several researchers have assumed an ecological approach to the investigation of the physical environment and young children's behavior. Prescott et al. (1975) and Rubin and Bryant in Rubin and Seibel (1979) looked at differences in behavior across programs. Shure (1963), Rosenthal (1974), Karlson and Stodolsky (1973), Shapiro (1975), Weinstein (1977), Rubin (1976), and Rubin and Seibel (1979) examined children's behavior within subsettings or with subsets of materials in one classroom. Morrison and Oxford (1978), Kounin and Gump (1974, 1979), Gump et al. (1957), Gump and Sutton-Smith (1955), and Gump (1964) offer specific evidence of the influence of the behavior setting on young children's behavior.

Prescott et al. (1975), in the *Assessment of Child Rearing Environments: An Ecological Approach,* examine the relationship between center structure and children's behavior. The authors carefully define attributes of both closed structure centers (characterized by clarity, dependence and restriction) and open structure centers (typified by ambiguity, independence, experimentation, variety, and personal teacher approach). They observe that children in closed settings spend more time responding to their environment and attending to restraints imposed on them, that they attend more to adults, receive more adult input, and recognize cognitive constraints more than children in open structure classrooms. Children in open structure classrooms have a significantly higher rate of all thrusting behaviors, as defined earlier in the discussion of softness.

> These findings led us to a concern for the *goodness of fit* between child and center. Our definition of a good fit for an individual child in a day care

program is that the adults in the center and the activities which they provide *enable a child to experience himself as competent and likeable and provide him with opportunities for enthusiastic and sustained involvement.* (Prescott et al., 1975, p. 59. Emphasis is the author's)

The authors maintain that good placements can be made in both open and closed structure environments. Case studies of children who are nonthrivers in their current placement are analyzed in terms of recommendations for placement in either more open or more closed settings.

Elements indicative of quality in any kind of center are delineated. It is suggested that children should spontaneously initiate and terminate activities more than 30 percent of the time, not be limited in their mobility more than 50 percent of the time, and remain in structured transitions less than 20 percent of the day, and that at least five components of the softness rating (defined earlier, Prescott, 1978) should be present. For closed structure settings the major detriment to quality is seen as the imposition of restrictions on children's movement and activity that cannot be counterbalanced by the positive aspects of the curriculum. Thus the authors advocate that closed centers be somewhat "open" in that requirements for conformity to rigid behavioral expectations be relaxed to some degree. High quality open structure centers are characterized specifically by low adult-child ratios in activity segments, incidences of children receiving help, a low proportion of unfinished activities, play areas with a variety and abundance of things to do, and teachers who "open up" the alternatives inherent in an activity segment.

Kenneth Rubin (1977) describes several studies of children's free play behavior in which he utilized a combination of the levels of social participation devised by Parten (1933) and the levels of cognitive play elaborated by Smilansky (1968). Not only does Rubin contribute observational categories that are highly relevant to the investigation of child-environment interactions, but he also reports some interesting relationships among free play behavior, materials used, age, and measures of cognitive development. Rubin looked for the incidence of five levels of play (functional, constructive, dramatic, socio-dramatic, and games with rules) when the child was engaged in solitary, parallel, associative, or cooperative play. He found differences in levels of play and social participation according to the engagement of the child in various activities. He also found that only certain aspects of social participation levels were related to the age of the child. Of special interest are his findings that older preschool children playing alone engage in high levels of constructive and dramatic play. Thus, with age, solitary play becomes more mature, a finding overlooked by research that uses only the Parten Scale. Rubin found significant positive correlations between the incidence of dramatic play and measures of spatial relations and classification skills. Correspondingly, low levels of dramatic play correlated negatively with these indices of cognitive development. Of major interest here is Rubin's finding that levels of social and cognitive play are related to materials in the preschool environment. Children using play dough engaged in solitary or parallel play 65 percent of the time, using a functional mode 75 percent of the time. Sand and water play were coded as 80 percent solitary or parallel play and 90 percent functional play, whereas painting and crayoning scored 82 percent solitary or parallel and 78 percent constructive play. Use of puzzles had a similar social play profile, but constructive play increased to 84 percent. Social interaction was scored 55 percent of the time for children engaged in house play and 75 percent of their play was dramatic or socio-dramatic. Cars and vehicles stimulated dramatic play 32 percent of the time and social participation 50 percent of the time. One finding that emphasizes the teacher's role in influencing the social and cognitive value of preschool activities is the fact that reading and number activities involved associative or cooperative activity 63 percent of the time. He attributes this finding to the fact that the teacher stimulated conversations and structured both activities as cooperative efforts.

Rubin and Seibel (1979) studied changes in children's activity preferences over a three-month period. Time spent on puzzles and play dough decreased significantly, while play with construction toys and with sand and water increased. These results are confounded by a physical design change that occurred. A wall was removed to allow full morning usage of the workbench, sandbox, and waterplay table. These activities had been restricted to one-half that amount of time in the earlier observations. Changes in play categories over time included the emergence of constructive play over both functional and dramatic play in the block area during the second observation period. When the children engaged in dramatic play with blocks, it was primarily cooperative, whereas constructive block play was characterized by solitary and parallel play. The authors conclude:

> It would appear as if the degree of "freedom" [in free play] is somewhat determined by the materials available to children. For example, group and dramatic play may be inhibited by the availability of art activities. Such activities appear to encourage non-social and constructive behaviors. . . . The present study's findings appear significant for those who plan educational programs for young children. For example, it was discovered that group-dramatic play was inhibited by the presence of sand and water, puzzles and art activities. This form of play has recently been suggested, by some, to contribute significantly to the development of social competence and perspective taking skills. (Rubin & Seibel, 1979, pp. 7 and 8)

Rubin and Bryant (Rubin, 1979) compared the play behavior of children attending a Montessori preschool and those attending a traditional nursery. They found that the Montessori students engaged in significantly more solitary and parallel constructive play and signficantly less cooperative functional and dramatic play than the traditional preschool children. In a study of carefully matched pairs of students, Dreyer and Rigler (1969) attempted to explore the hypothesis that young children acquire the cognitive constructs which the materials in a Montessori school are intended to provide. The authors found the traditional nursery school children to be significantly more creative on a nonverbal creativity test. These children approached the test situation in a markedly more social manner; they used significantly more functional terms to describe objects; and they portrayed people in their drawings significantly more frequently. Montessori students were more task oriented in the test setting; they used significantly more physical attributes to describe objects; and their drawings included many more geometric shapes. The authors feel that the study lends support to the ". . . notion that differing preschool educational environments yield different outcomes" (Dreyer & Rigler, 1969).

Karlson and Stodolsky (1973) delved more deeply into the ways children utilize the Montessori curriculum. In a series of 5-minute observations, children were found to exhibit significantly different patterns of involvement with activities. Children's activity preferences were analyzed in an attempt to predict their gain scores on subtests of the Wechsler Preschool and Primary Scale of Intelligence. Involvement in the following activities accounted for 76 percent of the variance in the gains made by the children: art, 13.5 percent; construction toys, 16.8 percent; blocks, 7.0 percent; sorting and matching, 16.6 percent; and math, 22.6 percent. Children's cognitive gains were significantly associated with the materials they used.

Shure (1963) observed children during free playtime in five subsettings in a nursery school. She recorded the population density; the mobility of children in and out of areas; the appropriateness of behavior to the location; complexity of social participation; positive, neutral, or negative affect; amount of constructive play with materials; and sex differences. She found that the highest social densities occurred in blocks and art (but this finding is confounded by the relatively large size of the areas) and that the most constructive use of materials occurred in the art and book areas. Blocks elicited the lowest rating in constructive use of materials. Games and blocks had the highest ratings for solitary child play whereas complex social interaction was found most frequently in the doll corner and at least half the time in the block area. Shure suggests that the high levels of functional manipulation and onlooker behavior in the block area were due to the high social density and levels of social interaction. She also speculates that the high level of social interaction in the doll corner may be a function of the small size of the area. Finally, Shure foreshadows future studies with the question: "Would a rearrangement or addition of equipment change some of the frequencies of the behavior found in this study?" (Shure, 1963, p. 990).

Carol Weinstein (1975, 1977) set about answering Shure's question. She recorded children's behavior within different areas of an open classroom, then modified aspects of the physical design and recorded the behavior again. She avoided Shure's problem of confounding space and numbers of children by comparing the expected social density (determined by the size of the subsetting) with the obtained usage by children, arriving at a more accurate rating of the popularity of learning areas. Her intervention consisted of providing workspaces, chairs, more display of materials, more accessible storage of materials, more low partitions, and a quiet private place for rest. Specific hypotheses concerning changes in children's behavior she formulated and tested for significance. Weinstein successfully modified the children's patterns of space usage, and this resulted in children occupying areas they had previously avoided. Second, she increased, as desired, the range of behavior exhibited in certain subsettings; and finally, she altered the frequency of specific behavior categories as predicted. This study presents yet another strong case for the influence of the physical environment on the behavior of children in educational settings.

Two more studies have applied an ecological approach to the investigation of young children's behavior in school settings. Shapiro (1975), observing the free play behavior of 274 4-year-old preschool children, noted a striking disparity between children's and teachers' preferences for activity areas. She speculated that the differences might result in a loss of spontaneous teaching/ learning interactions. Children populated the block and doll corner areas 37 percent of the time, but only 17 percent of teacher-child interactions occurred in those areas. However, the art areas where children spent 21 percent of the time averaged 35 percent of all teacher-child contacts. The author suggests setting up more independent art activities so that teachers are available for interaction and observation in the active block and housekeeping areas.

Rosenthal (1973) observed the involvement of children in various activity settings during thirty-seven free play periods. The most popular settings included art, blocks, and special activities, while puzzles, books, kitchen, and sand were the least popular. Art and role-play activities had the greatest holding power over children. Children averaged twenty activity shifts per hour with only 3 minutes of unoccupied time.

> Descriptive and statistical analyses consistently implicated setting variables as more significant predictors of the content and course of free play life than the demographic variables of sex, race and age (Rosenthal, 1973, p. 4004 A)

This author (Perkins, 1980; Phyfe-Perkins, 1980a) compared children's behavior in two architecturally similar, philosophically "open" (Prescott, 1975) day care classrooms that varied on four dimensions: the arrangement of semi-fixed features, the display and type of materials, the scheduling of activity segments, and the behaviors of adults. Classroom 1 was characterized by enclosed activity centers; a wide variety of labeled and available manipulative materials and a rotating series of thematic play materials in the block corner; a 2-hour period of free play; and adults who watched, helped, or participated with children for half their time in the classroom. In contrast, classroom 2 featured undefined activity areas and two major paths that interrupted children's play; fewer and less appropriate materials in the block and manipulative areas; a 45-minute period of free play, as well as more scheduled, formal, teacher-led segments; and adults who spent only 22 percent of their time watching, helping, or participating with children. According to predictions made by the author, children in Center 1 were found to have significantly higher levels of the following categories of behavior: focusing on task, constructive play, and total verbalizations. Children in classroom 2 were significantly higher on the dimensions of waiting, unoccupied and antisocial behavior, as predicted. The dimensions of autonomy did not discriminate between the two centers, presumably because they were both "open structure" centers.

In an attempt to modify behavior in the second center, space was rearranged to eliminate the disruptive traffic patterns, a quiet room was added, and materials were supplemented and rearranged in the manipulative and woodworking areas. As predicted the levels of constructive play and focusing on task increased significantly, but there was no reduction in unoccupied or waiting behavior, perhaps because children continued to spend a large amount of time (20 percent) in teacher-led group activities.

All the ecological studies tend to point in one direction—that the early childhood subsettings, especially the materials provided in them, have a strong influence on the children entering the area. Children in housekeeping corners are frequently talking to each other and engaging in dramatic play. A well-equipped block corner seems to offer children opportunities for building and for cooperative dramatic play. In the art room children are often more subdued, less social, and busy with their creations. It seems that if centers not only select materials that match the children's interests and developmental needs, but also arrange semi-fixed feature space to promote play, the activity centers can channel behavior in appropriate and educational pursuits.

Taking a careful look at the creation of educational activity settings by preschool teachers, Lounin and Gump (1974) studied 596 lessons taught by thirty-six teachers and recorded on videotape. The lessons was conceived of as a signal system that varied in terms of continuity, intrusiveness and insulation. Children's on-task behavior constituted the dependent variable. The most successful lessons had a single continuous signal system that was "insulated" from distractions.

Kounin and Gump describe such a system:

> Let us consider the case of an individual construction lesson. The teacher provides each child with scissors, paste, a sheet of paper, and magazine pages showing pictures of food and suggests that each child make a collage of desserts. After a child begins such an activity, the major and persisting external signals come from the changing conditions of his materials. He selects a picture, but it must be cut from the page; the remaining space on the paper and the pages of pictures signal selecting another dessert, and so on. A continuous signal system occurs as one action and its immediate result provide impetus and guidance for the next action. The signal system and all individual-construction lessons thus provide continuous signals; they should induce high involvement provided each child has appropriate materials and is capable of grasping the goal and of carrying out the necessary participatory actions.

The signal source here, resting as it does on the results of each child's own actions on his own materials, produces a tight, closed behavior environment circuit. This closed circuit insulates the lesson and shields each child from foreign inputs (distractions, other children's deviancies) which may serve as stimuli to inappropriate behavior. Such a format, in addition to continuity, contains a high degree of *insulation*. (1974, p. 557)

The lowest *off-task* behavior was found in such construction tasks, followed by sequenced signals from a single continuous source such as listening to the teacher or a record. The lessons with the highest off-task scores included teacher-led recitation; role play, group discussion (characterized by multiple and shifting signals from children); and singing and body movement (characterized by high intrusiveness of props). Although some teachers can "handle" activities like group discussion or singing better than others, Kounin and Gump's research begins to analyze why these activities are difficult to manage if the goal is on-task behavior.

Kounin and Doyle (1975), following up on this inquiry, looked at pairs of high and low task involvement lessons taught by the same teachers within the same signal system format (e.g., teacher reading, teacher demonstration, and individual construction). In the analysis, the degree of signal continuity discriminated significantly between high and low task involvement of children in the same type of lesson taught by the same teacher. However, teacher regarding and teacher demonstration formats involve a different signal system from that of individual construction. In the former, the continuity of the teacher's signal emission is paramount and the amount of child recitation allowed significantly discriminates high and low task-involvement lessons. In order to tease out the distractors in the individual construction format, the authors scored lessons according to continuity detractors and continuity enhancers. These variables successfully distinguished between high and low task involvement, whereas amount of child recitation did not. This study concludes that teachers must attend to different aspects of their roles in order to enhance various activities. In individual construction teachers need to provide sufficient materials and be sure each step calls forth the next step in the project. In teacher-led formats teachers must employ a constant signal emission system avoiding the pitfall of numerous or lengthy child inputs.

Morrison and Oxford (1978) looked at a kindergarten class in order to see if continuous central signal emission and individual projects would produce more task-oriented behavior than whole class restriction. They found that students were significantly more passive, distractable, and nontask involved in class recitation than in the other two conditions. This finding is interpreted as supporting Kounin and Gump's theory that continuous signal emission, whether from teachers or well-organized materials, produces more on-task behavior.

Looking at the qualities of different day camp activity settings, Gump and others suggest detailed explanations of differences in children's behavior in different settings. Boy campers exhibited significantly more hostile acts in the dining hall than in cookouts and more aggression in cookouts than in swim (Gump, 1964). In a comparison of boy campers' social interactions (sharing, helping, asserting, demanding, and attacking), Gump and Sutton-Smith (1955) found significantly more interactions occurring during swim than in crafts. Gump, Schoggen, and Redl assert that

> Certain features of the activity-setting which support or provoke the behaviors and experiences that occur within it are clear. When props and performances are so organized that the valued actions are delayed or in short supply, an activity setting is likely to produce competitiveness whether it is in cookouts or boating. And a setting which requires performances directed at individual tasks is likely to produce lowered interaction whether it is crafts or library reading time. (1957, p. 43)

Recently, Kounin and Sherman speculated about the qualities of preschool activity settings that influence the length of time children remain involved in them. Settings with the lowest indices of holding power (clothing, displays and vehicles)

> all have a restricted range of constituent standing behaviors that are typically executed in a repetitive fashion without yielding clear indications of something being accomplished or altered as a result of the child's action. (1979, pp. 3, 4)

However, other settings with higher holding power (art, role play, books, and sand) seem to either offer a variety of expected behaviors or result in a clear sense of progress or an actual product.

Doyle (in Kounin & Sherman, 1979) found that activity settings differed widely in the amount and type of social interaction among children inhabiting them. The highest levels of socially occurred in preparation-clean up (70 percent), role play, and large muscle "multiple-niche" (e.g., equipment with places for two or more children). Audiovisual displays, small model props, "single-niche" large muscle settings, and puzzles maintained the lowest levels of social interaction—as low as 9 percent for puzzles. In addition, Doyle found that friendly cooperative prosocial behaviors occurred most frequently in role play, "multiple-niche" large muscle, preparation-clean-up, and waterplay. Such behavior was seen the least in science props, displays, art, and puzzles.

Houseman (in Gump, 1978) found that social interaction involving any kind of conflict occurred significantly more often on the climber (large muscle "multiple-niche") in the kitchen housekeeping area and with large blocks. Houseman identified factors that precipitated conflict. In the block area the blocks and the floor area are communal property. Conflicts arose because children wanted the same blocks or space. In addition a group might build a structure and "defend" it against those who had not participated in its construction. In contrast, activities that directed the child toward individual tasks, such as art, clothing, snacks, or lunch, had a very low rate of conflict-oriented social interaction.

Thus, it seems that behavior settings need to be analyzed for dysfunctional factors with respect to children's behaviors. The preceding studies suggest that rather than concentrating on getting a child to adapt to various educational subsettings, teachers should search for clues in the structure of the setting. Children may be deviating from an expected pattern of behavior because the setting does not really support the expectations that teachers or adults hold for it.

CONCLUSION

This review has attempted to provide a summary of research that relates the physical environment of the early childhood educational setting to the dependent variable of children's behavior.[1] This criterion, rather than gains in intelligence or achievement, was selected because of a belief in the importance of the child's interaction with the world as the major means of a child's growth and development. The paper intended to support the position that at least some of the variability in children's behavior in the preschool can be associated with the environment provided. Adopting such a point of view may encourage teachers and administrators to look for sources of desired and undesired child behavior in an area they can affect, namely the educational setting. Although children come to school with various agendas, the environment they encounter *does* help shape their interaction with it.

Of special importance in an understanding of the influence of the physical environment on behavior is the need to analyze space to see if it provides for a full range of children's behavior. Can a tired, unhappy child retreat to some private cozy area and regroup forces, or does the space provide only continued stimulation and frustration? Can shy children find small enclosed areas where they can flourish with one or two other children, or are such children found on the perimeter of activities, watching or playing by themselves?

Perhaps the skill of arranging the early childhood environment to support the maximum involvement of children with materials and with each other is a skill that can and should be taught. In reviewing the studies summarized here, it becomes clear that systematic observation of children at play in the educational setting is crucial to an analysis of the environment. Examining where the most social interaction, including aggression, takes place can be done at the same time as recording what level of cognitive activity occurs during each scheduled activity period (Perkins & Weinthaler, 1979; Perkins & Swaminathan, 1978). How much of the time do children wait, during transitions, for adults to pass out materials or for their turn in a small block area? Teachers and administrators might begin to look for such restrictions on child behavior that are imposed by the arrangement of the space and materials.

---

[1] See Moore et al. (1979) and Cohen et al. (1979) for a series of design recommendations for children's centers and play areas that are based on a review of the literature.

Although certain activity settings generally elicit characteristic behaviors among children, there can be no one set of prescriptions for the otpimal arrangement of space in early childhood settings. Each particular group of children enters into an analysis of characteristic patterns of child environment interactions. Some behaviors may be engendered by stresses in the children's home lives, but the provisions made for the children at the center can direct and absorb their frustrations and confusion. At this point it is important to stress the role of adults as an ecological factor in the early childhood environment (see Phyfe-Perkins, 1980b). Although the arrangement of the physical space and materials can promote behavioral expectations, teacher behavior and program format constitute major variables in the early educational setting.

In designing the physical space of the preschool, teachers need to consider the interrelationships among activity settings. If more cooperative, constructive, and dramatic play is desired, can the room(s) absorb the increased activity and noise that will likely result in expanding or adding appropriate materials to the block and housekeeping corners? If materials are taken out of closets and displayed on low shelves, are there sufficient workspaces nearby to absorb the children who are drawn to the displays?

Planning to enhance child-environment interactions involves a study of the ecology of the preschool. Reducing a characteristic behavior in one area may lead to its appearance in another less appropriate area. There is interdependence of behavior throughout the classroom. The final criterion for good planning may be expressed as follows: Do the behavior settings provide for and support developmentally appropriate activity of all the children enrolled? Perhaps the goal of studying and working with the physical environment was best stated by Pervin:

> A "match" or "best fit" . . . of individual to environment is viewed as expressing itself in high performance, satisfaction, and little stress in the system whereas a "lack of fit" is viewed as resulting in decreased performance, dissatisfaction, and stress in the system (1968, p. 56)

REFERENCES

Barker, R. G. *Ecological psychology: Concepts and methods for studying the environment of human behavior.* Stanford, CA: Stanford University Press, 1968.

Barker, R., Dembo, T., & Lewin, K. Frustration and regression: An experiment with young children. *University of Iowa Studies in Child Welfare,* 18, No. 1. Iowa City; University of Iowa, 1941.

Berk, L. E. Effects of variation in the nursery school setting on environmental constraints and children's models of adaptation. *Child Development,* 1971, *42,* 839-369.

Bloom, Benjamin. *Stablility and change in human characteristics.* New York: John Wiley & Sons, 1964.

Body, M. K. Patterns of aggression in nursery school. *Child Development,* 1955, *26,* 3-11.

Bott, H. Observations of play activities in the nursery school. *Genetic Psychology Monographs,* 1928, *4,* 44-88.

Bridges, K. J. B. Occupational interests in three year old children. *Pedagogical Seminary,* 1927, *34,* 415-423.

Bridges, K. M. B. Occupational interests of four year old children. *Pedagogical Seminary,* 1929, *36,* 551-570.

Brophy, J. E., Good, T. L., & Nedler, S. E. *Teaching in the preschool.* New York: Harper & Row, 1975.

Campbell, F. Preschool behavior study. *Architectural Psychology Newsletter,* August 1979, *3* (1), 59.

Canter, D., & Kenny, C. The Spatial Environment. In D. Carter (Ed.), *Environmental interaction.* London: Surrey University Press, 1975.

Cockrell, D. L. A study of the play of children of preschool age by an unobserved observer. *Genetic Psychology Monographs,* 1935, *17.*

Cohen, S., & Lezak, A. Noise and inattentativeness to social cues. *Environment and Behavior,* December 1977, *9* (4), 559-573.

Cohen, U., Hill, A. B., Lane, C. G., McGinty, T., & Moore, G. T. *Recommendations for child play areas.* Milwaukee; Community Design Center Inc., University of Wisconsin, 1979.

Day, D. E., & Sheehan, R. Elements of a better preschool. *Young Children,* 1974.

Day, D. E., Perkins, E. P., & Weinthaler, J. Maturalistic evaluation for program improvement. *Young Children,* June, 1979.

Deutsch, M., Early social environment: Its influence on school adaptation. In F. Hechinger, (Ed.), *Preschool education today.* Garden City, N.Y.: Doubleday & Co., 1966.

Dodge, D. T. *Room arrangement as a teaching strategy.* Washington, DC: Dodge, 1978.

Doke, L. A., & Risley, T. R. The organization of day care environments: Required vs. optional activities. *Journal of Applied Behavioral Analysis,* 1972, *5,* 405-420.

Drew, C. J. Research on the psychological-behavioral effects of the physical environment. *Review of Education Research,* 1971, *41,* 1, 447-464.

Dreyer, A. S., & Rigler, D. Cognitive performance in Montessori and nursery school children. *Journal of Educational Research,* 1969, *62,* 411-416.

Eastman, C. M., & Harper, J. A study of proxemic behavior: Toward a predictive model. *Environment and Behavior,* 1971, *33,* 418-437.

Ellis, M. J. Play: Theory and research. In G. Coates (Ed.), *Alternative Learning Environments.* Stroudsburg, Penn.: Dowden, Hutchinson and Ross, 1974.

Emmerich, W. Evaluating alternative models of development: An illustrative study of preschool personal-social behaviors. *Child Development,* 1977, *48,* 1401-1410.

Fagot, B. I. Variations indensity: Effect on task and social behaviors of preschool children. *Developmental Psychology,* 1977, *13,* 2, 166-167.

Farwell, L. Reactions of kindergarten first and second grade children to constructive play materials. *Genetic Psychology Monographs,* Vol. VIII, Nos. 5 & 6, 1925.

Fitt, S. The individual and his environment. *School Review,* August 1974, 617-620.

Gramza, A. F. Children's preferences for enterable play boxes. *Perceptual Motor Skills,* 1970, *31,* 177-178.

Gump, P. V. Environmental guidance of the classroom behavioral system. In B. J. Biddle & W. J. Ellena (Eds.), *Contemporary research on teacher effectiveness.* New York: Holt, Rinehart, & Winston, 1964.

Gump, P. V. Intra-setting analysis: The third grade classroom as a special case. In E. Williams & H. Rausch (Eds.), *Naturalistic viewpoints in psychological research.* New York: Holt, Rhinehart, & Winston, 1969.

Gump, P. V. School Environments. In I. Altman & J. F. Wohwill (Eds.), *Children and the environment.* Plenum Publishing Corp. 1978.

Gump, P. V.. Schoggen, P., & Redle, F. The Camp milieu and its immediate effects. *Journal of Social Issues,* 1957, *13,* 40-46.

Gump, P. V., & Sutton-Smith, B. Activity-setting and social interaction: A field study. *The American Journal of Orthopsychiatry*, October 1955, *xxv*.

Hall, E. T. *The hidden dimension.* New York: Doubleday & Co., 1966.

Harms, T., & Clifford, R. M. *Day care environment rating scale.* Frank Porter Graham Child Development Center, University of North Carolina at Chapel Hill, 1978.

Harms, T., & Cross, L. *Environmental provisions for day care.* Frank Porter Graham Child Development Center, University of North Carolina at Chapel Hill, 1977.

Herring, A., & Koch, H. L. A study of some factors influencing the interest span of preschool children. *Journal of Genetic Psychology*, 1930, *38*, 249-279.

Hulson, E. L. An analysis of the free play of ten four-year-old children through consecutive observations. *Journal of Juvenile Research*, 1930, *14*, 188-208.

Hunt, J. McV. *Intelligence and experience.* New York: The Ronald Press Co., 1961.

Hutt, C., & Vaizey, M. J. Differential Effects of Group Density on Social Behavior. *Nature*, 1966, *209*, 00.

Irwin, D. M., & Bushnell, M. M. Replant your learning garden. *Day Care and Early Education*, February 1976, *3*, 33-46.

Ittleson, W. H. In H. M. Proshansky, L. G. Rivlin & H. Winkel, (Eds.), *An introduction to environmental psychology.* New York: Holt, Rhinehart & Winston, 1974.

Ittleson, W. H., Rivlin, L. G., & Proshansky, H. M. The use of behavioral maps in environmental psychology. In H. M. Proshansky et al. (Eds.), *Environmental psychology.* New York: Holt, Rhinehart, & Winston, 1970.

Johnson, M. W. The effect on behavior of variation in the amount of play equipment. *Child Development*, 1935, *6*, 56-68.

Kagan, J., Kearsley, R., & Zelazo, P. *Infancy and its place in human development.* Cambridge, MA: Harvard University Press, 1978.

Karlson, A., & Stodolsky, S. Predicting School Outcomes from Observations of Child Behavior in Classrooms. Paper presented at AERA annual meeting, February 1973, New Orleans.

Kawin, E. The function of toys in relation to child development. *Childhood Education*, December 1934, 122-124.

Kohl, H. On finding private spaces. *Grade Teacher*, January 1970, *87*, 10.

Kounin, J. S., & Doyle, P. H. Degree of continuity of a lessons signal system and the task involvement of children. *Journal of Educational Psychology*, 1975, *67*, 159-164.

Kounin, J. S., & Gump, P. V. Signal systems of lesson settings and the task related behavior of preschool children. *Journal of Educational Psychology*, 1974, *66*, 554-562.

Kounin, J. S., & Sherman, L. W. School environments as behavior settings. *Theory into Practice*, Spring, 1979 (prepublication draft).

Krantz, P., & Risley, T. *The organization of group care environments: Behavioral ecology in the classroom.* Lawrence, Kansas: University of Kansas. ERIC Document Reproduction No. ED078 915, 1972.

Kritchevsky, S., & Prescott, E. *Planning environments for young children: Physical space.* Washington, DC; National Association for the Education of Young Children, 1969.

Lewin, K. Environmental forces in child behavior and development. In C. Murchison (Ed.), *A handbook of child psychology.* Worcester, MA: Clark University Press, 1931.

Lewin, K. *Field theory in the social sciences,* New York: Harper & Row, 1951.

Loo, C. M. The effects of spatial density on the social behavior of children. *Journal of Applied Social Psychology*, 1972, 2, 372-381.

Mack, D. Privacy: A child's need to be alone in the classroom. *Teacher*, February 1976, *93*, 52-53.

Mangurian, R. A celebration of space. *Day Care and Early Education*, 1975, *3*, 14-16.

Markey, F. V. Imaginative behavior of preschool children. *Monographs of the Society for Research & Child Development,* 1938, *18.*

McDowell, M. S. Frequency of choice of play materials by preschool children. *Child Development,* 1937, *8.*

Montes, F., & Risley, T. R. Evaluating traditional day care practices: An empirical approach. *Childcare Quarterly.* 1974, *4,* 208-215.

Moore, G. T., Lane, C. G., Hill, A. B., Cohen, U., & McGinty, T. *Recommendations for child care centers.* Milwaukee; Community Design Center Inc., 1979.

Morrison, S. B., & Oxford, R. L. Classroom Ecology and Kindergarten Students Task Related Behaviors: An Exploratory Study. Paper presented at the annual meeting of the American Educational Research Association, Toronto, Canada, 1978.

Moyer, K. E., & Gilmer, B. Attention spans of children for experimentally designed toys. *Journal of Genetic Psychology,* 1955, *87,* 187-201.

Murphy, L. B. Sympathetic behavior in young children. *Journal of Experimental Education,* 1936, *5,* 79-90.

Murphy, L. B. *Social behavior and child personality.* New York: Columbia University Press, 1937.

Nicholson, Simon. The theory of loose parts. In G. Coates (Ed.), *Alternative Learning Environments.* Stroudsburg, Penn.: Dowden, Hutchinson, and Ross, 1974.

Norum, G., Russo N., & Sommer, R. Seating patterns and group task. *Psychology in the Schools* 1967, *4,* 276-280.

Osmond, H. Function as the basis of psychiatric ward design. *Mental Hospitals (Architectural Supplement),* April 1957, 23-29.

Parten, M. B. Social participation among preschool children. *Journal of Abnormal Social Psychology,* 1932, *27,* 243-269.

Parten, M. B. Social play among preschool children. *Journal of Abnormal Social Psychology,* 1933, *28,* 136-147.

Peck, J., & Goldman, R. The behaviors of kindergarten children under selected conditions of the Social and Physical Environment. Paper presented at the annual meeting of AERA at Toronto, March 1978.

Perkins, E., 1980.

Perkins, E. Phyfe & Swaninathan, H. Data collection in the naturalistic evaluation of early childhood education. Paper presented at the annual meeting of the American Education Research Association in Toronto, Canada, March 1978.

Perry, G. *Cross-cultural study on the effect of space and teacher controlling behavior.* ERIC Document Reproduction No. ED131 351, 1977.

Pervin, L. A. Performance and satisfaction as a function of individual environment fit. *Psychological Bulletin,* 1968, *69,* 56-68.

Pfluger, L. W., & Zola, J. M. A room planned by children. In G. Coates (Ed.), *Alternative learning environments.* Stroudsburg, Penn.: Dowden, Hutchinson, and Ross, 1974.

Phyfe-Perkins, E. *An ecological assessment of two preschool environments.* Paper presented at the eleventh annual meeting of the Environmental Design Research Association in Charleston, S.C., March 1980.

Phyfe-Perskins, E. *The ecology of adult and child behavior in the preschool setting: A review of research.* Presented at the annual meeting of the American Educational Research Association in Boston, Mass., April 1980.

Pollowy, A. M. The child in the physical environment: A design problem. In G. Coates (Ed.), *Alternative learning environments.* Stroudsburg, Penn.: Dowden, Hutchinson, and Ross, 1974.

Preiser, W. F. E. Work in progress: The behavior of nursery school children under different spatial densities. *Man Environment Systems,* 1972, *2,* 247-250.

Prescott, E. Is day care as good as home? *Young Children*, January, 1978, 13-19.

Prescott, E., Jones, E., & Kritchevsky. Group Day Care as a child rearing environment: an observational study of day care programs. Pasadena, Calif., Pacific Oaks College, 1967. (Eric Document Reproduction Service no. Ed. 024 453).

Prescott, E., Jones, E., & Kritchevsky, S. *Day care as a child-rearing environment*, Vol. II. Washington, DC: National Association for Education of Young Children, 1972.

Prescott, E., Jones, E. Kritchevsky, E., Milich, C., & Haselhoef, E. Assessment of Child Rearing Environments: An Ecological Approach Parts I & II. Pasadena, CA: Pacific Oaks, 1975.

Price, J M. The effects of crowding on the Social Behavior of Children. Unpublished doctoral dissertation, Columbia University, 1971.

Proshansky, H. M., Ittelson, W. H., & Rivlin, L. G. The influence of the physical environment on behavior: Some basic assumptions. In H. M. Proshansky, W. H. Ittelson, & L. G. Rivlin (Eds.), *Environmental psychology: Man and his physical setting*. New York: Holt, Rinehart & Winston, 1970.

Quilitch, H. R., & Risley, T. The effects of play materials on social play. *Journal of Applied Behavioral Analysis*, 1973, *6*, 575-578.

Rosenthal, B. A. An Ecological Study of Free Play in The Nursery School. Doctoral dissertation, Wayne State University, 1973. [Dissertation Abstracts International, 1974, *37*, (7-A), 4004-4005.]

Rubin, K. H. Play behaviors of young children. *Young Children*. 1977, 16-24.

Rubin, K. H., & Seibel, C. G. The effects of ecological setting on the cognitive and social play behaviors of preschoolers. Paper presented at the annual meeting of AERA, San Francisco, 1979.

Santrock, J. W. Affective and facilitative self-control: Influence of ecological setting cognition and social agent. *Journal of Educational Psychology*, 1976, *68*, 529-535.

Shapiro, S. Preschool ecology: A study of three environmental variables. *Reading Improvement*, 1975, *12*, 236-241.

Sheehan, R., & Day, D. Is open space just empty space? *Day Care and Early Education*, December 1975, *3*, 10-13, 47.

Sherman, L. W. An ecological study of glee in small groups of preschool children. *Child Development*, 1975, *46*, 53-61.

Shure, M. B. The psychological ecology of a nursery school. *Child Development*, 1963, *34*, 979-992.

Smilanski, Sara. *The effects of sociodramatic play on disadvantaged preschool children.* New York: Wiley and Sons, Inc., 1968.

Smith, P. K. Aspects of the playgroup environment. In D. Canter & T. Lee (Eds.), *Psychology and the built environment*. England: Architectural Press, 1974.

Smith, P. K., & Connolly, K. J. Patterns of play and social interaction in preschool children. In N. B. Jones (Ed.), *Ethological studies of child behavior*. London: Cambridge University Press, 1972.

Smith, P. K., & Connolly, K. J. Toys, space and children. *British Psychological Society Bulletin*, 1973, *26*, 167.

Smith, P. K., & Connolly, K. J. Social and aggressive behavior in preschool children as a function of crowding. *Social Science Information*, 1976, *16*, 601-620.

Smith, P. K., & Green, M. Aggressive behavior in English nurseries and play groups: Sex differences and response of adults. *Child development*, 1975, *46*, 211-214.

Sommer, R. Studies in personal space. *Sociometry*, 1959, *22*, 247-260.

Sommer, R. *Personal space: The behavioral basis of design*. Englewood Cliffs, NJ: Prentice-Hall, 1969.

Srivastava, R. K., & Good, L. R. Patterns of group interaction in three architectually different psychiatric treatment environments. Research Report, Environmental Research Foundation, Topeka, Kansas, March 1968.

Tizzard, B., Cooperman, O., Joseph A., & Tizzard, J., Environmental effects on language development: A study of young children in long stay residential nurseries, *Child Development*, 1972, *43*, 337-358.

Tizzard, B., Philps, J., & Plewis, I. Play in preschool centres—I. Play measures and their relation to age, sex and I.Q. *Journal of Child Psychology and Psychiatry*, 1976, *17*, 251-264. (a)

Tizzard, B., Philps, J., Plewis I. Play in Preschool Centres—II. Effects on Play of the Child's Social Class and of the Educational Orientation of the Centre. *Journal of Child Psychology and Psychiatry*, 1976, *17*, 265-274. (b)

Updegraff, R., & Herbst, E. K. An experimental study of the social behavior stimulated in young children by certain play materials. *Journal of Genetic Psychology*, 1933, *42*, 372-391.

Van Alstyne, D. *Play behavior and choice of play materials of preschool children.* Chicago: University of Chicago Press, 1932.

Weinstein, C. S. The effects of a change in the physical design of an open classroom on student behavior. Unpublished doctoral thesis, Harvard University, 1975.

Weinstein, C. S. Modifying student behavior in an open classroom through changes in physical design. *American Educational Research Journal*, 1977, *14*, 249-262.

Weinstein, C. S. The physical environment of the school: A review of research. *Review of Educational Research*, December 1979.

Weinstein, C., & Weinstein, N. The effect of noise in an open-space school on reading comprehension. Paper presented at the annual meeting of the AERA in Toronto, Canada, March 1978.

Wright, M. E. Constructiveness of play as affected by group organization and frustration. In R. G. Barker, J. S. Kounin, & H. F. Wright (Eds.), *Child behavior and development.* New York: McGraw-Hill, 1943.

Zifferblatt, S. M. Architecture and human behavior: Toward increased understanding of a functional relationship. *Educational Technology*, 1972, *12*, 54-57.

8

Day Care
as a Resource to Families

Nancy E. Travis

Joe Perreault
Save the Children, Inc., Atlanta, Georgia
Child Care Support Center

With increasing numbers of women in the work force and with changes in the traditional family's make-up, day care is becoming more and more a partner in the child-rearing process. Such a partnership involves shared goals, planned communication, and mutual trust between parents and caregivers. Some day care programs achieve this relationship by chance and some by plan. This paper attempts to look at the relationship of parents to child care programs from a historical point of view and to offer suggestions on how a true partnership can be implemented.

A HISTORY OF DAY CARE

The day care movement in the United States has always grown in the shadow of the much larger movement to promote healthy child growth and development. Many day care leaders acquired their inspiration to serve children from the researchers and educators who pioneered the nursery, kindergarten, and pre-schools of this country. Similarly, day care leaders learned many valuable lessons about working effectively with parents from these same sources; yet day care emerged as having its own unique role to play in child rearing and family life and has contributed many insights into the variety of role relationships parents seek from the programs which serve their children. To understand the concept of day care as a family support service, it is helpful to review the history of day care and the role of parents.

Immigration and Industrialization

The first day care centers, which emerged during the late 1800s and continued through World War I, were sponsored by settlement houses and funded by affluent community-minded citizens and were designed for children of the working poor. As a part of the broader settlement house movement, these centers helped to meet a whole range of needs of families coming into cities from Europe or Asia and later from other parts of the United States such as the rural South and Appalachia. Services ranged from providing recreational programs and well-baby clinics to helping families find housing or obtain food, clothing, and fuel. Classes were offered in child care, preparation for citizenship, cooking, nutrition, and whatever else was needed to assist in survival. Thus the primary focus of day care was a social service. At the same time, there was a growing awareness of the potential for development in the young child and the opportunity for a professional role in offering advice and instruction to parents on the task of child rearing. This new-found knowledge in child development and parent education was eagerly adopted by most centers.

By the beginning of World War I, however, the growth of such centers had declined because of the decrease in numbers of immigrants to the United States.

Child Growth and Parent Education

Parent education for middle-class families had a period of growth and popularity between 1925 and World War II. The establishment of nursery schools at places like Merrill Palmer Institute and Bank Street College and the funding by the Abby Rockerfeller Foundation of Child Development Centers at universities such as Iowa, Minnesota, Stanford, Yale, and others in the early 1920s brought new knowledge and interest in the area. The cooperative nursery movement was another thrust that encouraged the study of child development by parents while their children were having a group experience. It was only at the end of this period, however, that any new day care programs were established. With the advance of the depression, WPA funds were used to establish "nursery" programs in many communities. These programs operated from 9 a.m. to 3 p.m. and included some working parents, but the real purpose was to provide good nutrition and adequate rest to deprived children while furnishing employment to out-of-work teachers and the new group of professionals from schools of child development and early childhood education. Again the focus of relationships with parents was on parenthood education.

The Crisis of War

Under the Lanham Act, passed in 1941, there began the first large-scale use of public funds to support the cost of day care. The principle goal of these expenditures for day care was to permit women to work in war-related industries, thus freeing men for combat. Many of the centers were staffed by teachers trained in the child development and parent education model but the strenuous times made it difficult to reach an ideal in teacher-parent communication. Women worked ten-hour shifts, six days a week. Their transportation to and from work was hampered by gas rationing; household shopping was time consuming; and many women were coping alone because their husbands were in the service.

Working Women as a Fact of Life

After the War, many women returned to a traditional role of homemaker and mother. Yet statistics on female participation in the workforce indicated a gradual but certain increase. What began as a trickle in the 1950s was confirmed as a flood by the late 1960s. In this new group of working women were many from low-income families who continued to need a broader kind of social program such as that provided by the settlement houses. Yet many more were middle- and upper-income women who sought to further increase their families' standards of living and who were influenced by the growing opportunity for women in professional careers and the supposed satisfactions of working outside the home.

The public funding of day care was discontinued in most communities after World War II. Yet to meet the demand for day care coming from various income levels, many independent day care organizations were established. Some were formed by nonsectarian nonprofit groups such as United Way and supported by charitable donations as well as parent fees. A larger number were initiated by church organizations which recognized that they had facilitites and some expertise in child care which could be applied to this emerging community need. An additional large thrust came from individuals, interested in the care and development of young children, who were willing to offer day care on a fee-for-service basis. They established for-profit day care centers, some of which did make a "profit" buy many of which simply provided the individual an opportunity to be with children while earning a very modest income.

The growth of day care services during this time was therefore an individualized kind of movement. Standards and practices were left to direct service staff and organizational sponsors to develop. Many academic institutions and nursery school leaders preferred to continue studying the developmental needs of children and viewed these newly formed institutions, whose tenuous funding made it difficult to hire highly qualified nursery teachers and whose long hours seemed to present less desirable teaching conditions, as low in status. The influx of more highly educated parents as well as the emphasis on purchasing a service at this time had a marked effect on the relationship between parents and day care programs. There was much less emphasis on parent education and a growth in emphasis on a businesslike relationship over the services being received by the child.

Yet it was also a period of the first full realization of the uniqueness of day care—family relationships. In individual day care centers, many astute teachers and directors began to recognize that the care of a child eight to ten hours a day was indeed different from the part-day nursery school role. Day care providers were partners in rearing the child and needed to develop a sensitivity to this shared responsibility. They had to learn to discuss with parents issues related to eating, discipline, naps, toilet habits, care during illnesses, and the many other aspects of child rearing which would be carried on by their program and which might involve conflicts in values between parent and day care programs that could be detrimental to the child. Similarly, the day care staff needed to know more about the needs of children of other than the nursery age, since many centers offered to care for infants and school-age children.

Social Change Catalyst

With the passage of the Economic Opportunity Act in 1965 and the establishment of Project Head Start, a new influence on the function of day care emerged. Head Start was designed to improve the functioning of low-income children in public schools (and, theoretically, throughout life) by involving them in a preschool program. Attention was given to health services, treatment of problems, nutrition, general child development, and especially the acquisition of cognitive skills. It was recognized early that in order to achieve these goals for children, parents would have to be involved in the process. Furthermore, Head Start was created in a climate of racial unrest and social turmoil, in which the poor and minorities felt that the larger institutions of society were not concerned about meeting their needs.

One of the strategies used both to reach Head Start's objectives with children and to make it possible for low-income parents to gain the skill and confidence to reform society was to encourage parent involvement. Parent involvement became a regular component of Project Head Start programs with its own budget and usually a staff person to assume responsibility. Parents were not merely exposed to parent education; they were encouraged or required to volunteer in the classroom, and many were hired as paid teachers in the program. They were encouraged to seek health services for themselves as well as for their children and to take a role in the actual operation of the program. Policy advisory committees made up of a majority of parents were a requirement. Parents were involved in setting policy, hiring staff, preparing the proposal which had to be submitted each year, and evaluating the program.

Parent involvement worked well in Head Start programs, particularly where mothers were not employed outside the home and were available for this intense level of participation. Encouraged by this success, day care advocates included a requirement for parent involvement in the funding standards for day care under Title IV and later Title XX of the Social Security Act. Similarly, when a comprehensive Child Development Bill was proposed in 1971 and again in 1975, the concept of parent involvement and parent control of the management of day care became a "do or die" issue for many of the leading day care political activists.

Incentive to Work and Services to Multiple-Problem Families

A major expansion of day care occurred in the late 1960s and early 1970s when public funds through Title XX of the Social Security Act were authorized to provide social services including day care for families experiencing social problems. Currently, more than a billion dollars a year is spent on day care from Title XX alone. Underlying this dramatic growth in day care services was a concern on the part of Congress and the country that the welfare system had grown too large. Day care was seen as a vehicle to move AFDC recipients into work training or paid employment and to decrease the welfare caseload. Along with this thrust was a rediscovery of the social service value of day care. Many families needed intensive social services and health services as well as day care. Parents participating in day care provided by Title XX were apt to be single parents, and a high percentage of them were current or former recipients of AFDC. Many were going to work for the first time and were trying to acquire job skills while caring for home and children. Others were physically or mentally ill and could not devote full capacity to their roles as parents and homemakers. Day care for families with such serious needs has required various kinds of supplemental resources, such as a social worker, health programs, and ongoing contact with other social agencies.

To many Title XX parents the day care center has become almost an extended family. Concern for the child's development is shared between staff and parents. Family-oriented social activities such as potluck suppers, watermelon cuttings, or ice cream socials provide an evening out at little cost for families without much money.

When asked about the kinds of things they would like to have from the center, parents sometimes express the desire to have activities for themselves— as persons, not just as parents. Classes in ceramics or sewing or how to be an effective consumer are well attended and enjoyed, and it often happens that the conversation turns to children and parenting. Such activities are usually optional, and not all parents attend.

CURRENT DAY CARE TRENDS

Recognition of Alternative Forms of Care

In the past ten years there has been a steadily increasing number of working women in the labor force and a corresponding increase in the need for child care. In addition to the rapid growth of Title XX day care there has also been an increase in day care services for middle-class families.

Although there have always been some private day care centers for families who could afford the tuition, many middle-class families have opted for other arrangements. In-home care has often been used, and care in the home of a friend or neighbor a common option. This latter choice was often referred to as baby-sitting, but it is now emerging as family day care.

In the past, many professionals saw family day care as a resource to be used when a day care center was not available; and they assumed that it would decrease when there were more centers available. It has now become evident that family day care is the true preference of many families. One reason that many parents choose family day care is that they prefer to select another family with the same general cultural background and similar values about behavior and discipline. They feel free to request certain eating and sleeping patterns which are compatible with those at home.

Because of this preference for family day care, and because it is a resource that is available in both urban and rural areas, there is a movement to organize homes into systems. Some of these are family day care agencies in which central administrative staff select homes, provide training, place children, and work to assure that the care provided is supportive of good child development.

In other instances providers themselves are forming associations and seeking training, sharing information and equipment, and advocating family day care. Because of this growing organization, family day care is beginning to receive more attention from professionals in the field and will probably continue to expand and improve.

The other large growth of day care in this decade can be seen in the emerging day care industry. In cities across the country day care chains are building new, attractive buildings located conveniently off major expressways between residential areas and places of work. They are attempting to provide good quality services but are caught between rising costs and the amount of tuition that families are able or willing to pay. It is still not completely clear whether the industry will be able to provide satisfactory care and still make a profit acceptable to investors. At the present time there appears to be a wide range in quality from one center to another.

Changes in the American Family

In addition to the fact that more women with young children are now in the labor force there have been other changes in the American family. The typical family is no longer a father who earns the living, a mother who is a full-time housekeeper, and two children. Such families make up only 20% of the population. There are many families with single parents—mothers or fathers—due to the high divorce rate. There are also many couples living together with children and without clear legal status. Furthermore, young families in our mobile society often live far from relatives and from the supports families can provide, especially in emergencies.

In spite of these changes there is still a belief that the family unit should be self-sufficient. In reality all families use some outside supports—schools, health services, recreation, to name a few. These are well accepted; but when mothers look outside for help in child rearing, some critics accuse them of shirking responsibility. These critics are often actually working to prevent the increase of day care.

Barriers to Good Parent-Caregiver Relationships

The heightened interest in the needs of the family has caused many institutions to reexamine their roles in relation to families. Day care programs have begun to realize that certain values and attitudes of staff or parents can constitute a major barrier to an effective working relationship.

Professionals in child development and early childhood education often identify so completely with the child that they do not really view the child as a family member. Most of them give intellectual recognition to the importance of the family but at the operational level entertain salvation fantasies. It is quite common to hear a teacher or caregiver say, "If it were not for the families we could do so much more for the children," or "We work so hard with the children and they seem to be making progress, and then they go back into the home and it is all lost." Caregivers do deal with parents who are immature or who have so many burdens and pressures on them that they do not carry out their parental responsibilities as well as might be hoped, but wherever possible the parental role should be supported and reinforced.

Day care providers have to be very much aware of their own values about the family and about the role of the mother as a worker. Many child care workers believe that all women should be at home with their children, and these feelings can be transmitted consciously or unconsciously. In a sense day care workers have resolved in a unique way the conflict between staying at home and working. They are in paid employment but are still engaged in a home-oriented task—that of rearing children. Thus it is not surprising that they may be critical of women whose work removes them completely from their children.

Another common barrier is an administrative one. Many programs have a policy that only the director or head teacher may talk with parents. Reasons given are that the direct caregivers are not qualified to do so and might in some way upset the parent or that there might be a breach of confidentiality. Yet often such supervisory personnel are not available very early or late in the day when parents are bringing or picking up their children.

Parents' perceptions of day care can also present a barrier. Many parents view the day care program as a "school." Sometimes their own early experiences with the educational system have made them reluctant to question school authorities. In some cases, the parents may feel unqualified to challenge the practice of a supposed expert; in other cases, the concern may be that day care staff will not accept criticism well and that it may affect the staff's relationship with the child or the child may be dropped from the program. It may be that some day care programs do react poorly to parental criticism, but generally day care programs are receptive to parental concerns and are willing to respond to them.

FUTURE DIRECTIONS AND RECOMMENDATIONS

Day care at the present time is still attempting to meet nearly all of the needs it has addressed historically and to include all the role relationships. It is true that many of those needs still exist and deserve to be met. However, our understanding of the nature of day care itself requires a different emphasis. Day care in the past was often seen as a solution to a temporary problem that would eventually be solved. In many cases it was designed to meet the needs of a specific economic and social class of parents. Any future definition of day care must recognize that day care has become a permanent support to family life in America and that parents' use of it is not limited to any social or economic group.

Wide differences in the kinds of services that parents need from day care must be recognized. Many families just need a place where their child can be safe, well-cared for, and happy during the hours that the parents must be away. They want consistent discipline, stimulating experiences, and positive social relationships for the child just as if the child were at home all day. They are interested in periodic parent conferences but do not look to the center for general information about child rearing nor for social contacts. They may well prefer not to be actively involved in the running of the center.

On the other hand, other parents view the day care center as a kind of extended family and will seek advice and reassurance from the staff, will enjoy participating in family-oriented social activities, or will want to participate in activities that enable them to learn new skills and help them grow as individuals. They may find participation in the administration of the center challenging and fulfilling to their sense of parental responsibilities.

To some degree day care programs can continue to widen their role relationship with parents and maintain a specialized approach; that is, programs oriented toward parent involvement, social services, etc., will continue to operate with this special emphasis. But it is, important to define these issues for parents before they enroll their children. At the same time, no matter what the special emphasis of the day care program, there must be a realization that the most appropriate response to a family is an individual one and that the same level of participation should not be expected from each family.

A Growth in Philosophy

At the conceptual level, there is a need for a definition of day care which integrates the many previous roles it has played and which accommodates a future that includes a supportive relationship with families and a greater diversity of forms of service and role relationships with parents. Similarly, the day care community must recognize that caregiving and nurturing are important functions. Day care providers need to accept the broader concept of day care as a partner in the child rearing process as well as a program with an early childhood education component. In our society, where more status has been given to education than to caring and nurturing, it has been easy for those in the field to emphasize education: Education in its broadest sense includes total development, but for many it means learning numbers and letters, colors and shapes—and much of the planning and in-service training in day care is focused on such activities. We would not argue against an educational thrust in day care, but we would suggest that "education" should be defined broadly and that academic preparation should not be emphasized to the neglect of other activities that contribute to preschool development.

Consumer Education

Parents need to select their child care arrangement thoughtfully. They should remember that they are still in charge of their child's life. Too often selection of a day care plan is not considered far enough in advance. Sometimes this is unavoidable if a return to work is a response to a sudden crisis, but in most cases there is time to plan and to make a thorough exploration of available options. Cost and convenience of location are often primary considerations, and they are realistic constraints.

The development of Information and Referral Services should be encouraged. In this way, parents can be advised about their options and can be given criteria to make good choices and to monitor the plan as it is carried out. Parents also need to know how to file a complaint if the situation warrants. Knowledgeable and concerned parents are the best hope for achieving and maintaining acceptable levels of quality.

Administrative Policies

With the growing appreciation of the importance and complexity of day care and its relationship to families, it is important that day care programs state clearly their goals and objectives.

It will facilitate successful carrying out of goals if these are written so that they are clearly understood by all concerned—board members, administrative staff, program staff, and parents. Having both written goals and written policies should enable a program to employ people who share a commitment to those goals and policies and to define the in-service needed for staff to carry them out.

Reexamination of the staffing practices of day care programs is another important administrative issue. Staff must have time assigned to interact with parents. In many current programs the fewest staff members are available in the early morning and late evening. These are the times that parents are readily available and are natural times to share information.

Parent-Caregiver Communication

All staff members should be capable of some communication with parents. If they are not able to do this when they join the program, it should be an early part of their training. Workers with negative attitudes toward parents should be counseled early in employment, and this basic problem should be discussed periodically during staff meetings.

All caregivers should be able to articulate the position of the program on such things as guidance and discipline; learning philosophies; simple childhood problems such as thumbsucking, bedwetting, sibling rivalry, not wanting to go to bed, etc. They should also know their own limitations and should be given help in knowing how to handle situations that are beyond their expertise. Parents who are having serious marital problems, problems with their jobs or in the community, etc., should be encouraged to talk to the director or the social worker if there is one. If the problem cannot be properly handled there, an appropriate referal should be made.

Clearly each day care program must analyze the different kinds of questions parents ask, define which staff members are capable of providing the information, and follow up with appropriate training. But a widening involvement of staff with parents is needed if each individual family is to gain a real support from day care.

CONCLUSION

There are many things that go into making a good day care program. The staff's commitment to children, knowledge of child development, and ability to carry out a successful program are extremely important. However, we also need to help people develop better interpersonal skills so that they can work successfully not only with children but also with their colleagues and the families they serve. A day care center is very much like a home. Children flourish best when there is harmony among the family members and where communication is open so that problems can be solved. Most of all, there needs to be a mutual commitment and a shared sense of satisfaction when things are going well and empathy when they are not.

This does present a very large challenge for those involved in the provision of day care. However, those people who are truly successful in working with children already have skills that can benefit the children's families—if they genuinely accept this as part of their role.

SUGGESTED READINGS

Authier, K. Defining the care in child care, *Social Work,* 1979, *24* (6), 500-506.

Powell, D. *The interface between families and child care programs: A study of parent-caregiver relationships.* Detroit, Mich.: The Merrill-Palmer Institute, 1977.

Travis, N., & Perreault, J. *Establishing a family day care agency.* Southern Regional Education Board, 1977.

Southern Regional Education Board, *Minutes. Task force on parent-caregiver relationships.* Unpublished memo, Atlanta, Georgia, August, 1976.

U.S. Department of Labor, Office of the Secretary, Women's Bureau. *Community solutions for child care: Report of a conference.* Washington, D.C., 1979.

9

School Curricula—
A Social-Psychological View

Philip Gammage
University of Bristol, England

Schooling is concerned with transmitting what society believes should be learned. Its main purpose is to "exchange ideas, resources, and people through a network of communication systems. The curriculum as taught is an example of such a communicaton system" (Skilbeck, 1976). But, as everyone knows, schooling is also used as a form of social control, a distributor of life-chances, added to which, as Silberman (1970) said, the teacher is concerned with much that does not exist in hard concrete forms: with procedures, with attitudes and feelings which act as mediators in the moving and changing process of socialization.

The socialization of the young, however, is not a one-way process, and education—as one part of the socialization process—is interpreted, selected from, adjusted to and internalized on the basis of the experience of the learner—that is, one not only teaches some *thing,* but some *one.* What is presented, the curriculum, has a transactional nature.

Curriculum arises from a history of perceptions of child-rearing and of culture; it operates within particular institutions which have real people as staff; it operates with today's children, not yesterday's; and it is institutionalized and ritualized as an artifact of the culture. Social psychology focuses on the interactions between individual psychology and social systems. The purpose of this paper is to bring the perceptions of a social psychologist to bear on curricula as currently taught *to* individuals and *by* individuals within the school system.

Much of what is taught in schools may strike one as hardly worth knowing as a child, let alone as an adult. Once, when I was a sixth-former, one of my friends studying economics estimated that 90 percent of what he was learning and had been learning over the past two years either was out of date, in strict utilitarian terms, or was related to the immediate goal of passing examinations. Now, of course, he could have been wrong—and children's views of what is useful are not the only criteria to employ by any means. Indeed, I would wish to strongly assert that a curriculum should always include an opportunity to study the "useless" as well as the useful.

Many people take an extremely "means-to-ends" view of the curriculum: They see the curriculum in the same way that they view an assembly line process in a factory. They apply the same criteria. Does the "product" sell; is it good value for the money? They take the view that education is of little or no value in itself. It leads somewhere; it gets you something. It makes you richer; it gives you prestige; or it (at very least) meets an expressed societal need. If it doesn't meet any of these requirements, you scrap it. Such views are often "heady" and persuasive stuff. Moreover, they fall into place with many an adolescent's views of relevance. Of themselves these views can lend great weight in the shaping of a curriculum. But of themselves they can easily become materialistic, shallow, and miseducative. I believe the curriculum in most schools represents at best an uneasy compromise between on one hand, the "cultural repository," traditional and ritualistic time-filling, utilitarian possibility, and, on the other hand, idiosyncratic, teacher-originated academic hobbies.

A teacher walking into the classroom is usually credited with knowing what ideas she or he hopes to deal with in the ensuing session. Experienced teachers will probably be acutely aware of the problems and pitfalls likely to occur in the sequencing of ideas. Such teachers will be aware of the constant need to be monitoring the response of pupils in order to alter and modify the level and "fit" of the material. Experienced teachers will be well aware that the shaping of much of the curriculum lies outside their hands. There are constraints upon teachers, upon their presentation, and upon their pupils' reception of their ideas. No matter how varied the pedagogical style, how attractive the packaging of knowledge, the content will be to a large extent determined by many factors totally beyond the teacher's control. For instance, the knowledge the teacher deals in will clearly be, at least in part, a portion of some existing cultural repository. It will have been shaped, altered, explored, and redefined by many minds and many social processes. Neither a particular subject nor the total school curriculum just "happens." Both depend upon a complex mixture of factors which interact in any given society. Those factors which influence the teacher's transactions with his or her pupils can be thought of simplistically in terms of relative immediacy in impact or of distance. Mr. Jones, in teaching classics on a Friday afternoon to a class of bored 15-year-olds, is likely to be most immediately concerned with holding their attention by convincing them of the utility of the subject or simply of the importance of "meal tickets" earned by passing examinations. He may wish to focus enthusiasm and encourage interest in aesthetic form for its own sake, but unless he is extremely lucky, the immediate constraints will dominate, and the lessons will be valued for pragmatic considerations rather than as part of long-term learning. Additionally, as is well known, any school curriculum as a whole will have been subjected to manipulation and reshaping as socially validated knowledge. Mr. Jones' Latin lessons, while still regarded as useful bases for further education, will for the most part be disregarded and only endured as prerequisite to professional entry or access to further education. In short, his Latin lessons will be considered by pupils, as well as by society at large, as having less immediate or obvious validity than, say, physics or mathematics, since the apparent instrumental use of the subject matter usually has some considerable bearing upon attitudes adopted toward that subject.

I think that any curriculum must combine hard-nosed analysis (appropos of societal relevance) with utopian imagination. Indeed, it is precisely the balance between those two extremes which is at the heart of most statements of educational aims. It is this balance too, which, in nonauthoritarian societies, can so depend upon teacher skills and imagination. As Shipman (1972) has said, eventually the curriculum consists of "accommodation and compromise, a mixture of horse trading and horse sense" (p. 145).

As a large number of educationists have pointed out, even where there is substantial agreement on the core of "teachable units" in a given curriculum, those elements taught are as much affected by the interaction (the transaction between teacher and taught) as they are by the actual content. One important element in the interaction is the teacher's understanding of the children's beliefs and values. Any system of schooling is embedded in a system of belief and values. When such a system is not in harmony with the beliefs and values of the children, or not able to draw upon some of their concerns, the curriculum is in danger of becoming at best ineffective and at worst almost useless. Thus knowledge of the values and attitudes of the children, while not the only information to be heeded, has long been considered essential for devising an effective curriculum.

One of the more disturbing imbalances in curriculum studies which I have noticed over recent years is the tendency for the field to become dominated by sociologists and administrators. In England, the recent thirty or so Open University units on curriculum design and development (E. 203 Educational Studies) reflected this domination. In that second level degree course only five percent of the contributions emphasized psychological issues (Gammage, 1976). Of course, to understand the curriculum one must assuredly look at the surrounding cultural, economic and ideological circumstances. But one must also look at the "recipients" and "actors"[1] in the learning process. As long ago as 1946, Jersild (1948) was attempting to apply many of the findings of human development and developmental psychology to specific curriculum problems.

---

[1] For instance, and to pursue the example given earlier, it is common for people to ascribe like or dislike for particular subject areas and for their associated success or failure in terms concerning *their* perceptions of the teacher: i.e., "I didn't get on with Latin because the teacher didn't like me, was unpleasant, etc."

Many discussions of the school curriculum hinge upon three closely inter-related questions. Some writers have seen them as a sort of education "trinity."

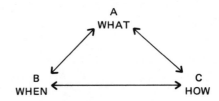

Figure 1. Basic questions of the curriculum.

Clearly, the "what" is extremely complex. Moreover, it is commonly discussed at two quite fundamentally different levels. Level A(1) concerns the culture as a whole: the purpose of schooling, the role of the school and of the teacher in a given society, as well as political and ideological views of that society's structure. Textbooks abound in this field: some with an avowedly political flavor, such as Dale (1976); some more obviously neutral in tone, such as Lawton (1975); some truly seminal in my opinion, such as Warnock (1977). But such books, while often extremely stimulating, tend, in my experience, to have little effect upon those engaged at the "chalk face." This may be a pity, but the practitioners are more concerned with level (A2), that is, with the "what" regarding the content of a particular program or series of programs in a given type of school. This level is more often dealt with my administrators, learning theorists, subject specialists, and curriculum theorists. "Recipe" books abound and appear to be well used (Nicholls & Nicholls, 1978; Warwick, 1975). While there is an obvious interrelationship between A(1) and A(2), as demonstrated for example in Nyrere's (1967) famous paper on in Bronfenbrenner's *Two Worlds of Childhood* (1970), practicing teachers can rarely afford the luxury of dwelling for too long on such connections, and they tend to move rapidly from content to timing, to the "when" of the curriculum process.

Indeed, when one makes even the most simplistic analysis of a curriculum in regard to content, one realizes that, for all the many and complex analyses of "what," it is the *"when"* which has often been the most fruitful factor guiding teachers. Let us examine this in more detail.

Although the "when" inevitably has overtones of both "what" and "how," it is generally discussed in terms of appropriate timing. Indeed, for many teachers of young children this has become the central feature of their curriculum planning, often providing, in limited terms, the rationale and justification for both *content* and *transaction*. Traditionally, psychologists have had a considerable amount to contribute here and have attempted to identify key issues. Evans (1975) and others have described such issues in relation to four sub-categories, roughly as follows:

B(1) *Sequencing the stages of human development and learning.* Psychologists of very different orientations have a lot to say here. Indeed, this might be regarded as the most fruitful strand in curriculum theory. Its effects on content have been considerable. One thinks immediately of Piaget, Kohlberg, Erkison, or Bruner, and their theories of child learning and socialization which appear to have had a direct effect upon the curriculum (e.g., Nuffield Maths, Science 5-13, The Middle Years Project, Health Education Project, Ypsilanti Language Curriculum, M.A.C.O.S., Nachalot Project, to mention but a few). Clearly, many such curricular packages or proposals have been based on theories of human development currently fashionable and employed as blueprints by the curriculum architects.

B(2) *Identifying appropriate learning strategies.* Referred to here are those theories relating the cognitive style of the learner to what is being learned. Notions of timing are not so appropriate here but tend to be employed as a part of the total explanation, sometimes with reference to developmental sequences. Though one may find evidence to suggest a considerable amount of research work in this area, I would assert that there has been little direct spin-off for the curriculum as yet.

B(3) *Sustaining motivation and enhancing feedback.* There is much diverse work by psychologists here. The principal theorists have been behaviorists, but among other major contributors have been some very dffferently oriented social psychologists, and even some psychodynamically orientated educationists, notably Morris (1972). Here, some of the Schools Council English/Humanities work is clearly also relevant. Several English Local Educational Authorities have recently concentrated on the issue, proposing revised systems of diagnosis and recording in the primary school (currently of the profile or log type).

B(4) *Isolating logical sequences of hierarchies within the structure of the subject, discipline, or area to be learned.* Gagné (1969) is one of the noted theorists here. His ideas concerning task analysis-taxonomy approaches to instruction (and it should be emphasized that Gagné sees instruction as only *one* aspect of education) center upon the arrangement of conditions which facilitate learning in regard to both vertical and lateral transfer. There are other theorists (particularly in the U.S.) who hold that task analysis yields suggestions concerning the appropriate sequencing and structuring of the material to be learned. As Gagné (1969) has pointed out, this is not a new idea. Its bases go back to Herbart and earlier. It is an eclectic thory drawing on work as diverse as that of Thorndike, Piaget, and Pavlov.

Closely connected with the "what" and "when" is the question of "how" one carriers out the transactions with the child. This does, of course, throw one back to considerations of the child's levels of cognitive development and sophistication. Teaching methods which appear suitable at one stage may not necessarily be suitable at the next. In this respect it may strike one as somewhat strange that, in England, one is likely to observe young children choosing, organizing, and selecting their learning experiences and sometimes even the material to be employed, whereas at secondary and higher[2] levels dictactic exposition and limited student choice are often the order of the day. Overall this is an aspect of the curriculum in which relationships and the quality of the transactions are coming more and more under scrutiny, an area where *mutuality* (to use Morris' term) has become of major interest to curriculum theorists and educationists in general.

Often, the most fundamental of all questions about the curriculum—"why?"—is left unasked and unanswered. Notably, it is omitted in most official pronouncements because it is so difficult to answer. Why teach this or that? Why this content as opposed to that? Why this timing as opposed to that? Why this method as opposed to that? Furthermore, the "why" of the curriculum underscores one of the major conflicts in the rationale for education with respect to both content and method. The two conflicting rationales are perhaps best set out as follows.

According to one view, education, and hence by implication the curriculum, is primarily concerned with preparing children to serve the future society. Hence, the immediate needs and interests of children must recieve secondary consideration to projected societal needs. Put in its extreme form, as Stalin is reported to have said to H. G. Wells, education is a "weapon" and teachers hold the front line in the battle for the mind and thus for the support of a certain sort of societal structure. Clearly, the line between indoctrination and education becomes very tenuous here. It is hard not to see the force of such views when reading the educational pronouncements of developing nations, or even when reading, for instance, the preambles to English Education Acts.

Opposing such a perspective are those who believe that education should be based on the immediate needs and interests of children; that is, that subsequent responsibilities and societal needs should be subordinated to the child's needs. For the curriculum to be effective, they argue, both content and transaction must be in tune with the potentialities of the individual.

Clearly the first view, in its extreme form, underlies a curriculum based upon an analysis of what a society requires generally in order to succeed or to provide for "satisfactory" adult role-playing. Such views are often, though by no means always, concomitant with overt politicization. Sometimes, as is the case of Freire's methods in Brazil in the early 1960s, education and particular curricula are used as tools for the expansion of political consciousness, for what Freire termed *concientizacao* or "consciousness raising." (Stress upon group identity, allegiance, and duty are, however, the more usual forms of politicization; see Bronfenbrenner, 1970).

---

[2]It has always struck me as rather curious that curriculum "theory" for the most part centers upon school rather than upon institutions of further and higher education. Is this part of the tradition that teachers of students over the age of 18 need no pedagogical training, whereas teachers of young children and adolescents do?

The second view is based upon the assumption that a "full" and "complete" daily existence during childhood is the best insurance for successful adulthood (a view with which I have *some* sympathy and one which gains a measure of support from various branches of psychology and even from biography). Great problems lie beneath such child-centered assumptions, however. What are the real "needs" of children? Who assesses them? How are they perceived?

In all, and putting aside the bulk of curriculum theory, any practical consideration of the social psychological constraints upon the curriculum would lead me to believe that the prime influences upon the curriculum are those depicted in the Figure 2.

In England, and to a small extent in North America, it would seem that primary/elementary schools have, by and large, been fairly successful in accommodating influences 1 and 5. This is partly because such schools are relatively small and intimate (the average English urban primary school has about ten to twelve staff members); partly it is an outcome of the long traditions of nonspecialist and polymathic teaching in such schools. Both factors have contributed to less parochialism in individual areas of the curriculum than is usually

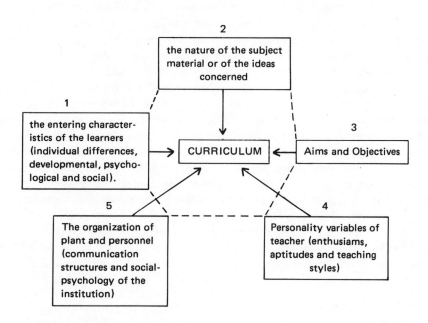

Note
Broken lines represent possible interaction
Solid lines represent major pressures

Figure 2.   Primary factors affecting the curriculum.

possible at later, more specialized stages of education. In such small schools the communication structure is much more informal than in secondary schools. If decisions concerning changes in pedagogy, style, and content are required, these can be effected quickly and simply. Different class groupings, team teaching, the sharing of common core "subject" concerns—all combine to produce less protective attitudes on the part of the teachers toward every particular curriculum subject. Added to this "looser framing" (Bernstein, 1971) are what many infant and kindergarten teachers would describe as the "facts of life," that children come to reception classes or first grades at such obviously diverse ability levels within a given curriculum. All this invites and indeed compels the primary teacher to concentrate continually upon the facilitation of *differential access* to the curriculum for different children within the same class or group. Additionally, and especially in English primary schools, traditions of "learning alongside the child" affect the role of the teacher so that his or her position is not that of the "fountainhead," sprinkling each child equally nor that of the "expert" whose expertise would be diminished by exploration or admissions of uncertainty. Rather, the primary teacher's talents, as Wilson (1962) put it, are spread pretty thinly, and modern teaching styles constantly tend to reinforce an awareness of width and shallowness rather than of depth.

It could be said, however, that primary schools have not done particularly well in respect to influences two and three. Frequently there has been weak or ineffective analysis of the discipline or knowledge area being taught. There have been some suggestions, too, that certain aspects of the curriculum are not as systematically developed as they might be—math, geography, and history being commonly cited, especially in connection with the more able child.[3] Some general concern has been expressed as to whether modern methods, such as integrated-day approaches, ensure sufficient development of the core curriculum; and in math in particular there is evidence, as shown in Land's (1963) early work and through the more recent work of Griffiths (1974), that the subject is not particularly well handled in the primary schools. Often, too, aims and objectives are expressed in vague and general terms such that translation to the day-to-day "system maintenance" of the school becomes well nigh impossible.

By 1979, all English Local Education Authorities, through their Advisory or Inspectorate services, had instituted working parties to carry out more careful analysis and evaluation with respect to influences 1, 2, and 3, and cumulative core subject profiles were already beginning to bear upon the shaping of basic skills curricula more directly (noticeably in Oxfordshire; in the Inner London

---

[3]D.E.S. (1975) Society makes its most conscious and concerted attempt at developing children's attitudes and beliefs through the school curriculum. These are made through policy documents centrally inspired "guide lines" and discussion papers (such as D.E.S. paper on the Curriculum, *Four Subjects for Debate* H.M.S.O. 1977), through systems of license and inspection, through local or provincial advisory systems, through public and externally validated examinations, through teacher training courses and textbooks, through research and development bodies (such as the Schools Council in the U.K.).

Education Authority; in the countries of Avon, Wiltshire, and Somersetshire, as well as in many others.) Even in the "ad hoc" and highly differentiated provision of preschool curricula (ages 2 to 5 years) the British Association of Early Childhood Education recommended (August, 1979) that their organization take steps to fund projects focusing research on more systematic early childhood curricula. The Department of Education Assessment and Performance Unit (A.P.U., established by the Department of Education and Science, 1975), somewhat akin to the American N.A.E.P., is likewise seriously occupied in the feasibility of more careful guidance and monitoring of the curriculum in middle childhood and adolescence. Norm- and criterion-referenced assessment are under active consideration. Both the Schools Council and the Regional Boards have also set up inquiries into, or courses on, assessment techniques (Macintosh, 1978). Accountability, continuity, and transfer from one stage of education to another have been serious concerns of both the recent Department of Education and Science major reports (D.E.S., 1978, 1979); and the earlier report underlines that one of the prime aims of the primary schools must be to ensure that curricula form a firm basis for succeeding stages, particularly in regard to basic skills. Articulation of the Curriculum therefore becomes an especially dominant theme in math, functional literacy, and science.

Education for children past puberty has, in both England and North America emphasized a gradually increasing specialization[4] in its approach. Consequently, such traditions, when combined with greater specialist knowledge of the teachers and the preoccupation with accreditation in terms of examinations (the "tickets" to success in most advanced technological societies), have led to greater success in the curriculum when dealing with influences 2 and 3. However, in my limited experience in a variety of countries (the U.S., Canada, the U.K., Spain, Australia) secondary stages of education have been woefully weak in providing differential access to the curriculum. "Rolling" timetables, variable time/subject commitments, free choice, and curricular "width" are not commonly experienced by the thirteen to sixteen year old adolescent. Frequently, such a child is still "grouped," "set," or "streamed" according to ability or according to a restricted choice of specialization and combination of subjects. Indeed, in the large comprehensive, collegiate or high school, there are many factors operating within the organization which make curriculum flexibility and dfferential access almost impossible to achieve. Communication structures become channelled and hierarchized, traditions and subject validation harden, and most students sit through identical portions or "gobbets"[5] of the subject. The different entering characteristics of the many students from a variety of primary institutions are not acknowledged except in the crudest of groupings. Those of

---

[4] In North America there is much greater emphasis on vocational aspects of education, particularly for age groups of 16 years onward in the collegiate and senior high schools.

[5] A process of sprinkling from a fountainhead, or of attempting to "wet each child equally," as a colleague put it.

us who are familiar with the problems of resource and remedial teachers, with the difficulties encountered by teachers of new subject areas (such as consumer education), are well aware that the introduction of a different aspect of the curriculum into an already frozen, crowded, and competitive situation may well lead to despair and conflict among the staff.

Those omnibus features grouped under influence 4 still need a great deal more research before even the crudest of generalization can be made about their effects upon the curriculum. Mutuality, concern, involvement, charisma, styles, and approaches—all affect the classroom climate to a great extent. We know that they can be important, but to what degree and in what context we know less. There is a long tradition of research in this area, but little conclusive to report beyond the rather trite reiteration that, in the last resort, what teachers teach is themselves, not the subject. It is interesting to note that (after a period of apparent disenchantment with psychodynamics and ego-psychology) college courses—at least those which I examined in England and some of those I observed in North America—are beginning to focus on the models of healthy personality as discussed in the theories of Allport, Maslow, Rogers, Fromm, and others. Maslow's theories, in particular, seem to form a prominent part of educational and social psychology courses for teachers. Most teachers are at least minimally aware of the work of Coopersmith (1967), Gordon (1966), Gergen (1971), and possibly of Rosenthal and Jacobson (1968). If the self-concept is as important as such writers would have us believe, then it clearly has great implication for learning and for curriculum planning. Certainly a major aim in any curriculum construction should be to provide chances of success for the child. How can children feel able unless they succeed? How will they go on learning in the face of repeated failure? If children develop the self-concept through interaction with those around them, then clearly teachers are needed who are capable of understanding and perceiving both their own and the child's views of the world.

In all, any social-psychological approach must serve to remind us of the context and process of interaction, of the competing forces in the socializing of the child. It must emphasize that school is concerned with socialization, and it must remind us that socialization is about the attitudes, feelings, and emotions of the person, as well as about the individual's cognitive construction of the world. But such an approach must also serve to remind us that socialization tends toward conservation and the confirmation of existing norms, values, and social roles. By implication, learning and hence the curriculum in schools is not merely the process of absorbing and storing facts; it is a part of human development, the development of the learners as persons. Thus, one returns to the point of emphasis in any social-psychological consideration of the curriculum. Knowledge transmitted is not necessarily knowledge received. To undertake transmission without reflecting on and attempting to ascertain the perceptions of the learner is to engage in grossly incomplete forms of curriculum planning. Image and perception are not necessarily congruent. The entering characteristics of the learners are vital ingredients, possibly *the* most vital ingredients, in the production of meaningful, well-matched, well-designed school learning.[6] I would be happier if current tomes on curriculum theory expressed this more clearly.

REFERENCES

Bernstein, B. On the classification and framing of educational knowledge. In Young, M.F.D. (Ed.), *Knowledge and control*. Collier Macmillan, 1971.

Bronfenbrenner, U. *Two worlds of childhood*. Penguin Books, 1970.

Coopersmith, S. *The Antecedents of self esteem*. Freeman, 1967.

Dale, R., et al. (eds.). *Schooling and capitalism*, London: Routledge and Kegan Paul, 1976.

Department of Education & Science, *A Language for life*, Her Majesty's Stationery Office, 1978.

Department of Education & Science, *Four subjects for debate*, Her Majesty's Stationery Office, 1977.

Department of Education & Science, *Primary education in England*, Her Majesty's Stationery Office, 1979.

Department of Education & Science, *Aspects of secondary education in England*, Her Majesty's Stationery Office, 1979.

Evans, E. D. *Contemporary influences in early childhood education* (2nd ed.). Holt, Rinehart and Winston, 1975.

Gagné, R. *The conditions of learning*. Holt, Rinehart and Winston, 1969.

Gammage, P. Human development and the curriculum. In Lawton, D., et al. (Eds.), *The child, the school and society*, E.203, units 5-8. Open University, 1976.

Gergen, K. J. *The concept of self*. Holt, Rinehart and Winston, 1971.

Good, L., Biddle, B., & Brophy, J. *Teachers make a difference*. Holt, Rinehart & Winston, 1975.

Gordon, I. *Studying the child in school*. Wiley, 1966.

Griffiths, J. *An exploratory analysis of attitudes towards mathematics*, unpublished M. Litt. Bristol: University of Bristol, 1974.

Jersild, A. T. *Child development and the curriculum*. New York: Teachers' College, Columbia University, 1948.

Land, F. W. *New appraoches to mathematics teaching*. New York: Macmillan, 1963.

Lawton, D. *Class, culture and the curriculum*. London: Routledge and Kegan Paul, 1975.

[6] See especially the work of Good, Biddle, & Brophy (1975), where, in referring to various studies of teacher effectiveness, they report work showing that different styles, methodologies and structures are required for different types of pupils at different age levels. And say "in general it appears that indirect teaching is probably effective, but only after students have mastered the fundamental tool skills and work habits required to assume responsibility for undertaking and maintaining their own learning efforts" (p. 76). And I quote: "the findings suggest that low SES students with minimal skills will progress most rapidly in the early grades in a carefully planned and teacher structured learning environment. . . . It should be noted, however, that although this appears the best *initial* strategy for teaching such students, the strategy becomes less effective to the extent that it succeeds!" (p. 78).

Macintosh, H. G. Training teachers in assessment techniques, D.E.S., *Trends in Education*, 1978, *3*, 28-34.

Morris, B. S. *Objectives and perspectives in education.* London: Routledge and Kegan Paul, 1972.

Nicholls, A., & Nicholls, H. *Developing a curriculum.* Allen and Unwin, 1978.

Nyrere, J. *Education for self reliance,* Government Publisher, Dar Es Salaam, 1967.

Rosenthal, R., & Jacobson, L. F. *Pygmalion in the classroom.* Holt, Rinehart and Winston, 1968.

Shipman, M. Contrasting views of a curriculum project. *Journal of Curriculum Studies*, 1972, *4*, 145-153.

Silberman, C. E. *Crisis in the classrooms.* New York: Random House, 1970.

Skilbeck, M. Appendix A. In J. Walton & J. Welton (Eds.), *Rational curriculum planning.* Ward Lock, 1976.

Warnock, M. *Schools of thought.* Faber, 1977.

Warwick, D. *Curriculum Structure and Design,* London: University of London Press, 1975.

Wilson, B. The teacher's role—A sociological analysis. *The British Journal of Sociology*, 1962, *13*, 15-32.

10

Preschool Education in Queensland, Australia— A Systems Approach

Gerald F. Ashby

Department of Education, Queensland, Australia

In this paper I address two major questions. First, what are some of the considerations involved in establishing a preschool education system? And second, what principles, derived from such an undertaking, may be useful to others in the years ahead? I consider both questions with reference to the state preschool system in Queensland, Australia. The answers that emerge are the result of my personal experience in the day-to-day planning, implementation, and management of the system's development from its inception. Whereas there are obvious dangers in reporting a project in which one has been closely involved, there are also advantages. On the one hand, bias and ego may lead to a confusion of aspitation and achievement, a tendency to paint an over-rosy picture. On the other hand, close involvement in an operation provides a unique lens through which to examine some aspects of early childhood education: the creation of a system from conception to actuality. Although I hope to avoid the danger, I also hope that the insights gleaned from the experience may prove helpful.

This paper is divided roughly into three parts. The first section describes the context within which the Queensland preschool system was developed. The second section introduces two case studies based on subprograms of the major program: the Pre-School Correspondence Program and the Class IV (small rural) School Project. In the third section I attempt to formulate a theoretical position based on the preceding sections.

At this point it should be noted that I was at the outset, and still remain, an early childhood educator (with a background in college teaching) who turned administrator, rather than an educational administrator who became involved in early childhood education. I think this distinction is important because of the differences in knowledge and attitudes associated with the two orientations. Undoubtedly, the development of the Queensland system was influenced by certain prior commitments to early childhood education in general, and pre-school education in particular. These have been explored elsewhere (Ashby, 1972). Of course, prolonged involvement in administration tends to generate a certain hard-nosed pragmatism, but one hopes that ideals are never totally sub-merged.

THE QUEENSLAND CONTEXT

In the course of campaigning toward the state election in 1972, the governing coalition parties announced that if reelected they would introduce a system of voluntary free preschool education for all 4-year-old children (the year before entry to primary school). While attendance at preschool would not be compulsory, universal access to such education was a policy objective. Responsibility for implementation was to be vested in the State Department of Education.

Following the reelection of the coalition parties, steps were taken to create a new divisional directorate within the Department of Education to carry responsibility for implementation of the policy. The government established the general framework for development. First, as far as possible, preschools would be located on the grounds of existing primary schools but would operate as part of the preschool directorate. Second, the standards for facilities and equipment would closely follow the standards set by the Australian Pre-School Association, and buildings would be built to suit preschool needs. Third, the teaching staff would consist of personnel specifically trained in early childhood education. Fourth, in general the curriculum would be of an accepted early childhood character and not a downward extension of the primary school curriculum. Fifth, attendance would be on a sessional basis, common throughout Australia, for five half-days each week. Sixth, parent participation and involvement would be encouraged. Seventh, government assistance to nongovernment, community-based preschools would continue, even after the introduction of state preschool facilities.

All of these aspects of the policy represented a major innovation in the field of preschool education in Australia in the early 1970s. Queensland became the first Australian state to adopt universal access to preschool education. Further, the decision to establish the preschool division at the level of a directorate, with senior positions of the same rank and status as existing divisions of the Department, broke a long tradition of locating preschool education at a fairly low level of administrative responsibility within some other section of the responsible division.

There is no doubt that the policy enunciated in 1972 enjoyed a high level of electoral and general community support. However, the task of developing an overall strategy for implementing the policy was complex. Two matters were of special significance in this regard: the geography and demography of Queensland, and the organization of education within the state.

A Brief Description of Queensland

Queensland occupies an area of 1.728 million square kilometres (667,000 miles) in northeast Australia (see Figure 1). In comparison with the United States, the area of Queensland is approximately equal to that of Texas, New Mexico, Colorado, Wyoming, and Montana combined. Also, the distance from the northern to the southern border of Queensland is approximately the same as the distance from the Canadian border of the U.S. to the Gulf of Mexico.

The population of 2.1 million (less than one-fifth that of Texas) represents approximately 15 percent of the Australian total. The greatest single population concentration is in the southeast corner surrounding Brisbane. Approximately 50 percent of the state's people live in this sector. A further 30 percent live in a string of coastal cities stretching north to Cairns, approximately 1,900 km from Brisbane, and in two major inland cities. The distribution of population coupled with the distances between centers in Queensland poses particular difficulties in the provision of services of all kinds.

The Queensland Education System

In Australia education is a state responsibility, although in recent years the Commonwealth (Federal) Government has played an important role through the provision of specific purpose funding. The Queensland Department of Education is responsible for the provision of education facilities and services for some 440,000 students throughout the state. This represents approximately 80 percent of the state's children in the compulsory school attendance age group. The balance are served by nongovernment schools, of which the Catholic system is the most significant component.

The department employs some 21,000 full-time teachers and a number of others on a part-time basis. Two other groups assist directly in providing educational services to schools. The first consists of a range of professional personnel such as psychologists, therapists, media specialists, and other professionals who provide specialist services. The second group consists of ancillary staff such as clerical personnel, laboratory attendants, teacher aides, groundsmen, janitors, and cleaning staff.

Control of all functions is vested in the permanent head of the Department, the Director-General of Education, who is directly responsible to the Minister for Education. The former is a permanently tenured public servant (as are all officers, including teachers, in the department), whereas the latter is a Member of Parliament, from the ranks of the governing political party. The Director-General is assisted by an immediate senior staff, including directors of divisions and a team of regional directors. Directors are responsible for various

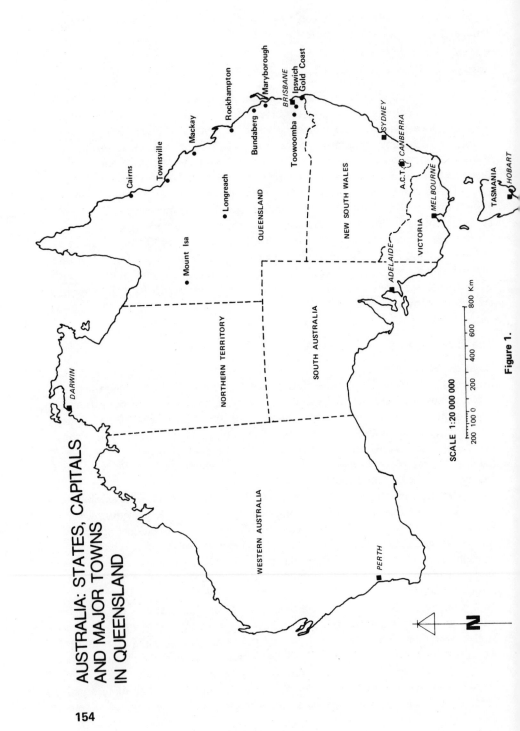

AUSTRALIA: STATES, CAPITALS
AND MAJOR TOWNS
IN QUEENSLAND

DARWIN

WESTERN AUSTRALIA

PERTH

NORTHERN TERRITORY

SOUTH AUSTRALIA

ADELAIDE

Mount Isa

Longreach

QUEENSLAND

Cairns

Townsville

Mackay

Rockhampton

Bundaberg

Maryborough

BRISBANE
Ipswich
Gold Coast

Toowoomba

NEW SOUTH WALES

SYDNEY

A.C.T. CANBERRA

VICTORIA

MELBOURNE

TASMANIA

HOBART

SCALE 1:20 000 000

200 100 0   200   400   600   800 Km

Figure 1.

N

154

QUEENSLAND: POPULATION DISTRIBUTION
AND EDUCATION REGIONS

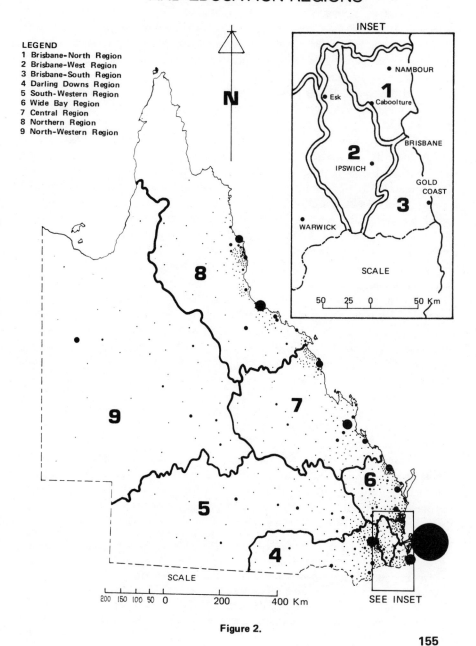

LEGEND
1 Brisbane-North Region
2 Brisbane-West Region
3 Brisbane-South Region
4 Darling Downs Region
5 South-Western Region
6 Wide Bay Region
7 Central Region
8 Northern Region
9 North-Western Region

N

INSET

NAMBOUR
Esk
1
Caboolture
2
IPSWICH
BRISBANE
GOLD COAST
3
WARWICK
SCALE
50   25   0   50 Km

8
9
7
6
5
4
SCALE
200 150 100 50 0   200   400 Km
SEE INSET

Figure 2.

155

school sectors (e.g., preschool) while Regional Directors have responsibility for all schools and operations within particular geographic areas (see Figure 2).

Visitors to Australia often comment (and frequently unfavorably) on the extent of government centralization in education and other areas of administration. In part centralized control is a product of the history of settlement of Australia. However, and more important, centralization represents an attempt to achieve degrees of equality in the provision of facilities and services across very large geographic areas. Planning and decision making must take statewide considerations into account and ensure that very small and isolated communities are not disadvantaged in comparison with more populous areas. Further, it should not be imagined that centralized control of policy planning and provision intrudes into the day to day functioning of schools. Substantial and balancing degrees of autonomy exist (and indeed must exist) within an organization such as the Queensland Department of Education.

Figure 3 depicts, in simple form, the structure of the school system within Queensland. Variations both in structure of and in age levels for progressing through school systems exist between States and these have posed intractable problems over many years. Compuslory schooling in Queensland is from six to fifteen years of age. However, most children enter Year 1 of primary schooling before they turn six. It should be noted that there is only one date for initial entry into school: at the beginning of the school year, in late January. Preschools cater to children in the year before entry into Year 1.

Queensland primary schools are classified in accordance with size. The number of pupils determines the distribution of resources and the type of staffing provided. Table 1 sets out the classes of regular primary schools within the education system. In addition to these schools there is a whole range of other facilities for children with special educational needs, including the handicapped and, more particularly, geographically isolated children. The latter group are assisted by means of a central correspondence school, located in Brisbane, which provides a full range of primary education. There are also a number of "Schools of the Air" which provide supplementary instruction to pupils on primary correspondence courses.

There are four main types of preschool facilities being developed by the Department of Education. Three types of facilities are designed to serve different sized groups of children on a sessional basis. The fourth type of facility is designed specifically to cater to particular groups of children having some particular need.

1. *Standard Unit*. This is a facility designed for a total of fifty children enrolled on a sessional attendance basis. In general a child attends five half-days per week, and two groups of twenty-five make up the total enrollment. Staffing for this unit consists of one teacher and a teacher's aide.
2. *Reduced Unit*. This is a facility designed for areas where the eligible preschool aged population is significantly less than fifty children, and likely to

THE EDUCATION SYSTEM OF QUEENSLAND

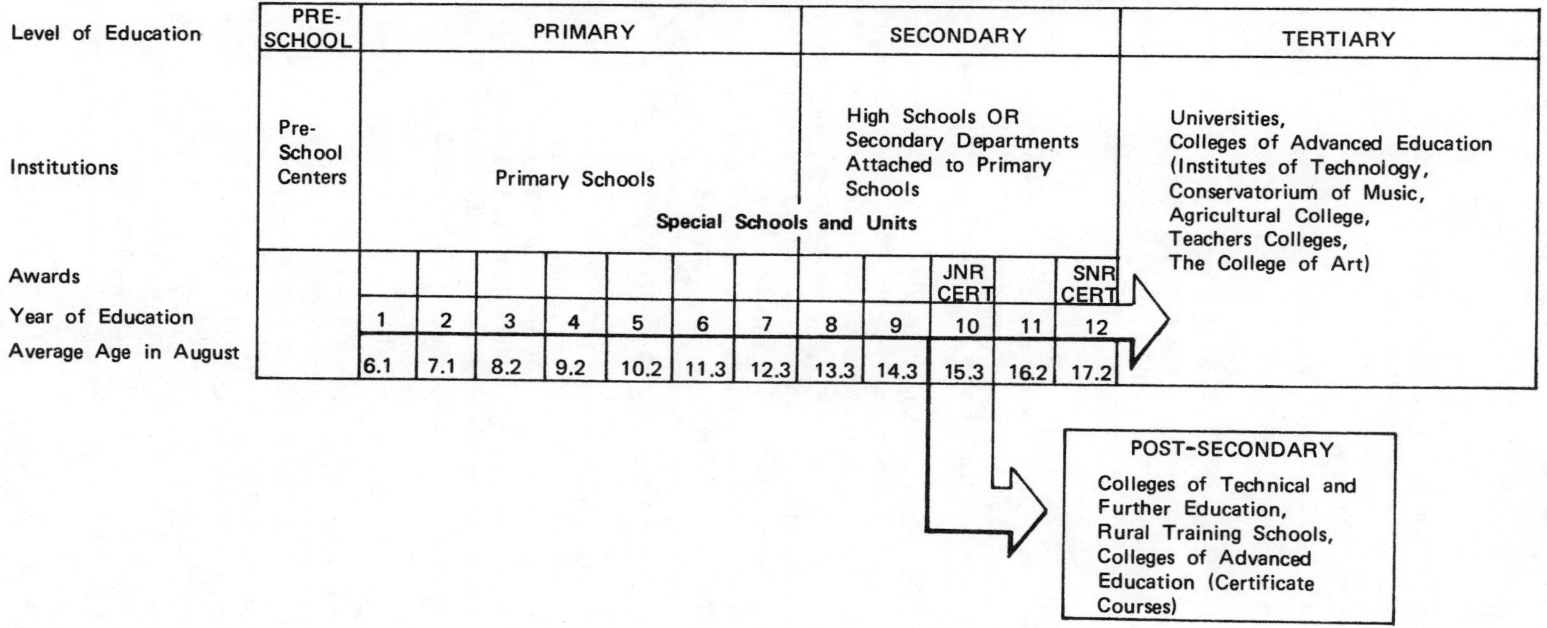

Level of Education	PRE-SCHOOL	PRIMARY							SECONDARY					TERTIARY
Institutions	Pre-School Centers	Primary Schools							High Schools OR Secondary Departments Attached to Primary Schools					Universities, Colleges of Advanced Education (Institutes of Technology, Conservatorium of Music, Agricultural College, Teachers Colleges, The College of Art)
		Special Schools and Units												
Awards										JNR CERT		SNR CERT		
Year of Education		1	2	3	4	5	6	7	8	9	10	11	12	
Average Age in August		6.1	7.1	8.2	9.2	10.2	11.3	12.3	13.3	14.3	15.3	16.2	17.2	

POST-SECONDARY

Colleges of Technical and Further Education, Rural Training Schools, Colleges of Advanced Education (Certificate Courses)

2 August 1979

Figure 3.

157

Table 1. Classification of Primary Schools in Queensland.

Classification	Enrollment
Class I	601 +
Class II	301 - 600
Class III	101 - 300
Class IV	37 - 100
Class V	21 - 35
Class VI	20

remain so. On average, reduced units are designed for total enrollments between twenty to thirty-five children. Depending on the sessional attendance pattern adopted in a particular center, which might include half day or full day attendance, the staffing consists of a teacher and, where necessary, a teacher's aide.

3. *Special Units.* These units are designed to serve the needs of particular groups of children (e.g., deaf, cerebral palsied, etc.). Each such unit incorporates features required for work with the particular group being served. As a general principle special units are built in association with preschool units enrolling nonhandicapped children to enable integration of the handicapped child into a regular group to occur. As these units may cater to children below 4 years of age the enrollment is flexible, but groups are kept to the smallest possible size. Staffing is dependent upon the numbers of children enrolled. The optimum adult/child ratio is approximately 1:4-5. This consists of a mixture of teachers, specialist consultants, and therapists and teacher's aides.

4. *Multiple Units.* Multiple units providing facilities equivalent of up to three standard units may be established on the one site. In certain circumstances a special unit might be added to this maximum. Where the need of an area is greater than that provided by three standard units, excluding a special unit (say five groups of twenty-five children = 150 total enrollment), additional facilities are established on separate sites. Staffing for each unit is one teacher and a teacher's aide.

Foundations of the Preschool System

At the time of the government decision to provide preschool education, the eligible population of 4- to 5-year-old children was estimated as 42,000. Of these, there were an estimated 8,500 children aged 4 to 5 years attending community preschools operated by various voluntary groups. The majority of existing preschool facilities were in urban areas with very few in small rural centres. Furthermore, within the urban areas there were disparities in the distribution of facilities. In general, because the voluntary organizations charged fees to supplement state government subsidies and had to raise considerable sums of money in order to acquire premises, availability tended to be restricted to more affluent communities.

Almost inevitably, a conflict emerged. Whereas voluntary organizations welcomed the Government's policy, they argued that it should be implemented in communities other than those where voluntary preschools existed. Conversely, parents within communities served by voluntary preschools did not want to be deprived of access to state-provided preschools. The resolution of this conflict was achieved through the development of effective communication and collaboration between the department and the voluntary organizations—something that took time.

As indicated, implementing the government's policy presented a number of immediate problems. These included:

> welding a new element into a large beaurcratic organization with its established procedures and networks;
>
> determining a basis for establishing preschool facilities throughout the state;
>
> establishing building design and equipment standards;
>
> establishing cost projections and methods of monitoring costs;
>
> establishing staff training programs;
>
> matching staffing programs to construction programs;
>
> formulating and disseminating the educational objectives of the preschool education system;
>
> securing and maintaining public acceptance of and interest in preschool education;
>
> developing appropriate administrative procedures for the conduct of preschools, the enrollment of children and such matters;
>
> establishing necessary support networks for teachers, parents, and children;
>
> devising and providing appropriate curriculum resources;
>
> establishing cooperative relationships with existing preschool services;
>
> ensuring cooperation from local school administrators.

Most of the immediate matters were overlaid by the pragmatic need to work toward speedy implementation of the election promise. It should be kept in mind that no data base existed concerning the setting up of a comprehensive preschool system within Australia. Such literature as was available was inappropriate in terms of either the assumptions involved or the context within which the system was to operate. Indeed, there was an absence of policy-orientated literature concerning early childhood education, and this influenced the adoption of a "formative" approach to planning and development. A fundamental principle that permeated all decisions was retention of maximum flexibility in determining both ends and means.

The Government sought quick and visible outcomes resulting from its policy. This both simplified and complicated matters. On the one hand, it facilitated such matters as site acquisition, design and construction timetables, staff build-up and materials procurement. Strong governmental support also ensured maximum cooperation from both the Department of Education and other state departments. However, great care had to be taken so that plans did not close off future options for delivering services or, indeed, wholly preempt the type of service offered. This necessitated a broad conceptualization concerning the type of system (albeit flexible and responsive to change) to be established.

There was an acute awareness that if things were not done right first time around, there might never be another opportunity. It is possible to build on success but failure seldom provides second chances.

Thus, beyond the immediate, practical concerns, a number of much broader issues emerged. These included:

establishing strategies for ensuring continuity between preschool and initial primary school programs;

articulating the administrative and professional relationships between preschool and primary school personnel;

creating provisions for children for whom conventional types of Australian preschools were not a viable consideration;

ensuring a smooth transition from the anticipated period of development of the system into a more stable, operational mode;

providing avenues for professional development of personnel and for career satisfaction;

instituting mechanisms for the maintenance of motivation among teaching staff and providing for their input into the system;

developing communication networks between personnel, other elements in the Department of Education, and other agencies;

initiating formal interagency mechanisms for the provision of particular services such as health and psychological services;

ensuring adequate and appropriate special provisions for particular groups of children such as the physically, sensorially, and intellectually handicapped;

ensuring adequate opportunities for parent and community input into the education process.

Thus, aspects of short-term and long-term planning had to be collapsed in ways that retained flexibility in terms of future development, and also ensured that quality was provided in the immediate context. Two early decisions, both of which illustrate the character of the planning, highlight the point.

The first example relates to a particular strategy for getting under way. Because of the distribution of population throughout the State it was accepted that in certain cases, both the facilities and the types of services provided would have to be radically different from those generally available within Australia.

This decision had a number of outcomes, two of which may be noted. First, it led to the creation of a portfolio of standard preschool designs intended to satisfy a wide range of community and environmental situations. The basic planning module was a "standard unit." A standard unit consisted of a facility designed to accommodate twenty-five children per session, there being two sessions conducted in each unit daily. Staffing of a standard unit was one teacher aide, plus voluntary helpers.

All architectural plans for both indoor and outdoor areas were developed around the standard unit module. Further, units could be aggregated to form multi-unit centers or reduced in area to serve lesser numbers of children. Standard designs could also be modified in terms of internal layout, but contained within the standard shell, in order to create specialized facilities for children with special education and other needs. Finally, the issue of furniture, equipment (both indoor and outdoor), consumable, and other materials developed around the standard unit. An immediate consequence was the increased capacity that this approach provided for monitoring and projecting costs, as information could be refined in an almost infinite number of ways.

A second outcome of the decision to focus initially on conventional preschool facilities was that it provided lead-time necessary to assemble data to assist in deciding what to do in areas served by small Class III and Class IV, V, and VI schools. In this regard, the search was for alternative modes of service delivery which would be consistent with the general philosophy of the evolving system. Two quite different approaches were developed. These were the Pre-School Correspondence Program and the Class IV School Project, both of which will be considered in more detail later.

The second example related to the decision to opt for what has come to be called a "flat" administrative structure. This approach was recognized as somewhat radical within a hierarchical bureaucratic organization, such as the Department of Education. The tradition of the "line and staff" pyramid was well established. However, a distinction was drawn between authority and responsibility. Although the delegation of authority, that is the formal process of distributing decision making and advisory functions within the hierarchy, was accepted, it was also believed that the shaping of advice provided opportunities for wide ranging participation in the decision making process, that is, that the individual teacher should enjoy the widest measure of professional autonomy consistent with the maintenance of the organization, and further, that it was important to distinguish between those areas of policy which the teacher was expected to implement and those areas where choice was vested in the teacher. Many implications flowed from emphasis upon the professional autonomy of the teacher. For example, the type of support services provided to teachers very clearly involved careful consideration. A peer-level advisory support system was opted for rather than the more conventional notion of a supervisory team. Thus, for example, advisory personnel were drawn from the ranks of teachers and returned to teaching after a fixed period of time. Advisers were teachers who could advise, assist, counsel, console, and even criticize, but always as peers. However, they could not demand or order and, more important, they did not form a supervisory cadre, which might become a self-interest group. A further implication was the fostering of a professional-colleague relationship between the preschool teacher and the principal and staff of the associated primary school. The possibility of the preschool being administratively the responsibility of the primary school principal was avoided. Although it was appreciated that many preschool teachers would be young and lack experience, it was believed that locking the preschool into the primary school might stifle growth and initiative. Further, administrative union could be effected at any future time, but, once done, would be difficult to undo if found inappropriate.

These two examples are not definitive in terms of spelling out all the implications that flowed from the decisions, nor are they representative of all of the decisions that were made. Suffice it to say, at this juncture, that there was a firm belief that if early childhood education principles were to penetrate the education system of Queensland, they required careful nurture and the optimum opportunity to demonstrate their potential for influencing, from below, practices of the primary school.

Perhaps the most significant set of early decisions revolved around the question of objectives. There is a seductive simplicity in stating system-wide objectives, including the idea of minimum competencies. These can comfort administrators by providing immediate answers to critics. Indeed, system-wide objectives may even be adopted by teachers for translation into programs! However, there is little point in proposing that the individual teacher should enjoy a wide measure of professional autonomy and then proceeding to spell out, in detail, what constitutes acceptable exercise of such autonomy. Further, it was firmly believed that there was not much merit in proposing that all preschools should be the same or follow the same curriculum. Rather, it was maintained that better results might be achieved by helping teachers to develop the kind of program best suited to their particular groups of children and communities.

However, there was a clear need to state publicly what the preschool system was about, and therefore a set of four statements was developed. These statements, describing the functions of a preschool rather than the objectives of preschool education are as follows:

1. To provide a bridge by which the young child can be assisted to make a transition from home to school;
2. To encourage parent interest and participation in the early education process;
3. To promote the physical and mental health of the young child;

4. To develop those abilities, skills, and attitudes which will aid the educational progress of the young child.

The shift in emphasis from objectives to functions may appear subtle, but it represented a significant trend away from the kinds of approaches which had dominated Australian preschool education for many years. In general, statements of objectives concerning preschool education consisted of beliefs about the nature of child development and the conditions necessary for optimum development. Although such statements are influential in developing educational programs, it is important to distinguish between the program and the organization (or institution) sponsoring the program: The purposes of the latter may be different from the former. Emphasis on functions was also a break with the Australian primary education tradition, which had been dominated by the prescribed syllabus for almost a century.

The basis and intent of each function was identified and elaborated upon in terms of conditions to be met by educational programs in Queensland State preschools. These conditions spelled out the broad thrust of the system. Thus, for example, the first function analyzed the mediating and socializing role of the preschool. The preschool was viewed as an aid to children (and their parents) in moving from one powerful socializing agent, the home, to another, the school. As a result the preschool was concerned with building upon and extending home learning, while at the same time gradually shifting the focus toward the styles of learning and experiencing promoted in the early years of primary schooling.

The statement of functions, and the elaboration, were widely promulgated both in the Education Depatment and in the general community. Because each function was capable of treatment at a variety of levels, the statement was perceived as the "philosophy" of the preschool system. Further, the statement of functions proved a major resource for teachers and others when explaining the preschool to the community and to colleagues from other levels of education. It had the prime virtue of simplicity. Thus, although a wide variety of programs were adopted by teachers, efforts were consistently made to use the statement of functions as a pivot around which the programs evolved. The outcome was that throughout the state, teachers presented a unified approach to colleagues in primary and secondary schools who were often skeptical—something that surprised many observers who anticipated that preschool education would be purely "play and happiness." Further, in subsequent years when more detailed analyses of curricula were undertaken, these functions still played a significant role in shaping the kinds of statements which emerged (Halliwell, 1977a, b).

The growth of the preschool system was rapid. Table 2 indicates the growth of the center-based program between 1972, when the policy was announced, and 1979. Such bald statistics do not indicate some of the novel areas that opened up for the preschool teachers: advisory work throughout the state; work in hospitals, media production, theatre-in-education, special education, research, and curriculum development activities; as well as the two sub-

Table 2. Preschool Division in Queensland, 1972-1979.

	No. of Centers	No. of Units	Enrollments[1]	Teaching Staff
1972	—	—	—	21[2]
1973	18	28	1,000	85[2]
1974	78	103	4,668	175[2,3]
1975	148	220	9,355	287[2]
1976	231	341	15,839	508[2,4]
1977	289	421	19,383	584
1978	329	493	22,490	653
1979	338	509	24,600	729

[1] Enrollments are effective as at National Census date of August 1 each year.

[2] Includes primary and high school teachers undertaking preschool training programs.

[3] From 1974 includes teachers on Pre-School Correspondence Program.

[4] From 1976 includes teachers deployed in Class IV School Project.

programs discussed in the next section. In addition, the geographic distribution of preschool facilities across the state presented to teachers ranges of community settings and lifestyles which were novel in terms of the Australian experience in preschool education, and this forced some reformulation of many long cherished ideas about what constituted a "proper" program for young children.

CASE STUDIES OF TWO SUBPROGRAMS

The center-based program was designed to provide access to preschool facilities for the majority of young children throughout the State. However, special approaches were needed to provide preschooling for children in the many small schools and in the Primary Correspondence School. (The latter had existed for some fifty years and in the early 1970s offered full primary education to approximately 1,600 children each year.)

The first special program was the Pre-School Correspondence Program, introduced in 1974. This was designed for children in areas served by Class V and VI schools (enrollment less than thirty-five) and those who would normally enroll for primary schooling with the Primary Correspondence School. The second program was the Class IV (Early Education Class) School project which was introduced in 1976.

Pre-School Correspondence Program

The Pre-School Correspondence Program (P.S.C.P.) was developed to cater to those children whose families lived in very isolated parts of the state. Such children were typically envisaged as progressing into primary schooling by way of the Primary Correspondence School or by way of very small one-teacher schools which had a total enrollment across all grades of fewer than thirty-five pupils. It was estimated that up to 1,000 children might be eligible for this program. However, because of poor communications in the outback, it was understood that not all parents would participate.

Essentially the P.S.C.P. was conceived as a home-based, parent-taught program consisting of multiformat materials, packaged and delivered by regular mail services and supported by a team of teachers based on the unit headquarters in Brisbane. However, when the idea was first developed in 1973, only scanty information was available to guide the construction of such a program. Furthermore, although primary and secondary correspondence schools had existed for many years in all Australian states and in New Zealand, there had been virtually no rigorous evaluation of the processes involved in designing and delivering such programs. Therefore, a conscious decision was made to adopt a formative development and evaluation approach to the P.S.C.P. This strategy permitted materials and processes to be tested while at the same time providing at least a minimal level of service. A fundamental concern of the planners was the retention of maximum flexibility within a functional structure which would permit both ends and means to be varied in accordance with experience and data.

A set of key statements was developed to describe the proposed program. The statements combined both intentions and aspirations and provided a basis for the development of materials, process, resources, and organization. Although the original set of statements has undergone many changes as a result of experience and increased knowledge and sophistication, the spirit of the original set has been retained. The program proposals were as follows:

1. To construct a home-based, early childhood education program, taking into account the variability of geographic and environmental settings and the special needs of the children and the families who would participate in the program.
2. To provide for the cognitive, affective, psycho-motor, and (in so far as is possible) social development of children consisting of learning experiences in the following areas:

   language arts and associated skills, including auditory and perceptual skills;

   appropriate concepts and skills from mathematics and the physical and social sciences, including the development of relevant problem solving and inquiry skills;

   motor skill development and coordination at both the fine and gross levels;

   imaginative thinking and creative expression through music, movement, dance and various art media.

3. To ensure that both the materials, and the guidance given to parents in their use, reflected the principle of learning proceeding on the basis of the child's

active involvement with people, objects, and events in the everyday environment, and interaction on a "one-to-one" basis with the "parent-teacher."

4. To support parents postively in the role of both teacher and parent and, in
   particular, to promote the acquisition of skills and techniques that facilitate
   the child's acquisition of a positive self-image, self reliance in learning, and a
   sense of growing competence.
5. To maximize, to the extent possible within a correspondence–style program, direct, warm, and positive communication between "unit-based"
   teachers, "parent-teachers," and children as a basis for individualizing the
   "core" program to meet particular family circumstances.
6. To ensure that the role of the teacher both in the "unit-based" and home
   situations is defined as "active" and "supportive": That the initiation of
   action through suggestion, instruction, and reinforcement and the sustaining
   of learning through warm interactions are treated equally.
7. To establish such support services as might be required to supplement the
   "core" educational program.
8. To provide such opportunity for peer group socialization as might be possible
   within the limitations of family circumstances and opportunity.
9. To endeavor to provide a smooth transition from the preschool program to
   primary schooling, whether this be by correspondence or attendance.

Using this framework as a basis, a program entitled "The Child and His
World" was created. The program was to cater to the preschool child within
the setting of rural Queensland. The program sequence, as illustrated in Figure
4, contained eight major units or segments. Each segment covered areas through
which basic attitudes, concepts, and skills, important for both present and later
learning, could be developed. Segments constituted a standard package, the
"core," which went to each participant. Variation was introduced by the child's
unit-based teacher in consultation with the parent teacher. Each segment contained two types of material: constant objectives and changing contents. The
constants included matters such as promoting language skills; eliciting and using
information; and promoting and sustaining interests in and utilizing the
resources of the home environment. The materials explored new content
throughout each segment which was related to the particular theme.

In each segment the theme is broken down into concepts and subconcepts.
For example, Segment 2, *Daily Living,* includes the concepts *My Family, The
House Where I Live,* and *My Day.* Each of these is further subdivided. *The House
Where I Live* explores such things as types of homes, places where homes are
situated, inside homes, and what happens in different parts of the home. Various
games and activities are suggested under each subconcept. These include stories,
poems, songs, puppet plays, indoor and outdoor activities, and creative activities.
At the same time reference is made to earlier work for reinforcement.

Segments are designed to cover activities for a specified number of weeks
and are dispatched each four to six weeks. Each package consists of story booklets, concept builders, activities and games, language experiences, cassette tapes,

Program Title: THE CHILD AND HIS WORLD

Segment Themes	Segment Components	
1. Self-Identification	*Segment News:*	Overview and highlights of content
2. Daily Living		
3. Environment	*Segment Booklet:*	Treatment of theme, concepts, activities, and highlights
4. Perception		
5. Classification	*Program Workbook:*	Outline of activities that can be completed and returned to unit-based teacher
6. Relationships		
7. Independence and Responsibility		
	Story Booklets:	Development of major concepts of the segment
8. Personal Relationships		
	Cassette Tape:	Stories, music, movement—related to segment
	Teacher Information Sheet:	Review of segment returned to unit-based teacher.
	Contact:	Parent information newsletter.

Figure 4.   Pre-School Correspondence Program—Segment Themes and Materials

and a magazine for parents entitled *Contact*. Feedback forms prepared by the unit-based teachers are completed by parents and serve to indicate the level of the child's activity in the various learning areas as well as parent reactions to materials. In addition to this type of feedback, parents are also encouraged to submit samples of children's work (e.g., artwork, collections, "stories," etc.), to make cassette tapes incorporating conversation with the child, and so on. These materials assist the unit-based teacher to obtain a more rounded picture of the child and of the family.

Cassette tapes included as part of the basic content of each segment contain stories, language exercises, and lessons in creative movement, song, and dance. These are designed to reinforce the concepts presented in written form. A basic equipment kit consisting of supplies of paints, crayons, books, and other materials is also provided to each child at the beginning of the school year.

A Resource Book for Parents, which is issued to all parents, further aids in extending and enriching the segment materials and provides ideas and suggestions for using equipment and junk materials available around the home. This book refers to materials for use in play, both indoors and outdoors, and assists parents in establishing interesting, attractive, and inexpensive play areas.

Each segment of the program provides a general base from which to work. Concepts and learning goals are identified, suggestions for ways of proceeding and supporting materials are also presented. In addition, an especially vital ingredient is the input from the unit-based teacher. The quality of the communication among teachers, parents and children is the most critical process involved in the P.S.C.P.

On enrollment each child is assigned to a unit-based teacher who works with the family for the year. Each teacher is responsible for approximately thirty families. Families are grouped on a geographic basis in order to facilitate teacher visits and to enable the teacher to gain a more initmate knowledge of the area. It is the role of the teacher to individualize the "core" program for each child by shifting a focus, providing supplementary materials, and providing guidance to the parent-teacher in the home situation. Naturally, this process assumes a close communication network between teacher, parent, and child.

Teacher, parents, and children exchange letters and cassette tapes, and it is the teacher's role to meet parent requests for advice and to provide ideas on how to proceed. In this regard, teachers are able to draw upon a wide range of supplementary resources which can be used to augment the "core" program for an individual child. These resources also include a substantial collection of materials for parents.

All unit-based teachers spend some time out in the field visiting the children and parents for whom they are responsible. Generally teachers visit the home and in many instances will stay overnight with the family. In addition, wherever possible teachers conduct small group workshops for parents and children. These may last from a half day to a full day depending on circumstances. Parents and children also visit the Pre-School Correspondence Unit when they come to the city. Finally, unit-based teachers act as facilitators by putting parents in touch with one another and assisting them to utilize other support personnel and resources.

In the P.S.C.P., emphasis is placed on providing the child with as much opportunity as possible for learning through "play" situations. Parents are encouraged to provide an interesting environment which allows the child the opportunity to discover, explore, create, and experiment through active involvement with concrete materials. The program continually emphasizes that learning occurs through the day to day experiences of the child and is not limited to specific times set aside in the "schoolroom." (Many parents who act as home supervisors on primary correspondence programs have a particular area set aside in the home for school lessons, hence the term "schoolroom.")

Parents are encouraged to work with their children when and where they are able, in their own way and according to their commitments. Many families living on cattle or sheep properties are very dependent on the "family work force" to share the responsibilities in the running of the property. Obviously, the role of the parent-teacher must be tailored to fit in the family needs. The growth of the P.S.C.P. since 1974 is shown in Table 3.

Table 3.   Pre-School Correspondence Program in Queensland.

	Enrollments[1]	Teachers	Other Staff
1974	280	10	4
1975	540	21	7
1976	825	38	11
1977	882	38	14
1978	852	38	14
1979	835[2]	37	16

[1] Enrollments effective as at National Census date of August 1 each year.

[2] Enrollment at opening school year, January 1979.

An Outreach of the P.S.C.P.: SPAN

It was recognized from the beginning that the P.S.C.P. could do little to serve the young child's need to interact with age-mates. Further, it was acknowledged that many children in geographically isolated areas often have only limited opportunities for such interaction. It was decided to explore ways of meeting this problem. SPAN[1] groups were the outcome.

These groups were conceived as parent-run playgroups which would meet as frequently as the participants wished. Unit-based teachers took the initiative in proposing membership to parents, but the major decisions were made by parents themselves. Parents organized meeting places and determined their own procedures. However, the Pre-School Correspondence Unit provided a range of support materials, including information booklets and cassette tapes. In addition, each group received an equipment kit which consisted of basic play and other materials for children. A newsletter was also regularly distributed to groups.

Each year the Pre-School Correspondence Unit organizes a series of workshops for parents. These are conducted in a number of provincial cities. Attendance is open to all parents who are interested in forming SPAN groups. Assistance is provided for both travel and accommodations. Workshops usually last about three days. They are designed to introduce parents to ways of providing activities and experiences for young children in small group situations. Participation in discussions, practical activities, and observations of children in a playgroup setting form the core elements of the workshops.

Communication and support services to SPAN groups involve a three-way process linking SPAN to the Correspondence Unit and with preschool advisory teachers who operate within the various education regions of the state. This last

[1] SPAN refers to the distances to be spanned by and social group in the Queensland outback.

linkage is important. While there is a close relationship between SPAN groups and the Pre-School Correspondence Unit it is important for parents to have the assistance of teachers who are regionally based and can offer on the spot support.

The growth of SPAN groups has been remarkable. In 1975, ten groups were in operation. By the end of 1978 there were almost ninety. However, a most significant development is the extent to which parents whose children are not yet eligible for the P.S.C.P. have come to be involved in SPAN. It is evident that through the use of appropriate resources, such as materials, support, and training experience, parents have gained confidence and skill in developing valuable experiences for both themselves and their children. There is also evidence to suggest that the benefits of such experience are by no means restricted to SPAN participants but infuse many segments of rural community life in outback Queensland.

P.S.C.P./SPAN Research Project

Since 1975 a major research project, of a formative kind, has been conducted in connection with the P.S.C.P. and SPAN Groups. This study initially formed part of a two-year international program monitored by the Centre for Educational Research and Innovation (C.E.R.I.) of the Organization for Economic Co-operation and Development (O.E.C.D.). The project was planned to elicit a wide range of information on various aspects of program design, delivery, and organization. The research was based on the assumption that flexibility of both ends and means was an important characteristic of a responsive and sensitive organization. A number of key generalizations have emerged to date.

First, within a home-based approach to preschool education, it is absolutely essential that close attention be paid to the interaction among the major elements involved in the network. Such an observation may appear trite and self-evident, yet it is very important. In the P.S.C.P. the prime elements are the unit-based teachers, the parents, the children, and the program materials. Careful analysis revealed that impediments to communication existed at all levels of operation: Materials were often not clear to parents; frequently too many ideas were presented, so parents felt overwhelmed; teachers often responded too slowly to parents' requests for help; help was not of the kind actually sought; parents were often unable to express their concerns or satisfactions, and therefore deprived teachers of feelings of job satisfaction.

It is essential to remedy such communication problems as quickly as possible. It may be helpful to see how this was accomplished when it was discovered, in an early study, that teachers were taking too long to respond to parents' communications. Often several weeks elapsed before a response went back to a parent. A number of matters were involved: Teachers were almost *too* diligent in attempting to gather or devise resources to assist the parent;

communication was written (because the research design required records of communication); resources were not indexed in ways that permitted teachers to easily access relevant materials; and mail distributions and time-lines were inadequately understood by clerical staff in the Pre-School Correspondence Unit. Reorganization of the library, instigation of procedures for heightening sensitivity to parents' requests, the use of audio cassettes, and other changes were introduced so that when the matter was reinvestigated later, the focus had shifted away from time elements to the more qualitative issues of tailoring information more accurately to suit the family situation and the teaching abilities of the mother.

Second, organization of the content of the educational program to be implemented in the home situation is less critical than initially believed. Shaping the program to meet the needs of the child, the parent, and the family situation is the critical factor; that is, no matter how superior the educational package, it will not be effective unless there is individualized monitoring—the selection of those materials and additional resources most relevant to each family.

Very early in the research project it became quite obvious to the research team that although the materials that constituted the P.S.C.P. could be improved, and indeed had to be redeveloped, concentration on the content of the materials would not produce the most satisfactory improvements in the program's quality. Indeed, it was tempting, initially, to consider a series of empirical studies to yield information on the abilities of children and parents, and adopt a "deficit-strength" model for developing materials. However, it was also apparent that because of the tremendous spread of background variables, including parental education variables, it would be more productive to concentrate on the processes of communication between teachers and parents, teachers and children, parents and teachers, and children and teachers, so that each could better provide useful feedback to the other. The concentration of the research upon processes has permitted the development of strategies for improving the quality of the educational experiences much more directly than attempts to devise the "ideal" package might have achieved.

Third, home-based preschool programs can have the same range of spin-offs as more conventional center-based programs. This is a perception and judgment rather than an empirical observation. The data indicate that both parents and children grow in a whole range of ways and that a number of qualitative changes occur within the family when the program attempts to meet the family's perceived needs, rather than focus on needs which are external. However, home-based preschool education is not a cheap alternative. Costing studies indicate that it costs about the same amount per child to deliver a home-based as a center-based program; the only significant savings is in capital investment.

Fourth, unit-based teachers in the P.S.C.P. have the same needs for professional enhancement and support as teachers in conventional preschool units. Because the unit-based teachers operated in an office-type setting surrounded by many other teachers it was initially believed that professional stimulation would present few problems. However, investigation revealed that this was not so. Maintenance of motivation depended on feedback and job satisfaction. Teachers' prime sources of satisfaction came from children and parents. Thus it was found essential to recognize the autonomy of the unit-based teachers by providing similar opportunities to interact directly with the children and parents in their groups and individualize the standard "core" program. Further, it was shown that one element in enhancement was the opportunity to engage in increasingly more sophisticated ways of implementing the program. Thus it is always necessary to explore ways of ensuring that teachers can experience satisfaction through job enrichment, no matter what the setting in which the teacher operates.

Class IV School Project:
Early Education Classes

It was noted previously that areas served by Class IV schools presented a particular problem with regard to the provision of preschool education. Class IV primary schools have enrollments of between thirty-six and one hundred pupils. Thus, the annual pupil intake into the first year of primary schooling could vary betwen, say, five and fifteen pupils. And although these schools represented just over twenty-five percent (258 schools) of all primary schools operated by the Department of Education, they enrolled only 6.5 percent (14,300) of all pupils. Analyses indicated that the catchment areas served by Class IV schools contained approximately 2,500 children who would be eligible for preschool annually.

Clearly, providing conventional preschool facilities of the unit type was not viable. The limited population in catchment areas reflected in the small numbers of children attending this group of schools made such provision impractical. Other options had to be considered. One was the possibility of establishing mobile preschools which could visit areas on an itinerant basis. However, the distribution of Class IV schools and the distances between them indicated that this proposition would not offer an effective solution except in a minority of cases. Another option was to permit all children who would attend a Class IV school to be eligible to enroll with the P.S.C.P. This was considered undesirable because of the consequences for the size of the Pre-School Correspondence Unit. With a potential enrollment of 3,500, it was believed that formalization of the management of the unit and loss of flexibility of the desired organizational structure were inevitable. Furthermore, it was believed that results might be better if a more direct input was made into the schools and their communities. A major element in the thinking about preschool provisions across the state was the conviction that through sensitive interaction among teachers, children, and parents it was possible to raise educational expectations and exercise influence upon both homes and primary schools. Thus, it was decided to attempt an experiment: to create within Class IV schools a special grouping of preschool children and those in the initial years of primary education. These groupings came to be known as Early Education Classes (E.E.C.s), a name parents gave to one of the first classes which began at a school in the far north of the state. An important difference between the Class IV school approach and the regular center-based approach was that in the former the preschool component was to be wholly under the educational and administrative control of the school principal.

The project was initiated in 1976 after a detailed study of Class IV schools throughout the state. The numbers of schools involved in the years since introduction of the plan are presented in Table 4. In moving toward the adoption of the E.E.C. approach, a number of considerations were taken into account: first, that the functions of the E.E.C. should be no different from those of the center-based preschools, although obvious differences in educational programs were to be expected; second, that if the E.E.C. was to be effective it would be essential to secure the support of both school personnel and the community served by the school prior to initiating any class; third, that schools would need to be provided with the necessary resources in terms of physical facilities, materials and personnel to enable them to function efficiently; fourth, that it would be essential to provide schools with adequate support in terms of in-service education opportunities and access to advisory services; fifth, that given both resources and support, schools should also be given the freedom to evolve their educational program within the frameworks of the preschool and the primary systems; and sixth, that close evaluative monitoring would be an essential component of the approach.

It should also be noted that as with the center-based approach to preschool provision, the E.E.C. concept was quite deliberately kept very flexible. Keeping open possible future lines of development remained an important consideration. However, more important in this project was the need to explore the dimensions of community, preschool, and school interaction. It was recognized from the outset that the project could fail in a number of ways. First, the preschool element could lose its essential individual-centered character. Second, the primary school component could fail to meet parent and teacher expectations

Table 4. Class IV School Project: Number of Early Education Centers in Queensland.

1976	19
1977	56
1978	79
1979	93

with regard to learning in traditional, basic areas. Third, the clash between pre-school and primary value systems (and they were recognized as having a number of quite different orientations) could undermine the project.

However, it was also recognized that positive gains could be achieved through a wholly integrated approach. First, successful integration of the two value systems, preschool and primary, could result in an upward influence being exercised upon primary school practices by the preschool. Second, an integration of preschool and the initial primary grades could result in greater flexibility with regard to accommodating individual differences among children. Third, if parents became extensively involved in the school through their preschool child, this pattern might continue through other levels in the school. Finally, upwardly mobile principals in Class IV schools would generally be transferred to larger schools (which would have preschool units associated with them), where their direct involvement in preschool education and enhanced under-standing of preschool children would be an asset. This last consideration was judged significant because of its system-wide implications, for it was from the ranks of principals that senior leadership positions within the Department of Education were generally filled. Thus, the potential impact of the infusion effect was seen as having implications well beyond the Class IV schools. In order to ensure optimum facilitating conditions, emphasis was placed on providing resources and support. Without these it was believed that initiative could become either bogged down or misdirected, and motivation thereby dampened.

One further point should be noted. In 1973, when considering the matter of preservice teacher education, it was necessary to provide advice to training institutions on the projected number of teachers required and the general nature of the training desired. With regard to the latter, institutions were encouraged to opt for preservice programs which combined preschool and primary school training, with an emphasis upon the early childhood period of 4 to 8 years of age. Thus, teachers available for appointment to Class IV schools generally had a preservice background in both preschool and primary teaching.

Detailed analyses of Class IV schools provided considerable information which permitted planning targets and cost projections to be established:

> Year 1 (first year of primary schooling) classes ranged from one to twenty-one children with an average class size of 8.75;
>
> Year 1 classes of eight or fewer children occurred in just over half the schools;
>
> Year 1 classes of sixteen or fewer children occurred in more than ninety percent of Class IV schools.

These data enabled certain estimates to be made concerning staffing needs. Using the existing primary school staffing scale, it was projected that some seventy additional teachers would be required to implement the whole project. (All other teachers deployed in such classes would require inservice training of

various kinds.) This estimate was based on the assumption that preschool attendance would remain sessional, and each pupil would therefore represent half a
full-time equivalent. Further, from detailed information concerning existing
school facilities, it was determined that three separate types of accommodation
needs would have to be met:

provision of a self contained classroom facility which would serve preschool and any other students that the school included in the E.E.C.;

creation of additional space by extending a section of the existing school;

remodelling of an internal section of the school to provide storage space
or other such feature.

Granted the provision of resources and support, each school faced a
difficult management problem in determining how the E.E.C. should be
organized. No guidelines for this work existed within the Queensland, or indeed
elsewhere in Australia. Differences in sizes of Class IV schools meant there were
wide variations in how the children were grouped. Teachers were responsible for
children in one-, two-, three-, or even four-year levels of the school. Therefore, it
was decided that when an E.E.C. was established at a school, the group should
consist of a maximum of twenty-five children with no more than preschool and
two other year levels. It was also decided that a full-time teacher aide would be
appointed to the group and that a strong emphasis would be given to voluntary
parent involvement in classrooms.

A further problem faced by schools was to decide on the pattern of attendance that most suited their situation. While half-day sessional attendance was
possible in some areas, it was not practical in others. Various options existed.
The children could attend either each morning or each afternoon or they could
attend for a full day for no more than five full days per fortnight. In the latter
case children might travel on the school bus. This system was tested extensively
in 1973 at regular preschools, and results indicated that a maximum one-way
trip of 45 minutes every other day produced no ill effect for most 4-year-old
children. However, each preschooler on a bus had to be under the guardianship
of an older child. Most E.E.C.s adopted the alternate day pattern, one important reason being that it gave the teacher time alone with the older children. The
most difficult problem, however, was in establishing the educational program. In
this regard schools were invited to develop their own approaches within the
frameworks of the preschool and the primary systems. Resources of various
kinds were developed to assist schools in this effort, but the final decision was
vested in the school with regard to structuring experiences and content, determining timetables, and managing the program.

At the end of the first year of the project an informal evaluation was
requested of school principals. No uniform patterning of an educational program was sought, nor did one emerge. Rather each school worked out its own
way of achieving a balance in the curriculum experiences provided. However,

all principals reported that whereas the work of determining the program was demanding and exacting, it was nevertheless professionally challenging. One principal wrote:

> The preschool children enrolled at this school have shown great development in social skills, language skills, premathematical skills and fine and gross motor skills. They are better prepared to enter Grade (Year) 1 than any other group of children 1 have seen, they are independent and self-assured, and working forward eagerly to next year's schooling. I have been excited by the development that has occurred in the children who have taken part in this pilot program and I commend the program to every Class IV Principal. (Tainton, 1977).

Of course, not all principals were equally excited. Some were concerned that the preschool children might become bored by the Year 1 program. Others felt that the presence of preschool children in the school added to their administrative burden. Also, a number of principals noted that early in the year parents expressed concern that Year 1 children in the E.E.C. would be held back by the presence of preschool children and the demands they made upon the teacher's time. However, by the end of 1976 all principals involved in the initial year of the project were positive in their support.

E.E.C Research Project

On the basis of the first year of the project and the informal evaluation, a formal research project was begun in 1977 and 1978. This study sought to probe the processes and interactions involved in the operation of E.E.C.s. It also examined perceptions concerning the E.E.C.s (Turner & Miles, 1979).

The design of the probe was multidimensional. All fifty-six E.E.C.s operating in 1977 were included, together with two control groups. The two controls consisted of equal numbers of regular preschools and Class IV schools without an E.E.C. In the Class IV schools both teachers and principals participated; only teachers in preschools participated. In addition, the views of teachers in the next higher class to the E.E.C., that is, the class receiving children from the E.E.C., were also obtained in both 1977 and 1978.

The major areas examined were the work program, educational aims, support services, teacher aides, and parent volunteers, and administration.

The main difference in organization patterns between schools with and those without an E.E.C. was in the grouping of the lower end of the school. In schools with an E.E.C., the grouping were generally preschool and Year 1, with the next class consisting of Years 2 and 3. In the other schools, Years 1, 2, and 3 generally constituted the first class. Differences were also noted between teachers in the E.E.C.s and those in the first class of other schools. The E.E.C. teachers were younger, reflected different preservice training backgrounds, and were generally similar to teachers in preschools. The principals at the two types of schools did not differ significantly from each other: they averaged twelve years in office and previously had been staff teachers for a number of years, generally at the middle and upper primary school levels.

In the area of educational programs the E.E.C. teachers and preschool teachers were very similar, and both were different from teachers in non-E.E.C. schools. E.E.C. and preschool teachers highlighted integration of learning, use of interest centres, and tolerance of greater movement within the room; they also evidenced substantial differences in the use of art and music activities as compared to teachers in non-E.E.C. schools.

The processes of acquiring and using information were also more heavily stressed by preschool and E.E.C. teachers than primary teachers. The latter gave much stronger emphasis to information acquisition. Whereas all teachers exhibitied evidence of considerable planning, a major difference was noted between the E.E.C.s and other Class IV schools. In the former, the principal was involved to a much greater extent in working with the E.E.C. teacher on planning. Keeping individual files on children's progress, planning integration in various learning areas, and more cooperative evaluation were all in evidence. Thus, although it would be true to say that by the end of 1978 no distinctive new educational approach had emerged in the E.E.C.s, there were clear signs of new processes coming into play which had potential for vitalizing schools.

It appeared that the advent of an E.E.C. changed the education program for primary children rather than for preschool children. In the area of aims there was little difference between teachers in the three settings or between principals. However, where differences occurred they were at the Year 1 level. In particular, the degree of emphasis on social and emotional development and on aesthetic skills in the areas of art and music was higher among E.E.C. teachers than among primary teachers. One outstanding difference was in the area of parental involvement, which was strongly emphasized by preschool and E.E.C. teachers but not by other teachers.

Principals of schools with an E.E.C. program and E.E.C. teachers were strongly supportive of the project. The majority of teachers in the next class were also supportive. However, both E.E.C. teachers and their principals raised a number of concerns about their own lack of knowledge. For principals, this lack was in the preschool area, whereas for teachers the need was for program information at the Year 1 and 2 levels of the primary school.

The matter of support services was probed both with regard to availability and appropriateness. In general, there was widespread satisfaction with the support given by preschool advisory services as compared with support from primary advisory services. Further, differences in the usefulness of various departmental publications were also noted. For example, *Links,* a magazine put out by the preschool division, was widely used and referred to, but certain other publications prepared to provide assistance in content areas in the primary school were almost unused.

Major differences were reflected between E.E.C. schools and other schools on the matter of parental involvement. Preschools and E.E.Cs reported substantially higher levels of parental participation than did other schools. Indeed, a feature was the extent to which parents were seen to play a vital role in working with children in the E.E.C. Differences in the use of teacher aides were also noted. In particular, aides in both preschools and E.E.C.s worked more in a colleague relationship with the teacher than in the other schools.

In the area of administration most principals found problems. Many of these stemmed from the slowness in refurbishing schools and installing new facilities. Most other problems were the "teething problems" inevitably associated with welding new activities or responsibilities onto existing ones.

Overall the evidence obtained from the review was positive but indicated areas in which greater effort was needed. This was particularly the case in the provision of more extensive inservice education for principals and E.E.C. teachers. Offsetting this, however, was evidence that self-motivated learning appeared to be a consequence of installing an E.E.C. at a school. Further, changes occurred with the advent of an E.E.C. in terms of the schools organization, changes in the Year 1 and 2 programs, and the extent of community participation in the school.

PRESCHOOL SYSTEM INSTALLATION

The foregoing description provides background for understanding the three-pronged approach to the provision of preschool education facilities and opportunities in Queensland. On the basis of experience to date it is possible to derive a number of tentative principles that emerge from this exercise. Before detailing these it may be useful to summarize certain major assumptions underlying the development of preschool education.

Assumptions Underlying the System

The first assumption concerns the nature of preschool education. Elsewhere (Ashby, 1972, 1976, 1979) I have argued that there are specific criteria which identify an educational program. These criteria revolve around the intentions and worth of the learning promoted and the state of the learner. Within the Queensland system it was proposed that preschools provide educative experiences at two levels: for children and for parents. Of course, each level has its own particular set of demands; however, the intent of each is to view learning within a continuum of experiences. For the child, the continuum revolves around the progressive shifts in the location of learning activities that occur over time, coupled with changes in relationships between the child and others, the number of other people encountered, and various developmental factors. For parents the continuum comprises the changing pattern of the relationship with the child and the forms of support required by the child over time. Any preschool educational program must make serious efforts to operate at each of the two levels and ensure that each grows out of the earlier developmental phases and orientates towards succeeding phases.

A second assumption concerns the particulars of program content, style, and process. The sensitivity of the individual teacher to local conditions and needs is an essential requirement in this regard. The educational program for children and families must be organized in relation to the people and the setting involved. For example, there must be avenues by which parents can have input into the program, and teachers must be equipped to both solicit and make use of this input. Considerable trust must be given to teachers to evolve and translate ideas into relevant educational experiences appropriate to the setting.

The third assumption is that the teacher must be invested with considerable autonomy by an organization (in the beaucratic sense) to take initiative and be responsible for the educational welfare and well-being of the children and the families who make up the community of the preschool. However, this particular assumption has a very considerable sting in its tail, as translation into action is reliant upon three critical factors: first, the resources provided to the teacher; second, the processes by which teachers are inducted into their role; third, the support services provided by the organization. If resources are inadequate, autonomy is constricted. If induction is inappropriate, autonomy is meaningless. If support is not available, autonomy falters.

A fourth assumption is that a preschool system should be comprehensive in the access provided to a range of services. However, it is important to recognize that comprehensiveness does not mean providing every kind of service. While the Queensland system was charged with providing preschool education, the Department of Education was given neither a mandate nor the statutory responsibility to provide activities such as child (day) care services (these were vested in another authority). But clearly it is not sensible to propose that preschools should exist within a vacuum, uncoordinated with other types of provisions. Articulation between agencies is essential. Further, any assumptions concerning the comprehensive nature of a particular service should be tempered by the need to avoid duplication or overlap with other services. Thus, the determination of priorities and the identification of those matters which a system will, and can, cater to are essential. Within the Queensland geographic context, a range of alternative delivery systems was required. There was no single model for preschool education that was appropriate across the whole state.

A sixth assumption is that action cannot always await the availability of soundly based research. Judgments have to be made. Further, in 1973, there were virtually no policy-oriented data available on system development in early childhood education relevant to the Queensland context. Therefore, it was assumed that all decisions and actions that were made had to be carefully analyzed in terms of their perceived long-term implications. In particular, it was assumed that the retention of flexibility, except in areas where this was not a consideration, was critical, and the blocking-off of future options was to be avoided. However, in view of the absence of an established data base it was assumed that appropriate structures would need to be established to provide necessary information and evaluative feed back. It was also assumed that the information sought should be formative, rather than summative, in character and be used to directly assist decision making processes.

A final assumption was that the maintenance of motivation among staff and the retention of quality was a major concern of the organization. There is a profound difference between a growing, developing organization and one that has become relatively static in terms of growth. Excitement is not a state that can be successfully maintained over long periods of time. Yet retaining enthusiasm, interest, and innovation is essential in any educational endeavor. Many factors may inhibit the capacity of an organization to maintain quality. The most significant of these factors are loss of personal identity due to increases in the numbers of people involved and loss of a sense of clear direction or purpose by the organization. Whereas early childhood educators are well known for their dedication, it was assumed that at some point the character of the system would undergo change and that this would require careful management. Specifically, it was assumed that although it might be possible to contrive ways of maintaining a high level of enthusiasm, as in management by crisis, these would be unsatisfactory over a long period, and less spectacular mechanisms would be more productive.

Some Principles Derived
from the Queensland Experience

It is difficult to judge the extent to which principles emerge from the Queensland experience or indeed to determine whether these principles might be relevant elsewhere. This is true in part because of the context within which the preschool system developed and in part because such matters involve judgment. Naturally, it is easy to point to various planning issues such as identification of target groups, definition of the services to be provided, and similar matters, for these issues are well recognized. For that reason, it would seem more profitable to elucidate some tentative ideas not so readily apparent. However, it must be stressed that in attempting to identify any principles, tentative or otherwise, there is a subtle but important shift, from the role of describer to that of judge, with all the inherent dangers that implies.

Principle 1. Preschool education is a blend of functions and processes rather than a body of knowledge. This is not to say that knowledge is unimportant, but rather that knowledge is useful only in so far as it is relevant to developmental and social needs and to community and professional expectations. Both ends and means are variables in preschool education which may be adjusted in responding to needs and expectations. The activity of responding is itself the application of processes to some particular situation. The processes selected are interpreted against an understanding of the functions to be served by the preschool. Thus, it is of critical importance that the functions to be served by preschool education be clearly defined, with responsibilities clearly assigned. In particular, preschool education should remain primarily educational in its intent.

This view has important implications for the organization of preschool education. Flexibility to respond to changing circumstances is an outcome of organization. The closing off of options in relation to modes of service delivery and the types of services delivered is a constraint imposed by the structure of an organization. The major effects of structure are reflected in the orientations and commitments of the people involved in organization. In the final analysis a flexible, responsive organization, as opposed to one that is integumented, depends heavily upon the judgment displayed by the teachers who work in daily contact with children, parents, and other community agents. Unless teachers are able to grasp the responsibilities that are vested in them and consciously respond to shifting needs and expectations of individuals and communities, the system becomes closed. Therefore, administration involves trust and, to that extent, risk taking.

In administrative theory "flat organizational structures are generally believed better able to cope with variation of both ends and means than conventional bureaucratic structures." However, "flat" structures are very demanding in terms of the access that they permit among all members of the organization. Expertise is a criterion of leadership rather than status. Thus, the most senior members of the organization must possess recognized expertise and must interact extensively with all other personnel. At the same time, leadership cannot be conceived as the prerogative of those in positions of senior responsibility. Rather, efforts must be made to nurture professional leadership and professional responsibility in each member of the organization. Thus, attention must be paid to the forms, style, and content of communication and above all the avoidance of a "them" versus "us" mentality.

Principle 2. The quality of education offered by preschool services is a reflection of the quality of support provided to those who deliver the services. Although at first sight this statement may appear a truism, it is no less important because of that. Support takes many forms, from aiding an inexperienced teacher to adjust in a strange new situation to challenging the experienced, successful teacher to engage in increasingly more complex and sophisticated tasks. Further, support must be both appropriate to the individual teacher and readily available when required.

A comprehensive network of support services includes specialists of many kinds. However, support services must focus on *one central task:* assisting the individual teacher. Support must never be at the expense of the teacher, nor must the teacher be threatened or overwhelmed by it. The basic element in any teaching team is the person who works directly with children and parents; therefore the object of support is to enhance the competency of the individual teacher while ensuring that appropriate provision is made for the individual child and family.

In addition to support persons, two other forms of assistance must be provided to teachers. First, they must be recognized as professionals in their own right. The designation of professional autonomy carries with it responsibilities which must be recognized and nurtured by the organization. Second, the teacher must have sufficient resources to permit programatic choice to be exercised. Professional autonomy is an empty concept if the teacher lacks even the most minimal resources to execute a program. Of course, it is possible to overprovide with resources which may then be unused. Therefore, teachers must be given choices in selecting the resources they want and encouragement to establish their own priorities, in consultation with the parents and other colleagues who constitute the preschool community. In a similar vein, in the programatic area it is possible to overwhelm the teacher through the constraints of too prescriptive a program. Although most teachers claim that they want a degree of prescription, they soon resent the impotency that may follow if they cannot make choices and demonstrate individuality within the program. Thus, care must be taken not to provide too little or too much support; similarly, care must be taken to ensure that what support is given is perceived by the teacher as being helpful.

Principle 3. The preschool is a transitional educational setting which mediates between other powerful social institutions. Major examples of these other institutions are the home and the school. The effect upon the preschool of occupying a mediating position is that its program, Janus-like, must look in two directions: into the home and into the school. A number of implications follow. First, it is not useful to regard the preschool as a place apart from other educative and socializing institutions within society. The preschool can only operate with a degree of success when it attempts to bridge gaps between the various objectives sought by such institutions. Second, it is not desirable or profitable to regard the child in the preschool apart from a continuum of development and experience. Too often programs and curricula appear to have been premised on an "as if" basis: as if the preschool can educate in ways totally unrelated to the ways homes, communities, or schools educate. Third, the processes employed within the preschool are the means by which bridges are established between the institutions that surround it. Fourth, the content of the processes employed must draw heavily upon the local environment; that is, the content must reflect local realities rather than those prescribed or determined remote from the place where they will be implemented. This is not to suggest that such determinations cannot be made but rather that they may suffer from a lack of relevance. Fifth, that differences between various types of programs, with regard to such factors as aims, intent, and strategies, are less significant than the interactions between people in the program. It is the interactions and the sensitivity of the individuals involved that determine what is learned in the preschool.

The above implications are not definitive. However, they highlight something about the function of preschool education. Primarily, it is important for the preschool to be seen as leading toward the school, if not drawing away from the home. The subject matter of the preschool is to be found not only through careful observation of children of preschool age, but of children in homes, in schools, and in the community.

Principle 4. On-going formative evaluations, which both monitor and change processes involved in preschool programs, are a necessary condition for systematic development. However, this mechanism does not focus only on observations of children's development. Indeed, it may well be that such observations are of lesser importance than observations of what teachers, aides, and parents do in the program. This is not to suggest that assessment of a child's progress is unimportant. Rather, the suggestion is that such observations may suffer from a circularity that fails to come to grips with the source of change. The child may respond, or not respond, to the environment created by adults in the preschool setting, but the setting itself may often be ignored as a serious object for study.

Evaluation of the kind that is being advanced here depends very heavily upon the professional competence and maturity of the teacher. The organizational structure in which the preschool operates must elicit and value evaluative input. However, it must be recognized that change is the outcome of evaluation and that the implementation of such change should not be unduly delayed. It must be accepted that change of the type being referred to leads to diversity and this must be accepted as both inevitable and valuable. The involvement of teachers and aides as the evaluators of what is provided—how and to what effect—is essential in order to promote professional growth and maintain the health of a program.

The four principles that have been identified can be put together into a tentative theoretical model which describes an approach to the planning of preschool educational services. This proposed model can be referenced to classical planning models which are cyclical in operation. Typically, these models propose a sequence of events which follow a pattern: establish goals; identify resources; consider alternative options; select strategy; implement strategy; evaluate outcomes; revise goals (and so back through the cycle).

Classical approaches are essentially "ends-means" oriented. However, when education is provided in a wide range of settings both ends and means have to be adjusted to match local needs and conditons. Further, to hold that there are alternative methods by which some particular goal might be achieved is also misleading. The methods by which goals are achieved have different impacts upon the outcomes achieved. Therefore, it would appear better to start from the premise that outcomes will vary from place to place or, indeed, in the case of education, from individual to individual. Such a starting place can be provided by a description of functions to be served rather than of aims. Functions vary from aims in that they describe a broad class of events by type of provision, rather than by some objectives to be achieved. Statements of functions indicate direction without specifying what aims and methods ought to be applied in meeting the function: These are determined by the people on the spot. Thus, responsibility for determining the educational program and its mode of operation rests with the individual teacher. This requires a high level of professional competence on the part of teachers. However, competence requires room to be developed. Clearly success contributes to increasing competence, but so too does the exercise of responsibility and the capacity to make mistakes, providing there is some learning as a result of mistakes. Therefore, if teachers are to accept responsibility they must be accorded a measure of autonomy and provided with support networks which sustain this.

Not all teachers operate at any one time at the same level of competence. Thus, support systems must be flexible enough to accommodate differing levels of expertise. Providing personal satisfactions and opportunities for enhancement for each individual is a difficult task. It cannot be orchestrated on the grand scale; rather, support must take various forms for different individuals: For some, involvement in projects of increasing sophistication is essential. For others, the opportunity to go through processes, tried by others but found wanting, is an important step in personal and professional growth.

It is essential that the basic resources also be provided. Unsatisfactory physical conditions and the absence of equipment and materials are dissatisfiers which can seriously interfere with the effective implementation of a program. However, it must be recognized that the elimination of a dissatisfying condition will not by itself lead to satisfaction and commitment to the program. Unless there are rewards that are experienced by the teacher personally, it is unlikely that manipulation of extrinsic conditions will heighten professionalism.

It will be clear that much is made in this sketch of the centrality of the teacher to the processes of preschool education. Indeed, it may appear that too much emphasis is given to the professional component in preschool education. Perhaps. But it should be remembered that a basic belief in the development of preschool education in Queensland was that flexibility in organizational structure, responsiveness to changing patterns of need, and sensitivity to particular local circumstances were educationally essential in the creation of a system. The cornerstone of the system is people; hence, the thrust of this paper has been directed to highlighting those steps by which an attempt has been made to develop a caring, involved, and committed teaching staff.

Over the past two decades there has been a tremendous amount of activity in preschool and early childhood education. A great proportion of that activity has been directed toward the development of appropriate curricula. Much less attention has been given to implementation of programs at the system level or at the local school or preschool level. Yet it remains a fundamental truth that the worth of a program is manifested by the benefits it confers upon those who participate. Evaluating changes in status over a period of time, whether in terms of I.Q. or any other measure, cannot tell the whole story. The ways individuals' lives have been affected by their experiences must be taken into consideration. The outcomes of participation in preschool education are difficult to assess and can seldom be known with accuracy. However, difficulties of measurement do not make more elusive outcomes any less real.

If preschool education is to be effective it must exert its influence at many levels: upon children, parents, teachers in primary schools, other community agents, and upon the teachers who work in the preschool. What is required is the application of knowledge from many disciplines to preschool education and the careful analysis of the implications of such knowledge for organizational structures and programs. Without recognition of this fact, preschool education ceases to be a process by which change is effected and becomes instead an isolated educational artifact. Such a result would be a sad commentary on the potential of preschool education as a vitalizing force within education and the community.

REFERENCES

Ashby, G. F. *Pre-school theories and strategies.* Melbourne, Australia: Melbourne University Press, 1972.

Ashby, G. F. Psychological and educational bases of preschool education. In M. Pool et al. (Eds.), *Before school begins.* Sydney, Australia: Wiley & Sons, 1976.

Ashby, G. F. Parents as continuing support in special education. In *Too late at eight.* Brisbane, Australia: Schonnell Education Research Centre, University of Queensland, 1979.

Halliwell, G. *An interaction model for early childhood education.* Brisbane, Australia: Curriculum Branch, Department of Education, Queensland, 1977 (a).

Halliwell, G. *Open framework approaches to developing programs for early childhood education.* Brisbane, Australia: Curriculum Branch, Department of Education, Queensland, 1977 (b).

Tainton, J. A. The First Year, *Links.* No. 3, 1977, Brisbane Information and Publications Branch, Department of Education, Queensland.

Turner, T. & Miles, J. *An evaluation of early education classes in Queensland.* Brisbane, Australia: Research Branch, Department of Education, Queensland, 1979.

REPORTS OF PRESCHOOL CORRESPONDENCE
PROGRAM RESEARCH PROJECT*

Ashby, G., McGaw, B., & Grant, J. *The Pre-School Correspondence Program: Background.* Report No. 1 (1975) (ED 129 431).

Ashby, G., McGaw, B., Perry, R., & Grant J. *The Pre-School Correspondence Program: An Overview.* Report No. 2 (1975, Revised 1978).

McGaw, B., Ashby, G., & Perry, R. *Interactions in the Pre-School Correspondence Program:* Report No. 3 (1975) (ED 125 765).

McGaw, B., Ashby, G., & Grant, J. *Parents' Perception of the Pre-School Correspondence Program.* Report No. 4 (1975) (ED 125 764).

Ashby, G., Boorsboom, E., & Rosser, S. *SPAN Playgroups for Geographical Isolated Pre-School Children: Theoretical Basis and Strategies.* Report No. 5 (1976) (ED 162 733).

Grant, J., Ashby, G., & Clemesha, B. *Teachers' Perceptions of the Pre-School Correspondence Program.* Report No. 6 (1978) (ED 151 101).

Grant, J., Ashby, G., & Clemesha, B. *Analysis of the Teaching Styles of a Sample of Parents in the Pre-School Correspondence Program. Part 1: Parent Interviews.* Report No. 7 (1978) (ED 156 322).

Ashby, G., Rigby, A., & Grant, J. *Evaluation of the SPAN Parent Workshop and the Operation of SPAN Groups.* Report No. 8 (1979).

*Published by Research Branch, Division of Planning and Services, Department of Education, Brisbane. Most reports are available through the ERIC system of the U.S. National Institute of Education, under the ED numbers indicated.